BRITISH PRIME MINISTERS
IN THE TWENTIETH CENTURY

BRITISH PRIME MINISTERS IN THE TWENTIETH CENTURY

Edited by
JOHN P. MACKINTOSH

VOLUME II
Churchill to Callaghan

ST. MARTIN'S PRESS
NEW YORK

Printed in Great Britain
Library of Congress Catalog Card Number 77-76542
ISBN 0-312-10518-5
First published in the United States of America in 1978

Contents

Contributors

John P. Mackintosh is MP for Berwick and East Lothian and Professor of Politics at the University of Edinburgh.

Paul Addison has been Lecturer in History at the University of Edinburgh since 1967. He is the author of *The Road to 1945: British Politics and the Second World War*.

Robert E. Dowse has taught in various universities in the UK and in America and Africa and is currently Reader in Politics in the University of Exeter. His publications include *Left in the Centre*; *Readings in British Politics and Government*; *Modernisation in Ghana and the USSR* and *Political Sociology*.

Robert Blake, who was made a life peer in 1971, has been Provost of Queen's College Oxford since 1968. He was a Conservative member of the Oxford City Council from 1957 to 1965; in 1967 he was elected a Fellow of the British Academy. His books include *The Unknown Prime Minister: The Life and Times of Andrew Bonar Law 1858–1923*; *Disraeli*; *The Conservative Party from Peel to Churchill*; *The Office of Prime Minister* and *A History of Rhodesia*.

Keith Sainsbury has been Lecturer and Senior Lecturer in Politics at the University of Reading since 1955. His publications include *The North African Landings, 1942: A Strategic Decision*; *British Foreign Secretaries Since 1945* (part author); and *Select Bibliography of International History, 1939–70*.

Lucille Iremonger has written the first modern biography of the Earl of Aberdeen, nineteenth-century Foreign Secretary and Prime Minister, to be published in 1978. She is also the author of *The Fiery Chariot*, a study of the psychology of leadership and achievement with special reference to British Prime Ministers; and has contributed political articles to the *Daily Telegraph* and other papers.

Brian Redhead is a journalist and broadcaster. He was Northern Editor of the *Guardian* from 1965 to 1969, and Editor of the *Manchester Evening News* from 1969 to 1975. He is currently Presenter of the Radio 4 'Today' programme and 'A Word in Edgeways'.

Preface

John P. Mackintosh

This book was originally planned as a single volume at the time when the controversy over the role of the Prime Minister and the nature of the powers attaching to the office were at their height. Then the work grew in size, a chapter had to be added on Mr Callaghan and it seemed better to divide the book into two volumes. The division at 1940 not only left seven Prime Ministers in each section but also seemed to be a sensible division in that the war marked changes in the philosophy of government – the commitment to a welfare system and to full employment – in the scale of domestic activity and in the ultimate decline in British overseas power, which deeply affected all domestic institutions.

Since this decision was taken, the second and third volumes of the Crossman *Diaries* have appeared with their wealth of material on the Wilson Governments of 1964 to 1970. There has also been the experience of two very different personalities in office succeeding Wilson, Mr Heath and his Government of 1970–74 and Mr Callaghan's period in office since 1976.

This extra written and actual evidence has both complicated and clarified the situation. The complication has come from the continued decline in the power of British government – and therefore in the power of the Prime Minister – in relation both to other countries and to major pressure groups within Britain. With the precarious condition of the British economy and Britain's diminished military strength, Mr Wilson was unable, for example, to impose his will on Rhodesia and by 1977 any attempts at British mediation in this case can only proceed if they have the patent support of the United States. Britain, even in Europe, is in the second division and in late 1976 only stemmed a serious flow on the pound by adopting economic policies acceptable to the International Monetary Fund.

Also in this period, three successive Prime Ministers have had to come to terms with the trade unions. Mr Wilson had to abandon his proposed legislation on industrial relations in 1969, Mr Heath faced a boycott of his Industrial Relations Act, confrontation with the miners and defeat at a general election precipitated by this conflict. Both Mr Wilson and Mr Callaghan, in the period since 1974, have accepted that a major case for their governments is that they can rule with the consent of the T.U.C. Though it is not always clear who is leading or dominating whom, the Conservative Party seems also to have concluded that it would be highly undesirable to try and govern in a way which would be unacceptable to such a powerful pressure group.

So both internally and externally, the weakness of British government and of its leader has increased. But there remains the very great power of the Prime Minister within the machinery of government. At the time of writing, Mr Callaghan has established himself as the key figure in his own administration. He was able, from the start, to deny Mr Jenkins, a contender for the leadership, his claim to the Foreign Office and to refuse to appoint any of Mr Jenkins' lieutenants. He has gathered the main decisions on economic policy into his own hands. When Mr Healey wanted to cut public expenditure and take a loan from the I.M.F., a majority of the Cabinet led by Mr Crosland opposed. It was the Prime Minister's decision to come down on the side of the loan that settled the matter. While Mr Callaghan has been content to let Dr Owen do the legwork on foreign affairs, when really important issues arise in relations with the United States or over Britain's role in the European Community, Mr Callaghan has again been the principal architect of the policy. It was his determination to hold to a rigid line on pay settlements that prevented a compromise being offered to the firemen at any early stage in their dispute.

Mr Heath was equally master in his own house. The Crossman *Diaries*, whatever the memories of other ministers (and Crossman himself could have a different recollection on each day of the week), still furnish a magnificent picture of the Wilson Government. Then the Prime Minister could be full of self-confidence, handling negotiations with Mr Smith, labour disputes or sallies into European politics as he felt inclined. Or he could have one of his fits of uncertainty and nerves, decide he cared little about the issue but a lot

about securing his position and therefore prefer to go round the
Cabinet table asking each member's view in the hope that a consensus
would emerge. But, as Crossman says, whichever side of the Prime
Minister's personality was uppermost, it remained a Wilson
Government. His opponents never united, never had any plan of
action and never mounted a serious challenge to him.

In all, now, this paradox over the power of the British Prime
Minister appears to be well understood; the complexities of
Crossman's accounts have helped to convey the real situation and the
simplistic versions – always wildly unreal – of either an uncrowned
monarch or of a man who simply chaired the Cabinet who had no
more power than his principal colleagues, have both been abandoned.
The reality is elaborate but, as Crossman noted, it is the Prime Minister
who gives the tone, character and content to a Government and it is
for this reason that I hope this second volume of *British Prime Ministers in
the Twentieth Century* will prove both interesting and instructive.

Winston Churchill

Paul Addison

Churchill made a better Prime Minster than was predicted by men in high places. When he succeeded Chamberlain in May 1940, forty years of active political life lay behind him. Throughout those years, his gifts and failings had been an unending source of discussion in Whitehall and Westminster. It was felt that 'Winston' was a known quantity. It was allowed that he possessed many of the elements of a genius, and that he was a most dangerous politician to exclude from power. When properly harnessed, and under firm control, he was a first-rate asset. But, as Halifax and Eden could agree in March 1940, 'however much people admire Winston's qualities, that admiration is constantly balanced by fear of him if [he] were loose!'[1] John Colville, who was a member of the Downing Street secretariat when Chamberlain fell from power, has said: 'In May 1940 the mere thought of Churchill as Prime Minister sent a cold chill down the spines of the staff at 10 Downing Street. . . . Our feelings . . . were widely shared in the Cabinet Offices, the Treasury, and throughout Whitehall.'[2]

Why was there so much apprehension about Churchill's succession to power? The mistrust he inspired has been investigated at length.[3] Whether or not his contemporaries were right, they were convinced that he was never quite in touch with political reality. He was liable, they said, to be carried away by his bellicose imagination into disastrous decisions. As the Liberal journalist A.G.Gardiner wrote on the eve of the First World War: 'He is always unconsciously playing a part – a heroic part. And he is himself his most astonished spectator. He sees himself moving through the smoke of battle – triumphant, terrible, his brow clothed with thunder, his legions looking to him for victory, and not looking in vain.'[4] In the minds of Churchill's contemporaries, the years 1914–39 reinforced this impression. The Antwerp raid, the Gallipoli expedition, his crusade against Bolshevism, his pyrotechnics in the General Strike, his fight against constitutional advance in India, his intervention on behalf of Edward VIII in the abdication crisis – all were cited against him as examples of folly. His critics maintained that he lacked principle as well as judgement. Ambition was considered respectable provided that it was pursued through steady adherence to a party and application to the duller tasks of office. By these tests, Churchill was widely held to be an opportunist, changing his party when it was expedient, and employing office as a means of securing the limelight. In a phrase, he was clever but unreliable. As the Permanent Secretary of the Colonial Office had written when Churchill became a junior minister in 1906, 'He is most tiresome to deal with, and will I fear give trouble – as his Father did – in any position to which he may be called.'[5]

When war broke out Churchill had been out of office for ten years, excluded from power after 1931 by three Prime Ministers. But his campaign against Nazi Germany had proved right, and he knew more about waging war than anyone else in politics. Chamberlain appointed him to the War Cabinet as First Lord of the Admiralty, well aware that he could no longer be excluded without bringing down the Government. Churchill was well placed. He could not be held responsible for the military weakness of Britain. But he was in charge of the navy, the one fighting service with a clear superiority over its German opposite number, and therefore the most aggressive. Such episodes as the Battle of the River Plate, and the seizure of the *Altmark*, alleviated the gloom of the twilight war, and built up Churchill's position. His superb style and presence delighted the House of Commons and the press. No sooner had he made one speech in the House, and one broadcast, than gossip identified him as the future Prime Minister.[6] Personally he was entirely loyal to Chamberlain, but his own drive bore him on, and he could not help eclipsing his Prime Minister in public estimation. Full of *joie de vivre*, he was already beginning to believe that the Germans were on the run, and he announced with a fine disregard for statistics that the U-boat menace was at an end.[7]

In September 1939 Churchill pressed the Cabinet to agree to the mining of Norwegian territorial waters, to disrupt Germany's winter supply route of iron ore shipped from Narvik. The Cabinet balked at the idea. After Russia declared war on Finland on 30 November, Churchill proposed that under the guise of aiding Finland, an allied force should seize Narvik and the orefields of northern Sweden. The Cabinet rejected the scheme after long argument. It was only after the defeat of Finland, when the new French Government of Paul Reynaud demanded action and proposed the mining of territorial waters, that Chamberlain and the Cabinet agreed.

Meanwhile Hitler had decided independently to invade Scandinavia. The decision to mine the leads was not in the end taken because of pressure from Churchill; and it was a coincidence that the mining of the leads was at once followed by Hitler's invasion. Churchill's responsibility for the *origin* of the Norwegian expedition was therefore extremely indirect, but he was at once unhappily involved in its conduct. The Cabinet had a sub-committee for strategy and operations: the Military Co-ordination Committee. On the eve of Hitler's invasion of Scandinavia, Chamberlain had appointed Churchill as chairman of this committee. During the first fortnight of the battle in Norway, Churchill's chairmanship provoked a major row in Whitehall. Ismay, the secretary of the committee, spoke despairingly of the confusion Churchill had engendered in the planning of operations, and Chamberlain was obliged to resume the chairmanship himself.[8] At the end of April it was announced that all British troops would be evacuated from central Norway, and a political crisis became certain. At this very moment Churchill had asked Chamberlain for more powers, and Chamberlain had been obliged to announce that in future Churchill would be responsible, on behalf of the Cabinet, for giving guidance to the Chiefs of Staff. On 7 and 8 May the House of Commons debated Norway, with Churchill winding up the debate forcefully and faithfully for the Government. The Labour party divided the House. The normal majority of Chamberlain's Government was about two hundred. But as the result of a rebellion among Conservatives who had previously remained loyal, the majority fell to eighty-one with thirty-nine Government supporters voting against Chamberlain, and many others abstaining. It was clear from the debate and the division that a National Government was essential. Chamberlain strove at first to establish one under his own leadership. But Labour refused adamantly to serve under him, while the

Conservative rebels announced that they would support only an all party administration. Chamberlain therefore had to decide what advice he should give the king about a successor. His Chief Whip, David Margesson, told him that the House favoured Halifax. At 4.30 p.m. on 9 May, Chamberlain, Margesson, Halifax and Churchill met to decide who should be Prime Minister. No doubt Chamberlain and Halifax hoped that Churchill, humbled by the Norwegian fiasco, would volunteer to serve under Halifax. He almost certainly would have done, had not Kingsley Wood and Brendan Bracken egged him on before the meeting to seize his chance of the premiership. Chamberlain in his opening remarks implied that Churchill was badly placed to win the confidence of Labour. Margesson said that unity was essential, but did not declare which candidate he favoured. By remaining silent for a few moments Churchill indicated that he wanted the job, and Halifax made a little speech of renunciation.[9] While it is true that Halifax was the Establishment candidate, Churchill the favourite of large sections of the press and public, there had been no strong movement for or against either of them. The political world calculated that in a grim situation Churchill or Halifax would each on his merits be an improvement on Chamberlain, even though Churchill was the bigger gamble: no saviour was expected.

At dawn on 10 May the Germans invaded the Low Countries. That evening George VI appointed Churchill Prime Minister, and he set about forming a new administration in an atmosphere transformed by the new emergency. Bowing to the strong current demand, Churchill appointed a small War Cabinet of five, only one of whom, the Foreign Secretary, was responsible for a department. Chamberlain, who remained the Leader of the Conservative party, and the Labour Leader Clement Attlee, were automatic appointments, and the other two members were their party seconds-in-command, Halifax and Arthur Greenwood.

On the Labour side, Dalton, Morrison and Alexander were appointed to ministries which they had been shadowing during the twilight war: Economic Warfare, Supply, and the Admiralty. There was an obvious need to represent the trade union movement directly, and the choice lay between the General Secretary of the TUC, Citrine, and the General Secretary of the TGWU, Bevin. Churchill chose Bevin, whom he admired as a result of dealings with him at the Admiralty. No one foresaw at that point how important the Ministry of Labour and Bevin would become.

Left-wing hopes that Churchill would purge the Conservative leadership of the men of Munich were disappointed. Chamberlain, as Lord President, was chairman of the most powerful committee on the home front, and clearly number two in the administration. Halifax remained at the Foreign Office. Kingsley Wood, who had backed Churchill in the succession crisis, became Chancellor of the Exchequer. Simon, although removed from active politics, achieved the summit of his ambition as a barrister as Lord Chancellor. Of the major pre-war leaders only Hoare was consigned to the wilderness, or rather to Madrid as special envoy. It was assumed that this would be a brief appointment, and Churchill was thinking of making Hoare Viceroy of India after his term in Madrid. The distinctively Churchillian appointments were few, since there were few Churchillians. Eden became Secretary for War, remaining outside the War Cabinet. Duff Cooper was rewarded for his resignation at Munich by his appointment as Minister of Information. L.S. Amery became Secretary of State for India and Lord Lloyd, an imperial diehard, Colonial Secretary. There was only one outstandingly Churchillian appointment. A new Ministry of Aircraft Production was carved from the Air Ministry and given to Lord Beaverbrook, a press lord and rogue elephant widely distrusted in all parties. But overall, the Chamberlainite ranks were largely undisturbed. Of sixty-six ministers in the outgoing administration, forty-four were reappointed in some capacity, and the casualties were the work of Margesson, who had been Government Chief Whip since 1931, rather than of Churchill.[10]

The Liberals under Sinclair, an old friend of Churchill's, were carried along like paper boats on the tide. Sinclair went to the Air Ministry, and the other Liberal ministers turned out to be members of the Other Club, which Churchill and F.E.Smith had founded in 1911.[11]

Churchill's reconstruction created the minimum of political disturbance, while bringing about profound changes in the administrative machinery. On the home front, the Treasury's dominant role in economic policy was ended. The Chancellor was excluded from the Cabinet, and the Permanent Secretary, Sir Horace Wilson, was removed from the many civil committees of which he had been a member. Attlee and Greenwood designed a new structure of six committees for domestic affairs, one of which, the Lord President's Committee, was overlord. The economic section of the War Cabinet was greatly expanded, thus establishing something like the pre-war planners' conception of an 'economic general staff'.

The other key administrative change was that Churchill took the title of Minister of Defence and began to run the war by himself. Under Chamberlain, the Cabinet had been continuously in charge of strategy and operations, acting on the advice of the Chiefs of Staff Committee. Henceforth Churchill and the Chiefs of Staff determined military policy, although for some time their recommendations were still referred to the Cabinet, and to its sub-committees, the Defence Commitee (Supply) and the Defence Committee (Operations). This preserved the form of Cabinet government.

The reconstruction of May 1940 was for Churchill only the first step in his consolidation of power. The governmental machine had yet to be mastered. Conservative MPs still cheered their leader, Chamberlain, while their response to Churchill was subdued. For a while, Chamberlain was able to veto any invitation to Lloyd George to serve in the Government. When Halifax plunged the War Cabinet at the time of Dunkirk into a long hypothetical discussion on peace with Hitler, Churchill was obliged to humour him. Highly placed officials were only slowly convinced that there was method in Churchillian madness. Cadogan, the Permanent Secretary at the Foreign Office, described him as 'too rambling and romantic and sentimental and temperamental. Old Neville is still the best'.[12] The Secretary of the War Cabinet, Bridges, was almost driven to resignation in the autumn of 1940 in protest against Churchill's methods of conducting business. In these months Churchill was extremely fortunate to be able to count on the loyalty of Chamberlain who could easily have made himself the focus of discontent. When fatal illness removed Chamberlain from office in October, Churchill was able to grasp the leadership of the Conservative party and thus undoubted supremacy in the Cabinet and the House. This set the seal on his authority. As he wrote after the war:

I should have found it impossible to conduct the war if I had had to procure the agreement in the compulsive days of crisis and during the long years of adverse and baffling struggle not only of the Leaders of the two minority parties but of the Leader of the Conservative majority. Whoever had been chosen and whatever his self-denying virtues, he would have had the real political power. For me there would have been only the executive responsibility.[13]

There was of course a more fundamental reason for the astonishing growth of Churchill's stature in the early months of his premiership. Hitler, by his conquest of the Low Countries and France, and his threat to destroy Britain, had aroused in this country a tribal feeling of great ferocity and uncertain direction, a potent mixture of fear and aggression: the fear was evident in the hounding of enemy aliens; the aggression, with undertones of comedy, in the mustering within a few days of a quarter of a million men in the Home Guard. What was it in Churchill that made him the almost unquestioned tribal leader in the moment of danger? The prose of his most famous speeches – glorious, heroic, historic declamations – struck home to the very heart of the patriotic child implanted by the educational system in the middle- and upper-class adult. Behind Churchill's voice could be heard school-room echoes, a recitation faintly remembered: 'Then out spake brave Horatius, the Captain of the Gate. . . .' It was all the more extraordinary that Churchill was also accepted and respected by the majority of working-class people, though some were bitter and would not forgive him his part in the General Strike. He benefited, no doubt, from the fact that unlike Chamberlain he was a ripe character drawn from the aristocracy, the sort of figure celebrated in music hall songs as a 'swell' and a 'nob'. He himself rounded out this impression with touches of showmanship like the cigar and the V-sign. As Orwell noted, he got across so well that his name became attached to anecdotes and funny stories, a sign of genuine popular affection.[14] The basic reason, however, why people of all kinds endorsed his leadership, was that they wanted above all else to beat Germany and end the war. Churchill was the supreme hatchet man: it was certain that day and night he was plotting to destroy Hitler. The aggressive tones and reassuring rhythms of his voice were perhaps as important as the actual words he spoke in conveying his one great purpose: 'You ask, what is our aim? I can answer in one word: it is victory, victory at all costs, victory in spite of all terror, victory, however long and hard the road may be; for without victory there is no survival.' By July 1940, opinion polls recorded that eighty-eight per cent of the public approved of Churchill as Prime Minister, and a similar level of support was sustained throughout the war. The highest point of approval, ninety-three per cent, was reached after the battle of El Alamein and the lowest, seventy-eight per cent, after the fall of Tobruk. In April 1945, three months before Churchill and his party were roundly rejected at the polls, ninety-one per cent declared their approval.[15] Churchill was, then, adopted by the mass of the public for a particular purpose, military victory, and rejected once it had been achieved.

A review of his premiership must include some estimate of his temperament and manner of dealing with people. The popular image of Churchill as the bulldog was certainly accurate in the sense that he was capable of great ruthlessness, closely allied to enormous egotism. When he needed to manage people carefully for political reasons he was capable of the most complete self-control; he treated his potential rival Cripps with kid gloves in 1942, just as he displayed the greatest persistence in wooing and cajoling Roosevelt. He flattered MPs in the House by paying them little attentions, and deferring in debate to their great constitutional responsibilities. But his subordinates in the administrative chain of command knew what it was to be roughly dealt with, especially in the depressing years of 1941-2. 'One felt at times,' wrote Ian Jacob of his military secretariat, 'that we were all part of the furniture, necessary, ready to be made use of, but not requiring any consideration.'[16] Having shouldered the burden of his country's military fortunes, Churchill's instinct when a battle was lost was to harry his soldiers into renewed action. He pressured his commander in the Middle East, Wavell, into too many offensives in the first half of 1941, and sacked him for not winning them all. He wore down the morale of his CIGS, Sir John Dill, and sorely tried the temper of his more robust successor, Alan Brooke. The naval historian Captain S.W.Roskill has written: 'Between 1939 and 1943 there was not one admiral in an important sea command ... whom Churchill, sometimes with Pound's support, did not attempt to have relieved.'[17] During this black period of the war, the careers of a number of men were permanently blighted. They were bound to recall the darker side of Churchill. But after Montgomery's victory in the desert, the war was an almost continuous success, and Churchill for the most part more benign. By the end of the war those who, like Alan Brooke, had stayed the course, were captivated by Churchill despite the blows he had dealt them. He was, as General Ismay observed, 'a child of nature with moods as variable as an April day'. Always inclined to emotional behaviour, he could radiate so many different feelings towards a colleague in the course of one day as to break down all sense of normality in his associates, leaving them in a state of dazed and admiring surrender. George Mallaby, who served as Secretary to the Joint Planning Staff from 1943–5, has described what it was like to observe Churchill when he was taking the chair at a meeting. When the discussion began, 'that child-like face became the reflection of the man – the set bulldog look ... the sulky look of a pouting child, the angry violent look of an animal at bay, the tearful look of a compassionate woman, and the sudden spontaneous smiling look of a boy'.[18]

As Mallaby points out it was always surprising, in view of Churchill's reputation as the man of blood and iron, to be reminded of the softer and more vulnerable aspects of his character. The psychiatrist Anthony Storr has argued, in a brief essay which throws a flood of light on Churchill's inner life, that he was an inherent depressive with little sense of self-esteem. Physically delicate by nature, he sought to conquer his depression through excessive aggression and ambition – but at the end of his life he failed, and relapsed into despair.[19] This frailer side of Churchill had been detected by a critical observer writing in 1920, when Churchill was preaching his crusade against Bolshevism:

> People have got it into their heads that he is a noisy, shameless, truculent and pushing person, a sort of intellectual Horatio Bottomley of the upper classes. Nothing could be further from the truth. Mr Churchill is one of the most sensitive of prominent politicians, and it is only by the exercise of his remarkable courage that he has mastered this element of nervousness. ... Some of his friends have seen him in a state of real weakness, particularly of

physical weakness, and for myself I have never seen him in a truculent or self-satisfied frame of mind.[20]

There were occasions in 1940–5 when his confidence faltered, as in January 1942 when Eden noted that he was 'inclined to be fatalistic about the House, maintained that the bulk of Tories hated him, that he had done all he could and would be only too happy to yield to another'.[21] Similarly in July 1942 when a motion of censure was introduced by the worthy backbencher Sir John Wardlaw-Milne, members were surprised when Churchill, the great warlord, exclaimed at his critic: 'You great hulking bully.'[22] Physically, Churchill still possessed in 1940, at the age of sixty-five, astonishing stamina. But a turning-point in his health occurred in December 1943 when he was on his way home from the Teheran conference, after critical negotiations with Roosevelt and Stalin, and fell seriously ill at Carthage with pneumonia and heart trouble. After this, he found the long hours of administration more tiring, and the mastery of detail more difficult. By the end of the war he was exhausted, and he never recovered in his second premiership the dynamism of the first.

To people who worked with Churchill, his inspiration was unquestionable. But while they found his personality a source of endless fascination, he was troublesome from the point of view of sound and rapid administration. Criticism has often been levelled against his practice of arguing out crucial decisions with tired advisers into the small hours of the morning. It has also been recalled how, in committee meetings, he tended to wander from the agenda, introduce red herrings into the discussion, and persist in stubborn *idées fixes*. He was temperamentally indifferent to the inconvenience his methods caused, and cunning in getting his own way. When a proposal he disliked was raised in Cabinet, he knew how to filibuster and sidetrack the issue. He would sometimes appear not to grasp the implications of an argument which in reality he understood very well. In controversial matters, he was happy for men to appeal to his reason, while he wore down their morale.

This formidable man exercised his authority most unevenly over the range of government activities. In matters of grand strategy he soon acquired the sole effective political authority. In five years he encountered only one challenge on this score from within the House – the motion of censure of July 1942 – and one from within the Cabinet, Sir Stafford Cripps' proposals for reform of the defence machinery in September 1942. After this neither the House nor the Cabinet counted in defence policy; the true check upon his authority came throughout the war from the Chiefs of Staff. In the sense that war is foreign policy carried on by other means, Churchill as Minister of Defence was also virtual dictator in external affairs. In foreign and imperial policy as more normally defined, he was undoubtedly the chief policy-maker, but in this area he worked through the Cabinet, and in partnership with his Foreign Secretary, as a constitutional premier. In the administration of the war economy and civilian affairs at home, the third main sphere of decision, Churchill tried to be as far as possible the absent Prime Minister. Economic management was delegated to the Lord President's Committee; the coordination of supply, after great difficulties, to a Minister of Production; post-war planning to the Reconstruction Committee. Churchill intervened frequently to settle particular questions – such as production priority for the bomber programme – which closely affected the conduct of the military war. He remained also Conservative party Leader, ready to pounce if someone were pushing through a 'controversial' measure, repugnant to Tory principles. But he was inclined to regard domestic affairs as a diversion from his true mission, military leadership.

In his daily conduct of the war Churchill kept late hours, and it is sometimes suggested that after midnight he assembled a palace government of irresponsible favourites – Cherwell, Beaverbrook, Bracken – who swayed his mind with dangerous advice and disrupted the normal machinery of government. The charge of 'government by crony' is easily overdone: in some ways Churchill's system was the very reverse. His self-appointed task as war leader involved the daily transaction of business through a group of key advisers and assistants: his personal secretariat of civil servants, the Defence secretariat, the Chiefs of Staff, particular War Cabinet ministers. Almost all these men were regular government servants or professional politicians in their own right, and to a remarkable extent Churchill took over the administrative personnel of the Chamberlain Government. His Defence staff, for example, headed by General Ismay and his two deputies Colonel Hollis and Colonel Jacob, was simply the former military wing of the secretariat of the Chamberlain War Cabinet. Churchill's radical innovation was to supplement the formal machinery of decision by drawing these men into a daily circus around himself. This deeply impressed the civil servants, who had never been treated by a Prime Minister as familiars. The War Cabinet Secretary, Bridges, wrote:

> There were no frontiers between home and office, between work hours and the rest of the day; work went on everywhere, in his study, in the dining-room, in his bedroom. A summons would come at almost any hour of the day or night to help in some job. Minutes would be dictated, corrected, redictated. One might find oneself unexpectedly sitting in the family circle or sharing a meal while one took his orders.[23]

This mingling of Churchill's private and public life gives a distinctive flavour to the recollections of his intimates. We can therefore all picture him propped up in bed composing minutes, with his cat browsing among the papers on the coverlet; we can see his doctor, Lord Moran, thrown into the company of the great and buttonholing them for his diary; we can imagine that night at Chequers in April 1941 when the Director of Military Operations, Sir John Kennedy, alluded to the possibility of losing Egypt, and Churchill flew at him in front of the assembled company: 'If they lose Egypt, blood will flow. I will have firing parties to shoot the generals.'[24] The drama and human interest of these sessions easily obscures the other side to them. They established a circle of people at the centre of the war effort, bound by intimate ties, who knew exactly the way Churchill's mind was working, and, to an increasing extent, how to handle him. This, despite the rows and bad feeling, gave British war policy a coherence which was notably lacking among the parallel figures on the American side. It is an error to think of Churchill's entourage as a court: it was more of a working party, designed to make the premiership effective by constant discussion and argument.

It did of course include the trio of personal cronies, Bracken, Beaverbrook and Lindemann. All were his creatures in the sense that they owed whatever position they had entirely to his patronage. All were bizarre figures who seemed out of place in Whitehall. Bracken was a renegade Irishman who had arrived in London in 1919, disguised his origins with tall stories, thrust himself into the role of Churchill's aide, and risen in the meantime to the proprietorship of a leading sector of the financial press. As a Conservative MP he gave selfless support to Churchill in his lonely battles of the 1930s, and during his premiership became Parliamentary Private Secretary in 1940–1, and Minister of Information for the remainder of the War. The extent and direction of his influence remain obscure. His chief function, it appears, was to advise Churchill on the human element in domestic politics. He darted about collecting news and gossip, detected political rumblings, and advised Churchill on how to square his critics and reward his friends. He was the unofficial patronage secretary, and Churchill expected him to give his opinion on major appointments, and fix up minor ones with the Government Chief Whip. Because Churchill trusted him, he could speak his mind, as when he counselled against the appointment of another old Harrovian: 'You only want _____ because he was at that bloody old Borstal of yours. I hope to God it won't be going "forty years on".'[25] It was Bracken who prevented Harold Macmillan resigning from the Government at the end of 1942, and found him employment as Minister Resident at Algiers. And when the Home Secretary Herbert Morrison released Oswald Mosley from internment in November 1943, Bracken had the task of bringing round Ernest Bevin, who was extremely angry and threatening to quit.[26] It is unlikely that Bracken influenced general policy, except as Minister of Information from 1941–5. In this role he was very much at home, since he understood Fleet Street and knew his fellow press proprietors extremely well. He was an excellent manager of public relations for Churchill's Government. When the Beveridge Report was ready, Churchill wanted to suppress publicity about it, in case this committed his Government to adopting it. Bracken saw that it was given world-wide publicity, realizing that it was an important weapon for allied propaganda.[27]

Of Churchill's relations with Beaverbrook, Bevin said: 'He's like a man who's married a whore: he knows she's a whore but he loves her just the same.'[28] Beaverbrook and Churchill had both been through the epic high-level intrigues which accompanied the rise and fall of

Lloyd George. Churchill needed affection, and Beaverbrook shared with him a common nostalgia for a shared past, lent him the warm gift of encouragement when he was troubled, and diverted him by his roguish charm as a raconteur of savoury stories. Bracken too was a companion in this sense, but with Churchill as the dominant partner. Beaverbrook, however, could and did dominate Churchill, and was therefore regarded as the Prime Minister's evil genius.

Politically, Churchill's patronage of Beaverbrook could only be a liability to him. The proprietor of the *Daily Express* was disliked by Conservatives as an intriguer, and loathed by Labour men for his brand of right-wing politics. Beaverbrook commanded no political following, but for the whole of 1941 he pursued a bitter quarrel over control of manpower with Bevin, the main pillar of the Government apart from Churchill himself. At the end of 1943, Churchill almost drove the Labour leaders into revolt by trying to make Beaverbrook Minister of Reconstruction.[29] Beyond this, there was a general atmosphere of hostility to the 'Beaver' on personal grounds. If such was the cost, whatever was the benefit of his presence?

His utility as an emotional buttress for Churchill has already been touched upon. Officially, Beaverbrook held the posts of Minister of Aircraft Production (to May 1941), Minister of State (May to June 1941), Minister of Supply (June 1941 to February 1942) and Minister of War Production (February 1942). Since August 1940 he had been a member of the War Cabinet. After frequent threats of resignation, he threw up the new post of War Production after only a few days in February 1942, and was then outside the Government until Churchill brought him back as Lord Privy Seal in September 1943, this time outside the War Cabinet.

Churchill put him in charge of aircraft production in the knowledge that he would break all the Whitehall rules in order to get priority for supplies to the factories. His business tycoon methods shocked the Air Ministry, but the historian of war production has confirmed that his methods worked, and speeded up the output of fighters in time for the Battle of Britain.[30] Beaverbrook's second main contribution was his championing of the needs of Russia in the War Cabinet, following Hitler's invasion in June 1941. There was a general belief in Whitehall that Russia would swiftly collapse. It would therefore be a prodigal waste to send any quantity of supplies to Stalin.

Beaverbrook thought that Russia would survive, and pressed as Minister of Supply for the maximum aid to be sent. He began to call for the launching of a Second Front in the West to relieve the pressure on the Red Army. In these policies he was opposed by the Foreign Office, the Chiefs of Staff, and the Labour leaders. While he was out of office in 1942–3 he campaigned for the Second Front and indulged in obscure political intrigues. In his term as Lord Privy Seal he fought a losing battle, supported by Bracken and Amery, to establish post-war imperial preference; Churchill, falling in with the advice of J.M.Keynes and American demands, endorsed the proposals adopted at Bretton Woods. Later Beaverbrook believed that he and his papers could win the 1945 election for Churchill and his party. After Churchill's broadcast warning that socialism would require a police force on the lines of the Gestapo, Attlee replied: 'The voice we heard last night was that of Mr Churchill, but the mind was that of Lord Beaverbrook.' Beaverbrook's contribution was a variegated one, but his part in the Battle of Britain and his championship of Russia outweighed all the debit items in his wartime career.

F.A.Lindemann ('the Prof') was Churchill's chief adviser in both economic and scientific affairs. In 1941 he was made Viscount Cherwell, by which name he is discussed here. Although he was a most powerful man, he was not a member of the Government until he was appointed Paymaster-General in December 1942. He had arrived in Whitehall by a curious route. By birth and character Cherwell was an aristocrat, whose father's family came from Alsace. By training he was a physicist, and when Churchill first met him in 1921, he had just taken command of the Clarendon laboratories at Oxford as Professor of Experimental Philosophy (Physics). Their friendship developed into a political partnership and Churchill was drawn into the celebrated .conflict between Tizard and Cherwell over air defence before the war. When Churchill became First Lord of the Admiralty he established Cherwell there as the head of a private economic intelligence unit which gathered statistics to demolish the arguments of other departments. In May 1940 this became the Prime Minister's statistical section, working solely for Churchill.

The administration of the wartime economy required a continuous series of decisions about the allocation of scarce resources. The overall planning of the economy was eventually shouldered by the Lord President's Committee, assisted by the staff of the economic section of the War Cabinet. The function of Cherwell's statistical section was to provide Churchill with the means of focusing upon particular problems. Churchill often wanted to enforce some priority in the allocation of manpower or shipping space, or in the distribution of resources for civilian consumption. The statistical section made inquiries on his behalf, and Cherwell presented the results in simple charts and briefs recommending decisions. Frequently Cherwell's team briefed Churchill against a proposal which one of his ministers was putting forward. 'You can see how embarrassing it was,' wrote Oliver Lyttelton, an old friend of Churchill's who became Minister of Production in 1942, 'for Ministers to be knocked about on matters of fact, when they had not even seen the figures that were being used *against* them.'[31] Churchill was especially anxious to keep up levels of civilian consumption, and employed the section to oppose proposals for more rationing, or the diversion of resources to military needs. Cherwell's unit represented the first systematic attempt in Whitehall to collect statistics for use in decisions, pioneering the ground ahead of the Central Statistical Office. It has not yet been assessed in any detail, but it certainly gave Cherwell scope to investigate almost any aspect of government business.

In the field of post-war reconstruction Churchill, who knew very little of what was going on, relied heavily upon Cherwell for advice. On 12 January and 14 February 1943 Churchill dictated memoranda intended to postpone and maybe even shelve the carrying out of the Beveridge Report, the great blueprint of the welfare state. Who advised him to do this? Cherwell had a hand in it, for he stressed the view that in the long run there would have to be a choice between the Beveridge scheme and other proposals for social improvement, since it would be impossible to afford them all. But his comments paled by comparison with the massive obstruction of the Treasury, the true enemy of the plan.[32] In general Cherwell's advice on post-war problems was liberal. He wrote favourable briefs for Churchill on the White Papers on employment policy and the National Health Service. Churchill himself was alarmed by the health proposals, and turned to Bracken and Beaverbrook for ammunition against them.[33]

Cherwell's role as scientific adviser is more of an enigma. Sir Charles Snow has delivered an account of his influence which, if true, would make the flesh creep. He dwells on the antagonism between Tizard and Cherwell. Tizard, he argues, was by far the better scientist, but Cherwell, through his position as Churchill's courtier, was able to exclude Tizard and grasp the levers of scientific power himself, with terrible consequences.[34] But is Snow right? Until we know more about the scientific war, the verdict must be: 'not proven'. For although Snow tries to clinch the argument by discussing the decision to mount the area bombing offensive against Germany, his account of this great issue is misleading. Snow has two points to make about the strategic bombing offensive. The first is that it was a bad policy, wasteful and ineffective. There is a great deal of evidence to support this. His second point is that area bombing was adopted as British policy because Cherwell was the chief scientific adviser. Cherwell, the argument runs, produced in March 1942 a memorandum which purported to prove statistically that bombing alone would destroy Germany's power of resistance, by rendering one third of her population homeless. Two other scientists, Tizard and Blackett, utterly refuted Cherwell's statistics, but nevertheless strategic bombing, according to the Cherwell policy, 'was put into action with every effort the country could make'.

This is wrong. The main reason for the adoption of strategic bombing was that it had long been the doctrine of the air staff, at that time under Portal. They laid down the policy afresh in a directive of February, before Cherwell's paper. The main influence upon Churchill in inclining him towards the policy was Air Chief Marshal Harris, who was appointed, also in February, as C-in-C Bomber Command. A controversy was developing between the air force and the navy about the use of bombers, with the navy demanding their secondment to a supporting role in the battle of the Atlantic. The papers of Cherwell and his fellow scientists were incidental propaganda in an issue which could never be decided on scientific grounds. This was apparent when, as a result of the Cherwell memorandum, a committee was set up to inquire into the effects of strategic bombing. The conclusions were indecisive. If the committee proved anything, say the official historians of the bombing offensive, it was that 'a decision about bombing policy could not be arrived at on the basis of academic investigations into the prospects of a strategic bombing offensive'.[35] It was the sort of question which had to be resolved by political instinct. Churchill – while not adopting the whole-hogging view that bombing alone would end the war – did decide that the strategic bombing offensive should rank second only to the invasion of Europe in the war. The responsibility, therefore, rests fairly and squarely with him and his fighting instinct.

Snow also argues that Cherwell delayed the introduction in 1942–3 of 'window', a device for confusing German radar which might have saved many bombers and crews. But the then Director of Scientific Intelligence at the Air Ministry, R.V.Jones, has pointed out that although Cherwell was probably wrong, his view only prevailed because of the weight of expert opinion which supported him at the time. Cherwell was not a dictator. In 1943–4 he argued that the impending German rocket attack was an intelligence hoax. Jones argued that it was authentic, and it was his opinion which Churchill and his advisers accepted. Churchill fully appreciated the problem of having one scientist in a pre-eminent position, and he made a notable attempt to overcome it. At one point in the war he called Tizard to see him. He explained that as a layman he was unqualified to determine scientific points when they were in dispute. He would therefore prefer an arrangement whereby Tizard and Lindemann submitted advice jointly. It was Tizard who pointed out to him that this was impossible. In scientific questions, authorities necessarily differed, and the only possible system was to have one final authority, and to rely upon his judgement. Churchill therefore continued to employ Cherwell, who understood how to explain scientific issues to him.[36]

This effort by Churchill to bring in Tizard, his friend's opponent, is one instance of a marked feature of his political style, his Whiggish instinct for breadth and tolerance. He was usually too big a man to bear rancour for the past, or to play favourites when it would upset the political balance. Thus while R.A.Butler had been an appeaser, and Macmillan a staunch Churchillian, Butler became a minister while Macmillan still laboured as an Under-Secretary – a situation repeated at a higher level in 1951, when Butler was made Chancellor, and Macmillan only Minister of Housing. And we have only to compare the general run of appointments in the war years with the record of the 1930s to see that Churchill and his advisers displayed a consistent skill in selecting the right man for the job. One example was the reshuffle which followed Chamberlain's resignation, when Morrison was made Home Secretary in place of Anderson, and Anderson Lord President in place of Chamberlain. Anderson had drawn up the plans for civil defence before the war, and as Home Secretary was now responsible for their execution. In the first shock of the Blitz, he became a scapegoat for much that went wrong. It was therefore adroit to replace him by Morrison, whose whole life had been bound up with London. Meanwhile Chamberlain's departure left a gap for another administrator of his calibre to run the home front. Anderson filled the bill brilliantly. Not only was he a renowned administrator, but he was not a party politician, and was therefore a safe man for home affairs. Nor was Churchill afraid to appoint to an office a man who had in the past differed from him over the very matters which he would now be handling. The Prime Minister was sure enough of his powers to believe that poachers could be turned into gamekeepers. He was therefore content to send Cripps on his mission to India in the spring of 1942, or allow the Labour leaders a large part in reconstruction.

In May 1940 Churchill was obliged to set up, against his own inclinations, a War Cabinet of only five members, four of whom had no departmental responsibilities. The theory was that ministers would be free to chair a series of key committees, and devote their minds to the whole range of Cabinet business. By January 1941 there were eight members of the Cabinet, four in charge of departments, and the committee system was in decline. In place of the various home front committees business was concentrated increasingly in one only: the Lord President's Committee. Problems of supply were an administrative headache throughout 1941, and a lasting solution was only found in the appointment of a Minister of War Production, who was essentially a coordinator of the programmes of the supply departments – the Admiralty, Ministry of Supply, and Ministry of Aircraft Production. With this innovation the machinery of Churchill's administration was at last settled.

On the military side, Churchill gradually emancipated himself from Cabinet control. At first he punctiliously referred major decisions to the War Cabinet and its sub-committees, the Defence Committee

(Operations) and the Defence Committee (Supply). But as his confidence waxed, the War Cabinet began to fade out of the picture. In the last two years of the war it was only once consulted on a strategic issue. The sub-committees also withered. The number of meetings held each year of the Defence Committee (Operations) was as follows: 1941, 76; 1942, 20; 1940, 14; 1944, 10; 1945, 4. Churchill much preferred, when he wanted political advice on a strategic issue, to invite selected ministers to attend his sessions with the Chiefs of Staff.[37] There were murmurings occasionally against Churchill's 'one-man band', but his Cabinet colleagues were content for him to conduct the war by himself. On one occasion when Churchill was in dispute with the Chiefs of Staff, and brought in the War Cabinet to support him, Bevin said bluntly that he knew nothing about the war and neither did the others: Churchill should get on with it, or get out.[38]

At the heart of the war effort was Churchill's relationship with the three Chiefs of Staff. He and they were linked by a secretariat under General Ismay, who attended every meeting of the COS (Chiefs of Staff) Committee as Churchill's representative. The Chiefs of Staff themselves had two important sub-committees working under them: the Joint Intelligence Committee, and the Joint Planning Committee, which tested and devised possible operations. Asquith and Lloyd George in 1914–18 had none of the good fortune of Churchill in inheriting this efficient machinery, which embodied and unified the professional wisdom of the three services.

There has been strong criticism of Churchill as a military leader. Sir Basil Liddell Hart wrote that 'his fighting instinct governed his course, his emotions swamped his calculations, and reason asserted itself too late. In brief, his dynamism was too strong for his statesmanship – and his strategy.'[39] The Alanbrooke diaries, the only intimate record so far of Churchill's dealings with the Chiefs of Staff, often convey the impression of a mad bull running at a gate: 'God knows where we should be without him, but God knows where we shall go with him!'[40]

A number of qualifications have to be introduced into this picture of a wild man checked only by the sober resistance of his advisers. To begin with it is wrong to judge Churchill as a strategist pure and simple. As Prime Minister he was subject to political anxieties which reinforced his natural aggressiveness. Thus it was politically very important to try to aid Greece by sending troops in March 1941, even if it was strategically absurd. And it was with the idea of deterring Japan from entering the war that Churchill sent the *Prince of Wales* and the *Repulse* to the Far East at the end of 1941, only to see them sunk after the attack on Pearl Harbour. The alarming scheme for a landing in Norway in 1941–2 was Churchill's response to the plight of Russia. It used to be argued that his opposition to the Second Front in Europe also had political roots in detestation of Russia and Balkan ambitions. We now know that in 1942 at least, Churchill's behaviour was the very reverse. He was so conscious of his obligations to Stalin that in the last three months of the year he badgered the Chiefs of Staff constantly about the need to launch an invasion of Europe in 1943.[41] Political ambition entered much more into the Far East. Churchill's long and fruitless campaign of 1943–4 to pressure his advisers into the capture of Sumatra was the outcome of an intense desire to recover face in the Far East after the humiliation of the surrender of Singapore.

While there were continuous arguments, there was also a broad consensus between Churchill and his advisers. In 1941 as he crossed the Atlantic in the *Duke of York*, he addressed three long and lucid minutes to the Chiefs of Staff, sweeping the strategic horizon for 1942 and 1943, and proposing an overall plan. The official historian says of these minutes: 'There was indeed little that was novel or spectacular in the plan proposed; it was a simple application of familiar principles of warfare. Where the Prime Minister's strength lay was in his ability to discern these principles clearly, and apply them correctly, on the vast scale of modern operations.'[42]

When there were disputes between Churchill and his advisers, the Prime Minister's authority was, in the last analysis, weak. He bullied them because he knew he could not command them. They held the ace. When Admiral Pound decided against the Norwegian exploit, he shook his head and Churchill was beaten.[43] The Prime Minister remembered how Gallipoli, and the resignation of the First Sea Lord Admiral Fisher, had ruined his career in 1915. He would not in the last resort dare to push through a military decision against the will of his professional advisers, in case when things went wrong the blame should fall exclusively upon him. He never overruled the Chiefs of Staff on a purely military question. Nor did he remove Alan Brooke despite his quarrels with him. Chamberlain had surrounded himself with like minds, but Churchill appreciated people who could stand up to him, and he behaved worst of all to men like Dill and Wavell in whom he could not detect the fighting instinct.

But he absolutely refused to yield any of his control over military affairs. From the fiasco of Dahar in September 1940 to the fall of Tobruk in June 1942, there was a long story of military defeat. By the beginning of 1942 a strong current of criticism was noticeable in the House and the press, and when Sir Stafford Cripps returned home from Russia, where he had been Ambassador, he was built up as the new leader who would restore inspiration and reform the Government. Churchill was obliged to give him a seat in the War Cabinet, and despite the failure of his Indian mission soon afterwards, Cripps remained a considerable force to reckon with. In July Wardlaw-Milne moved his vote of censure on the central conduct of the war, and although only twenty-five MPs voted against the Government on that occasion, Churchill was aware that any further military setbacks would jeopardize his position. He was therefore alarmed when Cripps took up the popular cry for a reform of the defence machinery. Cripps proposed to take away from the COS Committee the planning of strategy and operations, leaving them with the function of executive command. Planning would be carried out by a separate War Planning Directorate of three. There was no thought in Cripps' mind of urging Churchill to give up as Minister of Defence, but his plan would have placed the Prime Minister under much stricter restraint, with two bodies instead of one to resist him. So uncertain was Churchill of his own position that he wrestled with these proposals – which he considered quite unworkable – through September. He could not afford a breach with Cripps before he knew the outcome of the forthcoming battle in the desert.[44] On 3 October Cripps handed in his resignation. Cunningly Churchill neither accepted nor rejected it, but awaited the news from the Middle East. Then came victory at El Alamein. Churchill accepted Cripps' resignation and appointed him outside the War Cabinet as Minister of Aircraft Production, a job he kept for the rest of the war. Cripps was the one man to emerge during the war as a genuine alternative type of leader. As an intellectual and former scientist, as the embodiment of left-of-centre progress at home, as a devout Christian who believed in the moral purpose of the war, Cripps combined all the appeals which Churchill most strikingly lacked. But he was too mild and innocent a figure to get the better of the Prime Minister.

Churchill admitted the existence of only one other contemporary statesman in Britain and the Commonwealth who rose to his own level and whose every judgement must be respected. This was Jan Christiaan Smuts, the Prime Minister of South Africa, and according to Churchill 'one of the greatest living men'.[45] Smuts, even more than Beaverbrook was a veteran of Churchill's own vintage. His own ambitions to dominate Africa, and Churchill's passion for the Mediterranean, gave them a joint interest in the Middle East and North Africa. Churchill's decision to sack Auchinleck in August 1942 owed much to Smuts: and in 1943 Smuts worked up Churchill in favour of various Mediterranean diversions from the Second Front.[46] Perhaps the secret was that this shrewd and hard Afrikaner not only gave Churchill the kind of advice he wanted to hear, and lent him his starchy respectability, but would never prove any kind of threat.

Smuts was one of the handful of men on either side of the Atlantic who knew about the plans to develop the atom bomb. At the end of the war Sir John Anderson, who had been responsible throughout for the 'Tube Alloys' project, urged that the Cabinet should be informed of the bomb so that it could discuss the vital question of the international control of atomic energy. Churchill, however, withheld the secret from the Cabinet.[47] This was not an example of government by secret circle so much as of normal practice, which Attlee was to follow in the case of the hydrogen bomb: the justification was the need to keep state secrets secret. On major political issues of the normal kind Churchill was punctilious in consulting the War Cabinet. He naturally referred to it the text of the Atlantic Charter, which he and Roosevelt had composed, and accepted an additional clause on social security. There was no time for him to call the Cabinet before his famous broadcast on the invasion of Russia, pledging aid to Stalin, but he consulted Eden, Cripps and Beaverbrook.[48] The Cabinet approved the doctrine of unconditional surrender before it was proclaimed at Casablanca, and in December 1944 fully concurred in the suppression of the Greek rebellion. But if he by-passed the War Cabinet over strategic decisions, and usually dominated it in questions of foreign and imperial policy, he was virtually at a loss to control its major sub-committees on the home front, the Lord President's Committee and the Reconstruction Committee. 'I feel very much,' he wrote to Attlee in November 1944, 'the domination of these committees by the force and power of your representatives.'[49]

It was a remarkable testimony to Churchill as a leader that although the party he represented was under almost constant attack from within the country during the war, this never damaged his position as war leader. This was amply demonstrated in the press. In all the military tribulations of 1941–2, as in all the controversy over the post-war future after Beveridge, the national press never questioned his title to the premiership. The war had inevitably revolutionised relations between Whitehall and Fleet Street. A Press Censorship Bureau under Admiral Thomson had the task of issuing D-Notices to prevent information of value to the enemy from appearing, but its relations with Fleet Street were excellent. What disturbed the press were the powers held by the Government under Regulation 2D to suppress any newspaper which the Home Secretary considered to be systematically publishing material designed to foment opposition to the war effort. In January 1941 Churchill and Morrison closed down the Communist *Daily Worker* and Claud Cockburn's *The Week*. This caused apprehension, justifiably, for in February 1942, with the wholehearted concurrence of Morrison, Churchill threatened the *Daily Mirror* with suppression. This was utter nonsense. The *Mirror* was a tonic for servicemen because it let off steam against spit-and-polish and the sergeant-major. Churchill, however, believed that it was undermining army discipline. The *Mirror* survived, greatly sobered, and the Government fell back on the technique of calling up columnists who were thought to show too little first-hand experience of military matters. Churchill was by no means alone in finding press criticism infuriating, for Morrison and Bevin also displayed intolerance. But he read all the daily newspapers with the closest attention as they were rushed to him from the presses, and perhaps attributed too much importance to them – in the First World War they had played a much more powerful role. Although *The Times* was traditionally the newspaper closest to the Government, Churchill was on distant terms with Printing House Square, and paid more attention to the *Manchester Guardian*. He praised it often, and took the greatest care in briefing its editor, W.P.Crozier. The *Guardian* was often critical of the Government, but Churchill regarded it as well informed and well disposed.[50]

He expected the House of Commons to give him support, and although he was nervous of its moods in 1941–2, he knew he was the undisputed master thereafter. There were several backbench revolts during his premiership, but only one in July 1942 against his leadership. One hundred and ten Conservatives voted against Bevin's Catering Wages Act on 8 February 1943, and in a tit for tat, ninety-seven Labour MPs voted against the Government's attitude to the Beveridge Report nine days later. However irritated Churchill might be at such goings-on, so far as the war effort was concerned they were noises off-stage. In March 1944 the Government was defeated by one vote when an amendment was brought forward on the Education Bill, calling for equal pay for women teachers. Churchill went down to the House the following day and announced that he had decided to make the matter the subject of a vote of confidence, and force the House to reverse its decision. This, he felt, would be a lesson to all the critics who failed to understand that there was a war on.[51]

As the war developed, Churchill's energies were drawn away from his initial task, the mobilization and defence of Britain, to the balance of world forces. Russia entered the war in June 1941, America in December. Henceforth he was continuously involved in the joint planning of Anglo-American strategy, and the prickly relationship with Stalin. In wartime, military policy embodied so many aspects of relations with other powers, that Churchill's sway in foreign affairs was virtually unchecked. His chief lieutenant was Anthony Eden, whom he appointed Foreign Secretary in December 1940. When George VI requested advice on who should succeed to the premiership if Churchill were killed, Churchill recommended him to send for Eden. The Prime Minister tended to dominate his Foreign Secretary, who was well over twenty years younger than himself. But Eden spoke not for himself alone, but for the Foreign Office, and he stood by its views when Churchill was taking a different line. On the eve of the D-Day landings Churchill wanted to repudiate de Gaulle as leader of the French. The Foreign Office had always thought well of de Gaulle and Eden, with the help of Attlee and Bevin, brought Churchill round.[52] A parallel occasion was the Morgenthau affair. The American Secretary to the Treasury urged Churchill to adopt his plan for dismantling German industry ('pastoralization') at the end of the war. Cherwell weighed in with the argument that Britain's post-war trade would benefit, and Churchill was persuaded. Eden and the Foreign Office had to restore him to reason by pointing out that the idea was improper and unworkable.[53] In the case of Yugoslavia Churchill in effect pursued a foreign policy which the Foreign Office opposed. He switched support from the right-wing guerilla leader Mihailovitch to the Communist guerrilla leader Tito, and established a military mission under his personal auspices. Churchill was concerned with military expediency, the Foreign Office with the spread of Communism. Another great Churchillian franchise in the heart of the Foreign Office domain was Harold Macmillan's sphere of influence in the Mediterranean, built up while he was Minister Resident at the allied headquarters at Algiers. As the Anglo-American forces conquered the Mediterranean, Macmillan guided the reconstruction of French, Italian, Yugoslav and Greek politics. The British Ambassadors to these countries were effectively under his direction.

Churchill was content to allow the Foreign Office to elaborate paper plans for the post-war organization of the world, knowing that power would follow in the wake of the forces he was directing. The key to the future balance of power lay in his cooperation with Roosevelt in winning the war. Churchill and Roosevelt entered into correspondence, at Roosevelt's invitation, while Churchill was at the Admiralty in October 1939. They met nine times in 1940-5 and were in each other's company for about 120 days altogether. They determined European strategy, Stalin being merely informed of decisions. Churchill's handling of Roosevelt was one of the summits of his achievement. In the first phase of their relationship, before Pearl Harbour, Churchill took the initiative in the subtle erosion of American neutrality. In the second phase, from Pearl Harbour to the Normandy landings in June 1944, Britain, and therefore Churchill, was the dominant military partner in the alliance – in 1943 Britain had almost three times as many men and four times as many ships in the Mediterranean as America. Thwarting the American desire for a Second Front, Churchill put all his skill into leading Roosevelt into the conquest of the Mediterranean and the invasion of Italy. After the summer of 1944, however, America rapidly overtook Britain as a military power in Europe, and Churchill's influence over strategy declined.

Churchill was unsuccessful in his attempts to persuade Roosevelt in the last weeks of his life of the dangers he saw in Russian expansion. Moreover his own attempt to negotiate with Stalin proved to be a failure. In the spring of 1944 the Red Army began to cross Russia's frontiers, and Churchill reacted with alarm. 'Broadly speaking,' he wrote to Eden in May, 'the issue is, are we going to acquiesce in the Communisation of the Balkans and perhaps of Italy?'[54] In the belief that through man-to-man discussions he could at least reach agreement for the containment of Russian power, Churchill flew to Moscow in October 1944, and reached his celebrated agreement with the Russian dictator on spheres of influence in the Balkans. Stalin agreed that Britain should have a dominant influence in Greece, and when British forces put down the Communist-inspired rising there in December, no word of criticism was heard from Russia. Churchill, who probably attached far too much importance to the vague agreement he had reached with Stalin[55], became convinced that the Russian ('that great and good man') had kept his word, and a lasting accommodation been reached. In this mood of optimism he attended the Yalta conference, at which Stalin promised free elections in Poland and the rest of eastern Europe. On his return, Churchill told the House:

> 'The impression I brought back from the Crimea . . . is that Marshal Stalin and the Soviet leaders wish to live in honourable friendship and equality with the western democracies. I feel also that their word is their bond. I know of no Government which stands to its obligations, even in its own despite, more solidly . . .'[56]

This was Churchill's Munich. A large area of Polish territory had been ceded to Russia on the understanding that the remainder was to be independent, and that Stalin had given his word. This miscalculation was perhaps a sign that Churchill's grip had weakened, for it was Stalin himself who had once said, in sincere tribute, that Churchill was the kind of man 'who will pick your pocket of a kopeck if you don't watch him . . . Roosevelt is not like that. He dips in his hand only for bigger coins. But Churchill? Churchill – will do it for a kopeck.'[57]

Absorbed in global problems, Churchill had not sought to provide leadership in domestic and post-war issues. It was the general assumption among politicians right up to the election itself that Churchill would be returned to power: his rejection appeared unthinkable. In 1943 he was hoping that Labour would join with him in the reconstruction period, and at that time Attlee, Bevin, Morrison and Dalton were all privately in favour of accepting. Dalton told Kingsley Martin, the editor of the *New Statesman*, that it would be 'total lunacy' to oppose Churchill at a general election. On six occasions between June 1943 and June 1945, BIPO predicted a decisive Labour victory[58], but no one seems to have taken much notice of opinion polls at that time.

It is generally agreed that one of the main reasons for the Conservative defeat in 1945 was the fact that Labour was identified with the goals of full employment and the welfare state, while the Conservatives were not. Part of the explanation for this lies in the fact that during the war Churchill and his political friends were absorbed in military and international affairs, while the Labour leaders were strongly represented on the sub-committees which dealt with post-war plans. Woolton, the Minister of Reconstruction, and R. A. Butler, the Minister of Education, were both deeply aware of the political importance of social policy, but Woolton was not at this time a Conservative, and Butler – the only leading Conservative to predict that his party would lose – was outside Churchill's circle. The whole outlook of the Conservative party could have been modernized and its image changed, had its leaders at that time been more deeply involved in their Government's own programme for the future. When the important White Paper 'Employment Policy' came before the Cabinet in May 1944, Churchill said that he had not read it, nor had he managed to read the note which Cherwell had written for him about it. But he had read the first sentence of Cherwell's note, which recommended acceptance, so he gladly gave his consent.[59] After the electoral defeat of 1945, the Conservative leadership had to bring in Woolton and Butler to educate them in the new ideas of 1942–5, ideas which had been developed within their own Government.

In the spring of 1945 it was expected that two years would elapse between the surrender of Germany and the surrender of Japan. Churchill hoped that Labour would stay in coalition for this period, and when Attlee was obliged by the Labour NEC to refuse his invitation to do so, Churchill insisted on a quick election on 5 July: Attlee had wanted an autumn contest. On 23 May 1945 Labour therefore resigned from the coalition and Churchill formed a caretaker government, with Butler as Minister of Labour, Macmillan as Secretary for Air and Bracken – to the delight of political commentators – as First Lord of the Admiralty. The story of the 1945 election campaign has been well told[60] and does not concern us here. Churchill felt no conviction in abusing Labour. 'I could never,' he had remarked, 'attack these men who have shared so loyally with me the burden and trials of our darkest days.'[61] The Conservative party, with a past it was happy to conceal, attempted to ride to victory on Churchill's coat tails, turning the election into a vote of confidence in the great man. Labour emphasized the issues and stood for a square deal in social and economic policy. Labour won 393 seats, the Conservatives 213. How many more seats would the Conservatives have lost but for Churchill?

The period of Opposition and the second premiership form an epilogue. As a result of the scale of the Conservative defeat, an extensive inquest was held, and the leadership broadened by the inclusion of Butler and Woolton. Churchill continued to take an Olympian view of his party and confined his leadership of the Opposition in the House to major speeches on important issues, leaving to others the daily conduct of hard fighting. He devoted much time to writing his history, *The Second World War*. The two great themes running through his speeches were European unity and the cold war. He launched the Council of Europe, and in 1950 advocated a European army 'in which we should bear a worthy and honourable part'. In the general election campaign of 1950 it was noted that the Conservative campaign was this time a collective one by party leaders, in contrast to the emphasis of Churchill alone in 1945.[62] In the October 1951 election 'Mr Churchill spoke less than any other leading figure in the campaign'. He was by this time considerably mellowed and his single broadcast was commented upon for its moderation and 'thought by many to have been his finest personal effort since the war'.[63] Because of the dispute with Persia, Labour tried to represent him as a warmonger who would take the dispute over the brink and send out British troops. But the scare failed.

W.N.Medlicott has described Churchill's third administration as 'by a long stretch the most successful peacetime ministry that the country had seen since 1918'.[64] If this is true, it must be in a very negative sense only. In 1945–51 the Labour Government carried through a series of great measures against a background which included economic collapse in Europe and the first great crisis of the cold war. The Churchill Government accepted Labour's legislative measures (except for the nationalization of steel), and even acquired a progressive reputation for having done so. Meanwhile, external conditions were relatively tranquil, and the era of chronic economic shortages was passing.

Churchill was elected with an overall majority of seventeen, a narrow margin which clearly dictated moderate tactics. Churchill devoted great care to selecting the Cabinet. It numbered sixteen, two fewer than Attlee's. He had a threefold aim: to restore the inner circle, reward the men of greatest weight in the party, and give the Cabinet as 'national' an appearance as possible. The junior appointments – 'Churchill hardly knows the names' – were made with the help of H.F.G.Crookshank, a senior figure in the party, and the Chief Whip.[65]

Churchill made himself Minister of Defence but quickly discovered that at seventy-eight he was too old to cope with the extra work, and Earl Alexander of Tunis was summoned from Canada. Other old familiars were plucked from their commitments and tenderly returned to the inner circle – Colville from the Lisbon embassy to be Principal Secretary, Ismay from private life to be Commonwealth Secretary and later first NATO Secretary General. But if Cherwell returned it was only briefly, and Beaverbrook and Bracken were absent. The Conservatives during the campaign had promised to build 300,000 houses a year, and Churchill shrewdly gave the job to Harold Macmillan, the man of *The Middle Way*. He was told that the job was a gamble but (tearfully) 'every humble home will bless your name, if you succeed'.[66] Naturally Eden returned as Foreign Secretary to the only department he had even been given the chance to master. It had been expected that Oliver Lyttelton would become Chancellor but Churchill opted for R.A.Butler, who was more acceptable to middle of the road opinion.

In time of economic troubles the Government needed a Minister of Labour capable of winning the confidence of trade unionists. Once again choosing astutely, Churchill selected Walter Monckton, a barrister long connected with politics but scarcely at all with the Tory party. Churchill's instructions were that he was to preserve industrial peace, a conciliatory policy, as Samuel Brittan describes it, of 'bringing the two sides together even at the cost of highly inflationary settlements'.[67] There were attempts at innovation. Churchill announced that three Cabinet ministers would act as 'overlords' to coordinate groups of departments: Woolton for food and agriculture, Leathers for transport, fuel and power, and Cherwell for research and development. The plan evaporated. Responsibility remained with the separate departments. The ministers were not to be held responsible to Parliament for the departments they coordinated, and when Woolton let this cat out of the bag, the scheme lapsed.[68] Churchill still distrusted the Treasury and established a watchdog to bark at it, the Treasury Advisory Committee. It gave the Treasury staff trouble for a time, and then faded away into the Cabinet Economic Policy Committee.

With the construction of his Government, Churchill's greatest work was done. For the first eighteen months in office, before his very serious stroke of June 1953, Churchill was still vigorous in Cabinet. 'He could be patient,' George Mallaby tells us, 'conciliatory, cunning, short-tempered, morose, procrastinating, contradictory, as the occasion demanded. He was always very pugnacious and never very business-like.'[69] He interfered far less with the departments. Anthony Eden worked patiently and successfully to wind up the Korean and Indo-Chinese wars, free now of Churchill's dominance. R.A.Butler and the Treasury, inheriting grave trading deficits and disappearing currency reserves, achieved through a combination of good management and better terms of trade an economic recovery. From 1952 the remaining rations and controls were removed, and the sales of cars and televisions rose. The Treasury sought a permanent solution to the problem of the pound by putting forward a plan called 'Robot' for a constantly floating exchange rate. After listening over a period to the arguments Churchill decided, on the advice of Cherwell and Salter, against it.

What direction did Churchill impart to his Government? The death of Stalin in March 1953 raised expectations of a more reasonable Russian foreign policy, and Churchill in a speech of 11 May 1953 suggested a summit conference. But President Eisenhower did not want to negotiate. Churchill disliked the McCarthyites and considered that the Americans were too inflexible towards Russia: 'They want to make enemies of Russia and to stir up her satellite states. That can only lead to a war. Malenkov is, I feel, a good man, I wish I could meet him.'[70] But this was impossible, for British dependence on the United States was established.

If the Americans blocked his policy of settling with Russia, at home he found himself lost for a theme. 'In the worst of the war I could always see how to do it. Today's problems are elusive and intangible.'[71] He played a significant part in sanctioning commercial television. A well-organized lobby of business interests made the running, and opinion in the party was rather divided. Churchill's relationship with the BBC had been a bad one before 1939 and he objected to its political tone: 'They are honeycombed with Socialists – probably with Communists.'[72]

The Prime Minister was curiously reluctant to follow through his speeches on European unity. The Labour Government had refused to join the European Coal and Steel Community, but the Churchill Cabinet was presented with the further option of the proposed European Defence Community. The moment the new Government was installed, Eden announced that British forces would not participate. In Cabinet, Macmillan and Maxwell-Fyfe argued that British exclusion would be a long-term disaster, while Eden and the Foreign Office, whom Churchill allowed to take the lead, saw no danger in the new European grouping. Only French rejection of EDC disposed of the issue. In place of EDC Eden proposed an extension of the Brussels Treaty Alliance; and under the terms of Western European Union Britain undertook to maintain in Europe a force of four divisions with a tactical air force, for fifty years. In all this Churchill lay fallow, originating ideas but no longer carrying them through. ' "Set the people free," said Mr Churchill. "What about our licensing system?" replied the ministers.'[73]

The extent of Churchill's illness after June 1953 was known to very few. Among them was his son-in-law Christopher Soames, who remarked that it was beginning to be noticed in the House that Churchill was getting deaf. 'He must pull out. He mustn't meet the new Parliament as Prime Minister.' Already the next general election cast a shadow, as Macmillan writes: 'We had a number of very able Ministers; but with the physical disabilities from which Churchill still suffered and the fact that the second most powerful figure was the Foreign Secretary, we felt that in home affairs we were drifting without the formulation of any fixed plan – without a new theme or a new faith.'[74]

Churchill harked back to the past nostalgically, but he did so in his conversation rather than his politics. After three years of conflict in Egypt, an agreement was signed on 19 October 1953 for the withdrawal of British troops. The Government was opposed on this issue by a group of diehards led by Captain Waterhouse and Julian Amery, 'the Suez group'. The Churchill who remembered Omdurman found this painful, but the Churchill who was Prime Minister recognised its necessity. The defence estimates were a chronicle of waning power. By 1953 defence expenditure was running at two-thirds of the level proposed by Attlee's three-year programme. Churchill adjusted to this as any Prime Minister would have had to, and even found himself proposing a toast to Nehru at an Old Harrovians' dinner.

Finally, Harold Macmillan urged Churchill that it was time for him to depart. There were other pressures, for Eden's friends 'were loud-mouthed in calling for Churchill's departure and suggested that if Eden's succession were to be long delayed he might become so frustrated that he would have passed the peak of his powers by the time that he entered into the joy of his inheritance'. [75] So on 5 April 1955 in the silence of a newspaper strike Churchill announced his resignation.

The second premiership was so great a contrast with the first that generalizations scarcely span the two together. By 1951 Churchill's skills of manoeuvre were unimpaired, but his capacity for mastering the flow of information, and driving through policies even within his chosen sector, were in steady decline. His second premiership was an honour bestowed on him at the end of his career in recognition of his first, by which he will always be judged.

Why had he made a better Prime Minister than men expected in 1940? Partly because, once in command, he was able to establish a congenial method of government. Partly because he knew his reputation and was determined to live it down. Partly because the old hands in Whitehall knew how to manage him. And mainly because, with all his faults, he was a much greater man than most people had realized. Yet it is difficult, for all his impact on history, to rank him among the innovators who changed or developed the office of Prime Minister. The experiment of abandoning Cabinet control of grand strategy was relevant only in wartime, and only then when there was a Churchill to act as Minister of Defence. The day had not yet dawned when a British Prime Minister could normally be expected to concentrate in his hands the responsibility for strategy in economic affairs. By drawing in outsiders to reinforce his position in Whitehall, Churchill was following in the footsteps of Lloyd George. By his use of the radio to establish himself with the public, Churchill was carrying on where Baldwin left off. His most important legacy to the future occupants of 10 Downing Street was quite simply the ghost of himself – the legendary leader who united the British in patriotism and sacrifice.

Notes

1. Halifax Diary, 18 March 1940. *Hickleton Papers*.
2. John Colville in Sir John Wheeler-Bennett (ed.), *Action This Day* (London 1968), p. 48.
3. Robert Rhodes James, *Churchill: A Study in Failure* (London 1970), pp. 46–7.
4. A.G.Gardiner, *Pillars of Society* (London 1913), pp. 57–8.
5. Ronald Hyam, *Elgin and Churchill at the Colonial Office, 1905–8* (London 1968), p. 502.
6. Harold Nicolson, *Diaries and Letters 1939–45* (London 1967), p. 37. Also Hamilton Fyfe, *Britain's Wartime Revolution* (London 1944), p. 15.
7. Donald MacClachlan, *Room 39* (London 1968), ch. 6.
8. Wheeler-Bennet, *op. cit.*, p. 48. Also *The Memoirs of Lord Ismay* (London 1960), iii.

9. For the change of Government see Laurence Thompson, *1940* (London 1967), ch. V. Also Halifax, *Fulness of Days* (London 1957), p. 219.

10. Nicolson, *op. cit.*, p. 86.

11. Sir Percy Harris, *Twenty Years in and out of Parliament* (London 1947), p. 151.

12. David Dilks (ed.), *The Diaries of Sir Alexander Cadogan 1938–45* (London 1971), p. 290.

13. Winston S. Churchill, *Their Finest Hour* (London 1949), p. 439.

14. George Orwell, *Collected Essays, Journalism and Letters* (London 1970), iv, p. 556.

15. Hadley Cantril, *Public Opinion 1935–46* (Princeton 1951), p. 106.

16. *Churchill by his Contemporaries. An 'Observer' appreciation* (London 1965), p. 86.

17. Captain S.W.Roskill, in 'RUSI Journal' (1972), p. 50.

18. George Mallaby, *From My Level* (London 1965), pp. 29–30.

19. Churchill, *Four Faces and the Man* (London 1960), pp. 203–46.

20. Churchill, 'A Gentleman with a Duster', *The Mirrors of Downing Street* (London 1920), pp. 108–10.

21. Lord Avon, *The Reckoning* (London 1965), p. 318.

22. I wish to thank Lord Butler for this anecdote.

23. *Winston Churchill, Memoirs and Tributes Broadcast by the BBC* (London 1965), p. 95.

24. Sir John Kennedy, *The Business of War* (London 1957), p. 106.

25. James Stuart, *Within the Fringe* (London 1967), p. 107.

26. Alan Bullock, *The Life and Times of Ernest Bevin* (London 1967), ii, pp. 186–7.

27. Francis Williams, *Press Parliament and People* (London 1946), p. 27.

28. Bullock, *op. cit.*, p. 178.

29. Henry Pelling, *Britain and the Second World War* (London 1970), pp. 182–3.

30. M.M.Postan, *British War Production* (London 1952), p. 116. For Beaverbrook through the war see A.J.P.Taylor, *Beaverbrook* (London 1972).

31. Earl of Birkenhead, *The Prof in Two Worlds* (London 1961), p. 215.

32. Winston S. Churchill, *The Hinge of Fate* (London 1951), pp. 861–2. PRO PREM 4 80/2 Memo of Kingsley Wood, 17 November 1942; Memos by Cherwell of 25 November 1942 and 11 February 1943.

33. PREM 4 96/9; PREM 4 36/3, Churchill minute to Eden, 10 February 1944.

34. C.P.Snow, *Science and Government* (London 1962).

35. Sir Charles Webster and Noble Frankland, *The Strategic Air Offensive Against Germany* (London 1961), i, pp. 337–9 for the Singleton inquiry. See also Michael Howard, *Grand Strategy* (London 1972), IV, pp. 20–4.

36. Private information.

37. John Ehrman, *Grand Strategy* (London 1956), vi, pp. 323–6.

38. Bullock, *op. cit.*, p. 108

39. Basil Liddell Hart, 'Churchill as a Military Leader', *Encounter* (April 1965).

40. Arthur Bryant, *The Alanbrooke Diaries: The Turn of the Tide* (London 1957), p. 290.

41. Michael Howard, *op. cit.*, pp. 208–10.
42. J.M.Gwyer, *Grand Strategy* (London 1964), iii, part I, pp. 336–7.
43. Arthur Bryant, *The Turn of the Tide* (London 1957), p. 262.
44. Winston S. Churchill, *The Hinge of Fate*, p. 497.
45. Churchill to Roosevelt, 21 May 1942. PREM 4 28/10.
46. W.K.Hancock Smuts, *The Fields of Force 1939–50* (London, 1968), pp. 377–8, 413–16.
47. Margaret Gowing, *Britain and Atomic Energy 1939–45* (London 1964), pp. 350–2.
48. Churchill to Attlee, 20 November 1944. PREM 4 88/I.
49. *Ibid.*
50. David Ayerst, *Guardian* (1971), pp. 544–7.
51. Lord Butler, *The Art of the Possible* (London 1971), p. 121.
52. Avon, *op. cit.*, pp. 452–7.
53. Llewellyn Woodward, *British Foreign Policy in the Second World War* (London 1962), pp. lv–lvi.
54. Winston S. Churchill, *Closing the Ring* (London 1952), p. 623.
55. Gabriel Kolko, *The Politics of War* (London 1968). pp. 145–6.
56. Winston S. Churchill, *Triumph and Tragedy* (London 1954), p. 351.
57. Milovan Djilas, *Conversations with Stalin* (London 1962), p. 70.
58. Cantril, *op. cit.*, p. 195.
59. Dalton Diary, 19 May 1944.
60. McCallum and Readman, *The General Election of 1945* (London 1947).
61. W.M.Citrine, *Two Careers* (London 1967), p. 229.
62. H.G.Nicholas, *The British General Election of 1950* (London 1951), p. 91.
63. D.E.Butler, *The British General Election of 1951* (London 1952), pp. 66, 99.
64. W.N.Medlicott, *Contemporary England* (London 1967), p. 522.
65. Harold Macmillan, *Tides of Fortune* (London 1969), p. 365.
66. *Ibid*, p. 374.
67. Samuel Brittan, *The Treasury under the Tories* (London 1964), pp. 173–4.
68. John P. Mackintosh, *The British Cabinet* (London 1962), p. 433.
69. Mallaby, *op. cit.*, p. 42.
70. Moran, *op. cit.*, p. 431.
71. *The Memoirs of Lord Chandos* (London 1962), p. 343.
72. Moran, *op. cit.*, p. 390.
73. Lord Woolton, *Memoirs* (London 1959), p. 376.
74. Macmillan, *op. cit.*, p. 529.
75. Randolph S. Churchill, *The Rise and Fall of Sir Anthony Eden* (London 1959), p. 192.

Clement Attlee

Robert E. Dowse

Sometime between 7.00 and 7.30 on the evening of 26 July 1945 Clement Attlee, the disputed Leader of the Parliamentary Labour party, in audience with King George VI, agreed to form a Government to succeed the caretaker administration of Winston Churchill. Behind this apparently placid and normal political succession lay almost fifty years of struggle for power by the Labour party. Immediately preceding it a 'plot' for power within the party had been foiled. After forming two minority administrations in 1924 and 1929–31, both of which had ended in a mixture of farce and electoral defeat, the Labour party had finally won a majority in the House of Commons over all other parties combined.[1] Twenty-two years of virtual Conservative dominance of the House of Commons had vanished, the lean years of opposition were over and with Labour in control the future could be faced hopefully, a future of greater social justice, of international conciliation and of decent living standards for the British masses.

The failed plot was one to unseat Attlee, or rather to prevent his ever obtaining access to power, the monarch's commission to attempt to form an administration. Herbert Morrison, the principal plotter, had a case but lacked support where it really counted and had enemies well placed to outmanoeuvre his every move. His case was a simple one. Firstly, he was the principal architect of the July victory and but for him it is quite probable that there would have been no election in July since Labour might well have remained in the Churchill coalition until after the defeat of Japan.[2] It was Morrison who had convinced, if convincing was needed, the national executive committee of the party on 21 May that further support for the coalition was not politic.[3] Secondly, it is a fact that following the fiasco of Ramsay MacDonald's 'betrayal' of 1931 the annual conference of the party had put restrictions on a Leader of the PLP in accepting office and dissolving Parliament. In

1933 it was decided that a potential Labour Prime Minister should consult the PLP prior to accepting office and Morrison, in urging this course on Attlee, was acting within the mutually understood limits which had been carefully worked out following MacDonald's expulsion from the party in 1931. It is also clear, however, that this was a bid by Morrison for the premiership.[4] Morrison's fatal weakness was the strength of his enemies and the lack of leverage of his 'friends'.[5]

Those actively involved in the attempt to replace Attlee were Harold Laski, Ellen Wilkinson and Maurice Webb who favoured Morrison, and Stafford Cripps who wished for an election by the PLP.[6] It is also clear that at least some members of the PLP, most of whom had had no voice at all in Attlee's selection as Leader of the PLP, wished for an election. An election in the PLP would have given Morrison at least a chance of becoming Prime Minister, but it was clear that once commissioned by the King to form a Government Attlee would have no difficulty in doing so.[7] The issue came to its crisis sometime during the afternoon of 26 July at a meeting in Transport House between Morgan Phillips (Secretary of the party), Attlee and Bevin; Morrison was at the meeting but was in a minority of one. During this time there were at least two messages, one from Cripps to Morrison stressing the need for delay and the other from Churchill to Attlee informing him that Churchill would resign at 7.00 p.m. that evening. The Prime Minister also informed Attlee that he would recommend that George VI 'send for Attlee and invite him to form a government'.[8] Bevin, Attlee's strongest supporter, then suggested that Attlee go to the palace and kiss hands. The affair was over; Bevin had decided and with his support Attlee was impregnable. The trick would have to be alienating Bevin from Attlee.[9] Had the issue been between Attlee and Bevin or Attlee and Morrison the outcome might have been different, but Bevin's automatic and unconcealed contempt for Morrison sealed his fate – to be always just below the top of the political pyramid.

When Labour formed its administrations in 1924 and 1929 it had an almost completely inexperienced top echelon and, indeed, in 1924 only Arthur Henderson and J.R.Clynes had held Cabinet office. In 1945 the party had at the top a range of collective experience unrivalled in its history and comparable to that of any administration in recent British history.[10] Morrison had been a successful Minister of Transport in the second Labour Government, and Minister of Supply and Home Secretary in the Churchill coalition. Bevin had enormous experience as a trade union leader which gave him an independent political base and had done a spectacularly successful job as Minister of Labour with a seat in the Cabinet in the coalition. Dalton was an Under-Secretary in the Foreign Office in 1929–31, and Minister for Economic Warfare in the coalition. Cripps was British Ambassador to Russia in 1940–2, Lord Privy Seal and Leader of the Commons and then Minister of Aircraft Production in the coalition. On a lower level A.V.Alexander, Lord Jowitt, Viscount Addison, Lord Pethick-Lawrence, Shinwell and others had all had varied governmental training.

Attlee, similarly, had been Leader of the PLP since 1935, had been an Under-Secretary in 1924, Chancellor of the Duchy of Lancaster and PMG in the second Labour Government.[11] During the Second World War he had served from 1942 as deputy Prime Minister and had a seat in the Cabinet from 1940. It was then with considerable justice that Attlee could later claim for himself 'full experience of high and responsible office' and of his field of choice for the administration that 'there was no lack of experience'.[12]

In 1945 one might legitimately question him, as Leader of the PLP, on the grounds of his obvious lack of political imagination and flair. One might doubt, as Laski had doubted, his popular appeal, but even this shortcoming was by no means obvious, as a glance at the newspaper cartoons of the time will demonstrate. As for lack of imagination that 'was, in the Labour Party, no disadvantage, for that party usually has too much of it'.[13] It was also an advantage that Attlee was associated with no cabal in the party. He had no debts to anyone, was close to no one, except Bevin, and did not interfere with his ministers' running of their departments – he left that to Morrison.

On one level at least, however, his qualifications for office were beyond dispute. He was not averse to getting rid of colleagues doing a bad job. If Henry Fairlie is to be believed that 'Ruthlessness is necessary in politics', then Attlee certainly had one of the necessary qualities.[14]

Not only had Attlee the advantage of a relatively wide field from which to select his administration, he had also the tremendous advantage of a large number of absolutely new MPs with no claims upon him for office of any kind. That is, there were few who could with much legitimacy expect office and form cliques from disappointed expectations; he could reward the old parliamentary wheel-horses without necessarily antagonizing the new generation. The Cabinet which emerged gave few elderly ladies the nightmares they were reported to have experienced in 1924 and again in 1929. It was broadly representative of the Labour movement of the 1940s. Manual workers were well represented in the Cabinet, less well represented in the numerous junior posts and were, of course, to decline as a powerful group in the party in the 1950s.[15] Their strength was a reward for the loyal support of the unions during the 1930s. Men such as Viscount Addison and Lord Pethick-Lawrence were from the Liberal generation which entered the party in the early 1920s.[16] The generation which had supplied political *cachet*, expertise and punch in the 1930s, such as Alfred Barnes, Emmanuel Shinwell, Arthur Greenwood and George Isaacs, was also well represented, as was the intellectual wing of the 1930 party with Hugh Dalton and Stafford Cripps. Of course the categories suggested above are by no means exclusive since, for example, Shinwell had a place in the administration not only for his role in the 1930s but also as a consequence of his popularity amongst the miners. The appointment of Aneurin Bevan was the only one that could be regarded as 'dangerous' as it represented the elevation of a left-winger to the Cabinet. He was also the only member of the Cabinet lacking previous governmental experience of some kind.

Mr Attlee clearly found the process of balancing the Cabinet, the chemistry of Cabinet-making, an intellectually stimulating one. Fitness for the post, status in the party were both important considerations, but a Prime Minister has also 'to balance the personalities, the weight of the responsibility of the particular office, also standing in the country'.[17] Attlee also considered some offices more appropriate for women, and even gave consideration to balancing 'the intelligentsia (with) a trade unionist to correct his outlook'.[18]

Whilst not quite a gerontocracy, the majority of the Cabinet were just under sixty years old in 1945, with Attlee aged sixty-two. But, given the fact that the PLP member usually started in Parliament later than the House of Commons average, 'it was unavoidable that ... the general age level among ministers was rather high'.[19] The average age of members of the 1945 PLP elected prior to 1945 was fifty-seven years whilst that of the new members was forty-five years; there had been a dramatic rise in the educational standard of the PLP and a startling change in the occupational background, with the liberal professions greatly increased.[20] Thus there was a yawning occupational and age gap between the Cabinet and especially the 1945 entry into the PLP. Given that this gap could be bridged, and doing so seems to have been the major preoccupation of Dalton, the Cabinet was well balanced as could be in a period of transition.[21]

But the most experienced administration and the most able leadership needs a programme, it needs an electorate aware of what is being undertaken and it needs a measure of good fortune. Labour had the first two. The party programme in the 1945 election represented a rather diluted version of various schemes mooted in the 1920s and 1930s with a strong dash of industrial efficiency and rationalization. As with its personnel the Government's programme was a reformist reaction to the horrors of inter-war poverty and social injustice. Nothing in the approach was novel. Commentators on the Government's pro-gramme and its policies – up to 1949 anyway – differ in how far back they place the reforms envisaged in the programme. Miliband, for example, argues that the 'new era did not begin in 1945, but in 1940, and in the years of war'.[22] On the other hand, writing mainly of the nationalization bills, Eldon Barry suggests that they may be seen as 'the anti-climax of the socialist movement which for seventy years had linked its ultimate objective with the achievement of specific nationalisation measures by parliamentary means'.[23] All were clear that within the party there was widespread agreement on the overall coverage of policy, and it was equally clear that unlike 1924 and 1929 the Government was going to introduce its home affairs programme.[24]

If the policy of nationalization, fairer shares, a vigorous attack on unemployment and a health service represented a compromise with party 'socialist' traditions – as it did – it must also be appreciated that it represented a platform uniting most significant sections of the Labour party. Possibly more than that, it represented a series of discrete proposals with which a large majority of the electorate would not quarrel.[25] The Labour victory was in a real sense a culmination of a debate which reached well beyond the structure of the party out into the nooks and crannies of British society, a debate which was carried on in the air-raid shelters, British Restaurants and even seeped through into the army bureau of current affairs. The servicemen's parliaments of 1945 had socialist majorities before the general election of July 1945. More than forty-five per cent of the entire adult population had listened to the election broadcasts, had heard Churchill rattle the bones of the Gestapo and had made up their minds on how to vote.[26] The programme was pitched just to the left of the suburbs!

Up to 1949 the Government's major failing in home affairs was a lack of imagination in allowing the propaganda battle, the fight for the sympathy, attachment and understanding of the people, to go almost by default. The nasty jokes about 'fiddlers', the Conservatives' vermin campaign and the silly jibes about Gambian chickens and East African groundnuts all went unanswered when the Government in fact had a perfectly reasonable case to present.[27] The Attlee administration allowed itself to appear ordinary and mundane, indeed more than a trifle grubby. Morrison had some flair – his Festival of Britain is an example – Cripps for a time struck a responsive chord amongst those British, possibly a majority, who took a gloomy satisfaction in belt-tightening, but as an administration it lacked the gesture or the imagination, for example, to capture the almost overwhelming enthusiasm that miners and railwaymen felt on vesting day. It failed to capitalize on, perhaps even distrusted, the ordinary workers' immense enthusiasm for nationalization, failed to involve the worker in any sort of participation in the new state-controlled industries. The administrators remained the same, only the pit-head showers and the signs on the coaches changed!

Initially then Mr Attlee was relatively fortunate, and in his low-keyed replies to Mr Churchill's radio allegations he fitted in well with the sober national mood. His Cabinet of tried and experienced worthies echoed closely the British tradition of cautious change. Yet from the beginning there were difficulties, not with the Opposition which was in confusion until well into 1946, but in the formation of the Cabinet and in foreign affairs.

The difficulty with the formation of the Cabinet was a very minor but technically interesting one since it illustrates well the role of the monarchy and the question of personality balance in constructing a

Cabinet. Bevin wished to go to the Treasury and Dalton wanted the Foreign Office, and at the audience in the evening of 26 July the King suggested that it be the other way round.[28] Attlee apparently initially suggested Dalton as Foreign Secretary and the King countered with Bevin. According to Dalton, Attlee was not on the morning of the 27th sure that Dalton would not have the Foreign Office – so the royal advice was not immediately decisive. Morrison also claims to have helped to change Attlee's mind; Dalton, for his part, writes that Morrison wanted the Foreign Office.[29] The crucial factor appears to be that until the fateful meeting in Transport House on the afternoon of 26 July Attlee had simply assumed that Bevin desired the Foreign Office, a position he wanted Bevin in.[30] On that afternoon Bevin indicated he wished to go to the Treasury, and it was with this in mind that Attlee suggested Dalton as Foreign Secretary to the King. The monarch's advice appears to have coincided with what Attlee really wanted, 'it was not a decisive factor in my arrival at my decision'.[31] It was not decisive because it was in accord with what Attlee wanted, and it is apparently the case that Francis Williams (Attlee's press aide), Richard Crossman and Ritchie Calder had also pressed for Bevin for the Foreign Office.[32]

Apart from the question of the role of the monarch, there is also the question of Cabinet formation in this episode. Firstly it appears that Attlee was deluged by advice: he did not act in the sort of vacuum that his own laconic remarks suggest.[33] Secondly, and more important, Attlee had to settle the vital problem of selecting three top offices to fit three top men, none of whom trusted the other and one of whom (Bevin) had a hatred for another (Morrison) verging on the pathological. Close contact between Bevin and Morrison was out of the question.[34] It is true that the Prime Minister might have considered Cripps for any one of the top posts in the Cabinet, thus enlarging his field of choice, but at the same time Cripps had a record of unreliability in the 1930s and he had challenged Attlee's leadership on the 26th. Of the others with visibility in the party only Arthur Greenwood, a much underrated man, could have been considered. But at the most this gave five men for the three top posts; the Prime Minister was not hindered by the attempts to control him already mentioned, but in fact he had a narrower effective choice at the top than is sometimes implied.[35] Below the top three offices in the Cabinet there is no evidence that considerations other than those Attlee thought prudent had any effect either on the choice of Cabinet or ministry. For example in selecting a Minister of Fuel and Power (Shinwell) Attlee had a very wide choice, and the fact that Shinwell had a post in 1924 in charge of the Mines department of the Board of Trade may have turned the scales in his favour. But he was not an inevitable choice, nor was it inevitable that he was given a seat in the Cabinet. It was, however, prudent with forty-one miners on the Labour benches to give them a token of the Government's absolute commitment to nationalization of the mines.[36]

On foreign affairs the Government almost immediately ran into trouble with the left wing of the PLP, with Mr Bevin's first survey speech as Foreign Secretary a major disappointment to the more idealistic section of the party. That there were going to be few changes from the previous policy had been reasonably clear at Potsdam when Bevin replaced Eden as a British delegate, but on 20 August 1945 the new Foreign Secretary made the British position clear: 'Anthony Eden might well have made precisely the same speech, though more gracefully.'[37] The interest here is not in the reasons for the Bevin policy since they are clear enough. Russian intransigence, the economic weakness of the UK did not permit an independent foreign policy,[38] and the fact that nobody had the slightest idea of what a socialist foreign policy would look like are factors which go far to explain Bevinism.[39] However, these considerations do not account for his survival when the bright, if somewhat vague, prospects for international peace and harmony held out in *Let us Face the Future* were shattered. He was criticized in the Cabinet by Shinwell, Bevan and Dalton for his handling of the Palestine situation and on the same issue he was attacked in Parliament, but he was never in danger because he had Attlee's backing. In fact 'Bevin always kept Attlee fully informed . . . and regularly sought his judgement, so that foreign policy was in a very real sense a joint affair'.[40]

It should also be stressed that Bevin 'reported fully to his colleagues'[41] but Attlee followed the 'traditional' arrangement of allowing the Foreign Secretary very considerable operational and policy autonomy.[42] Bevin was a part, a crucial part, of the 'inner

Cabinet' consisting of Attlee, Morrison, Bevin, Dalton and Cripps which could resist any other combination. Thus on the acceptance of the conditions of the American loan in September and November 1945, 'Bevin, Cripps and [Dalton] were in firm coalition . . . Alexander, Bevan and Shinwell were most unhappy though none of them pressed their objections so hard as to threaten resignation'.[43] This inner group could resist any combination of Cabinet or ministerial colleagues should the necessity arise and could resist, if it arose, very considerable pressure from the PLP.[44] In fact pressure from the PLP on foreign affairs was by no means important to the Government since 'So long as the Government's domestic policy is unaffected by Mr Bevin's foreign policy, he will be supported by that solid phalanx of Labour MPs who do not worry about events across the channel.'[45] And, on most important issues of foreign affairs the Government had no fear of defeat since the left very rarely called for a vote in the Commons and, anyway, the Conservatives supported Bevin.[46]

The Government could resist considerable pressure from the PLP because it was broadly united, but more to the point is that it took care such pressure did not arise too frequently.[47] This was in part a consequence of the Government's hewing relatively closely to its promises of the 1945 election; on the whole no reformist socialist could object in principle – he might well in detail – to Labour's domestic policy. With all its defects from a left-wing point of view it was one of the great reforming ministries of British history. The Government's legislative programme was the heaviest in British parliamentary history, and if its priorities might be challenged its work could not; and in order to get a programme of such complexity through Parliament the Government had to control its own backbenchers as well as the parliamentary time-table.[48] The relative peace within the PLP was also due to an extensive formal consultative network established between the Government and the Parliamentary party by Morrison.[49] This network consisted mainly of a liaison committee, a large number of MPs organized into area and functionally specialized groups and the meetings of the PLP once a fortnight.

The liaison committee consisted of the Chief Whip, the Secretary of the PLP (not an MP), a Labour peer elected by his colleagues, Morrison and two members elected by the PLP. Its job was to maintain a formal channel of communication between Government and party and to arrange for ministers to attend meetings of the backbench groups.[50] The groups, there were twenty of them in 1945, broadly corresponded with ministries such as Defence, Finance, Health etc.[51] Members belonged to as many or as few as they chose, but their primary function was to acquaint MPs with a department but not to give them a role in policy formation. They 'provided us with teams of experts'.[52] However, only in a few cases did the groups have much impact on policy and some MPs felt that 'they are a means of keeping the rank and file occupied with trivial tasks so that their influence could be minimized'.[53] This is perhaps too sharp a conclusion, however, since it is clear that the civil aviation group was significant, and Dalton *established* a group on finance, 'my group', consisting of Evan Durbin, Hugh Gaitskell, Christopher Mayhew, Tom Williamson, George Benson, Jim Callaghan, William Mallalieu, George Brown and Douglas Jay.[54] 'Some other members were added by the Whips, after consulting me.'[55] Despite the authoritarian tones (evident throughout the autobiography) it is obvious that Dalton did discuss confidential matters with them and 'consulted them about policy, putting various alternatives before them – for tax changes, for example – and inviting their preferences'.[56] And it is quite clear that through the group Dalton was able to encourage and support men who might otherwise have been left drifting and who were to form an important section of the party in the 1950s.

Dalton's group was a small and intimate one, unlike that of foreign affairs which was large and from which a considerable amount of semi-private information was leaked to the press, thus making Bevin more reluctant than ever to discuss frankly his ideas on foreign policy before the backbenchers. The fact that left-wingers were on the committee also did not endear it to him.[57]

The fortnightly meetings of the PLP were frequently attended by Attlee and other ministers and the policy of a department might be called into question, but ministers never conceded to the PLP the right to interfere in departments, nor did they allow it a policy-making function in any formal sense. But here a general consideration must be that it would be extremely foolish for a Labour Government deliberately to antagonize its backbench support even if sure that in the end the loyalists would swamp the PLP in a vote. In fact matters did not often, or were not allowed to, proceed to a formal vote for and against a particular minister's policy since 'the Government will shift its position in advance of the meeting if it fears that strong sentiment is developing against its policy'.[58]

One other important consideration behind the relative quiet of the period on Labour beckbenchers should be noted. It is that the left-wing lacked a parliamentary leadership, its only figures of stature being in the Cabinet and hence gagged by collective responsibility. During 1946–7 the *Keep Left* group, organized by Richard Crossman, maintained a running attack on the Government in the 'privacy' of the PLP and sometimes on the floor of the Commons. In most cases they were able to get only limited support in the PLP since, anyway, the Government could always muster sixty to seventy votes in the PLP almost irrespective of its case. Additionally the parliamentary left 'lacked coherence and organization . . . after 1945'.[59]

Not only did the left lack an organizational basis, it also fell down on the score of its representatives among the PLP as a whole. It was predominantly composed of the 1945 and subsequent entry and whilst it had occasional support from the large group of trade unionists it was overwhelmingly non-trade unionist. The PLP opposition was not random since it tended to consist of the same group with some fresh adherents on different issues, but it was able to obtain a serious percentage of trade union support only once and that was on a question of home politics.[60] This was the reduction of the Government-suggested eighteen-month period of compulsory national service in March 1947.

In November 1946 Mr Attlee at a meeting of the PLP announced a Governmental decision to impose an eighteen-month period of compulsory enlistment in the armed forces. The PLP accepted the decision, but the plan was forced to a vote in which fifty-four voted against, and two weeks later in the Commons one hundred MPs abstained from supporting the Government in the lobby. On 31 March when the Bill was before the Commons, eighty members of the PLP signed an amendment urging its rejection. On 1 April seventy-two members of the PLP voted against it, twenty abstained and fifty remained away from the Commons. Two days later the Government reduced the proposed period from eighteen months to one year, and shortly after the Bill went through with little trouble.[61]

MacGregor Burns attributes the change of front to the 'Government estimating the strength of dissent and independently making a concession', but at no time was the Government likely to be defeated in the PLP, and certainly not in the House. In retrospect it is possible to interpret the concession as a reaction to difficulties not only in the PLP but *also within the Government itself*. At the time the Government was committed to 'manpower' budgeting and there was an estimated manpower deficit of 630,000 workers. A ministerial committee on economic planning composed of George Isaacs (Minister of Labour), Cripps, Morrison and Dalton was unanimous in recommending not only against strengthening the forces but actually cutting them down.* This was not accepted by the Cabinet, from which both Bevin and Morrison, who supported the cuts, were absent. In this it was swayed by A.V.Alexander, the Minister of Defence, a member of the Cabinet and deputy chairman of the defence committee. Since Attlee appears to have taken a mildly pro-defence stance, it is likely that Alexander was backed by political heads of the service departments and by John Wilmot, the Minister of Supply and an ex-officio member of the defence committee. Thus there was something like an equilibrium of forces with the defence committee ranged against the economic planning committee, with Morrison, a member of both, away ill and without the opportunity to effect a compromise. There had been serious quarrels in Cabinet and Cabinet committees on the issue of expenditure on defence and at the same time it appeared that the dispute would broaden out into a fissure. In this situation there was everything to gain from a compromise and very little from a hard line.

It is interesting and significant that the dispute broadened and hardened when the primary coordinator for home affairs, Morrison, was ill and when Bevin, who would have given weight to one side or another – almost certainly defence – was also away from the Cabinet. Attlee's second administration was to collapse soon after a similar fissure was allowed to develop. But one major point is that these were exceptional circumstances, and normally the Government was too

---

*The structure of the Cabinet and its committees will be discussed below.

strong or too careful to allow itself to be dragged into a dispute with its own back bench.[62] Another is that in introducing compulsory military service in peace time the Labour Government was flying in the face of a party tradition which did not favour the military. Unlike almost everything it did between 1945 and 1949 in home affairs, conscription had not been even hinted at in *Let us Face the Future*. It was outside the consensus which had been hammered out within the broad mass of the party over the years: 'Thanks to this consensus, *and within its limits*, the party could act effectively, harmoniously and coherently.'[63]

It is noteworthy that Labour had never been able to develop a socialist foreign policy, other than one of faint approval for small nations and an anti-Versailles and pro-League of Nations and United Nations stand. Its 1945 programme was noticeably vaguer on foreign than on home politics, and the majority of the PLP was simply not interested in foreign affairs in any serious way. The Government might get a bad press in *Tribune* and the *New Statesman*, there was even a Cabinet dispute on Bevin's handling of Palestine, but the backbench dissidents never had a chance to put real pressure on the Government's foreign policy because they failed to persuade the PLP to stand against the Cabinet on a single issue. Had they been able to, on Palestine, it is possible that caught between its own backbenchers, some unhappiness in the Cabinet and very considerable pressure from the Truman administration, the Government might have yielded.[64]

The organization and personnel of the Government was such as to allow it to be quite sensitive to its parliamentary and national constituency. Attlee himself was quite clear about the role of a Prime Minister in the Cabinet: 'He has got to collect the voices of his Cabinet. He's got to reflect the views of his party. He's also to some extent to reflect the views of the country as a whole.'[65] On the level of ideas Attlee had few and tended to be wary both of ideas and of people with them. He operated best on the level of procedure and administration; he was it was suggested by an intimate friend 'the chief administrator of the British revolution'.[66] A Prime Minister should be a leader but, so to speak, an anticipatory leader going where the consensus led him, not attempting to reshape the ideas or attitudes of his followers. He should be, as Attlee was in Rose's phrase, 'a non-aligned politician'.

As with almost any other leadership posture, Attlee's had its advantages and drawbacks. The advantages are quite clear. In a 'federal' party such as the Labour party, the Cabinet helps to cement the disparate groups together and Attlee on the whole was quite prepared to recognize this and make the Cabinet a broadly representative body. It also meant that business was gone through with expedition and efficiency when there was broad accord in the Cabinet. On the whole there was such accord in the Cabinet when the policies it had inherited were in process of enactment up to 1949, when the party could live on its intellectual capital, but when this capital ran out, as it manifestly did, Attlee's mode of leadership simply reflected the bankruptcy of the party.[67]

Attlee's ideas on the conduct and organization of the Cabinet and its committees were not novel since he had formed them in part during the 1930s and in part whilst serving his period in the war time Churchill Cabinet.[68] He was attracted by the idea of a small Cabinet of 'overlords' but, typically, 'was well aware that considerations – both political and personal – would make it difficult to adopt'.[69] He had, however, far fewer reservations about a system of non-departmental ministers 'for the supervision of particular groups of ministers and to have men in the Cabinet free from absorption in departmental detail and available for considering major policy'.[70] He also favoured the use of Cabinet committees, but again with caution since 'excessive resort to committees tends to slow down action by discussion of matters that should be decided by ministers themselves'.[71] His ideal size for a Cabinet was 'probably about, at most, sixteen' which meant the exclusion of purely administrative ministers, for example the Postmaster General or, normally, Fuel and Power.[72]

Within the Cabinet Attlee was not generally inclined to strong leadership, leaning usually towards the consensus and favouring informed brevity rather than principled diatribes. He kept total control of the agenda and firm control over the appointment of Cabinet committees and their chairmen, thus indirectly also controlling policy.[73]

Initially his Cabinet was of the normal type with twenty ministers, seventeen of them departmental, with Attlee himself as Minister of Defence. Eleven ministers were not in the Cabinet (excluding the four Law Officers) and only one of these was non-departmental. Thus he excluded a larger number of ministers than would have been the case pre-war, but there were more ministries in 1945 than in 1935. Had all the new ones been included the Cabinet would have numbered about thirty so, for example, Aircraft Production, Town and Country Planning and Food were left out.[74] In the reorganization of the British defence system of 1946 a separate Ministry of Defence was established with its own minister which permitted the exclusion of the three service ministers.[75] Following the nationalization of the coal mines and the debacle of Shinwell as Minister of Fuel and Power in the winter of 1946–7 that department was also dropped.

Two principal coordinators, without departmental responsibilities, were appointed; Mr Greenwood as Lord Privy Seal was responsible for the smooth coordination of the social services as chairman of the Cabinet social services committee. Morrison, as Lord President of the Council, chaired a Lord President's committee with an extremely wide-ranging scope, including all matters not covered by other committees plus, prior to the reorganization of 1947–8, the 'internal economic policy and the supervision of the general development of the nation's economy. It could be described as a sub-Cabinet'.[76] Mr Attlee in his capacity as Prime Minister and Minister of Defence (up to 1946) chaired the defence committee which also was a coordinating committee including A. V. Alexander (Minister of Defence), Morrison, the three Service Ministers, Ministers of Supply and Labour and the Chancellor of the Exchequer.[77]

There were a number of other standing committees established in 1945. A small one on legislation, chaired by Greenwood, which included the Law Officers, the Lord Chancellor and the Whips, had the job of superintending the general progress of Bills through the Commons. In the reorganization of 1947 the functions of this committee were transferred to Morrison chairing a future legislative committee which assessed the legislative priority of Bills. Morrison also headed a committee on the socialization of industries which included ministers from departments involved in nationalization. Attlee also took the chair at the committee on India and Burma and a colonial affairs committee was under Greenwood's supervision. Both were abolished in 1947.[78]

A number of temporary or *ad hoc* committees were set up to deal with pressing problems as they arose – housing committee, National Health Service, food supplies and a fuel committee. All of these were chaired by the Prime Minister, who clearly moved into an area when something was going seriously wrong.[79] Ministers not in the Cabinet served on both types of committee since leaving them out would have been politically dangerous.

A number of points should be made about this system. Firstly, it was a continuation of the one 'developed by Sir John Anderson in Mr Churchill's War Cabinet, and continued by Mr Attlee'.[80] Secondly, the burden of membership of both committees and Cabinet was clearly a staggering one, but some very senior ministers were also departmental chiefs: Dalton, Cripps, Bevin and Bevan to mention only the most obvious. Dalton, at least, did not regard them as an unmixed blessing, complaining in July 1946 that 'we ministers are spending far too much time in Cabinet committees'.[81] And Bevan found that in his negotiations with the representatives of the medical professions, prior to the passing of the National Health Bill, his 'freedom of manoeuvre in consultations' was impeded because 'he appeared as the representative of the policy-making authorities rather than as the authoritative policy-maker'.[82] Thirdly, it is evidently the case that in the event of a disagreement on a committee or between comittees that Attlee would be 'dragged' in to mediate or make a decision. Thus on the manpower committee, chaired by Bevin, there was a policy disagreement on demobilization which resulted in a letter from him in November 1945 to Attlee, hinting at resignation, and requesting Attlee's support.[83]

But the really major trouble with the system as it operated prior to the reorganisation of 1947 was that there was a proliferation of committees and a consequent blurring of responsibility for economic policy. In January 1947 on top of the Lord President's committee and its sub-committees was grafted the ministerial committee on economic planning consisting of Cripps, Morrison, Dalton and Isaacs, the Minister of Labour. The combination of bad luck (the worst winter for a century) and lack of coordinated planning for economic development forced a change of machinery. 'The management of the economy in the first ten months of 1947 had shown an unparalleled incompetence' and something had to be done.[84] The simple fact of the matter was that whatever his political virtues may have been Morrison, whose Lord President's committee was responsible for economic coordination, was not up to the job.[85] On the other hand it was clearly impossible to coordinate the work of men as powerful as Cripps at the Board of Trade and Dalton at the Treasury; it was not a matter of coordination but of giving power to one man. A better machinery and, more important, a concentration of economic power emerged in part as a consequence of the Cabinet crisis of 1947 and in part as a result of Dalton's resignation following the Budget leak in November 1947.

The political crisis of 1947 stemmed from the precarious economic condition of the country exacerbated by Britain's overextension in feeding its sector of Germany, the sterling convertibility condition of the 1945 American loan, and the feeling among some of his Cabinet colleagues that Attlee had not taken a firm enough direction in changing the economic planning organization.[86] The lead was taken in April by Cripps who wished, initially, for Bevin to take charge of economic planning, for Dalton to go to the Foreign Office and Morrison to be taken away from economic planning.[87] Morrison, for his part, blamed the economic crisis on Dalton at the Treasury.[88] Bevin, in conversation with Dalton, criticized Morrison and Cripps who 'was more than half-way to Moscow' and he also turned momentarily against Attlee who 'was very weak and Bevin often had great difficulty in getting him to make up his mind'.[89] In addition, Dalton reports that Bevin's PPS had told Bevin that a large number of MPs wished Attlee replaced by Bevin, and unlike the 1945 plot this one was from the right of the PLP and had trade union backing. The major difficulty for the plotters was that Morrison would not join a cabal to replace Attlee with either Bevin or Cripps since he had a claim to the throne, and any other position would *de facto* represent a decline in his fortunes.[90] And Cripps would not serve under Morrison.

On 9 September 1947 Cripps had an interview with Attlee in which he suggested that Attlee resign and become Chancellor, that Bevin replace him and double up as Minister of Production and Dalton go to the Foreign Office. Attlee then delivered his master stroke by suggesting that Cripps take over as Minister of Production, and at the same time proposed a constitutional innovation. He thought that the Inner Cabinet (Attlee, Dalton, Cripps, Morrison and Bevan) should be made public and take a great deal of detail from the Cabinet.[91] That this proposal robbed Herbert to pay Stafford worried none except Morrison.[92] In September 1947 Cripps became Minister for Economic Affairs with general responsibility for economic policy and took from the Lord President the whole apparatus of economic planning including an economic planning board, an economic planning staff and an economic information unit.[93] Clearly, the major political problem would be relations between Dalton at the Treasury and Cripps at Economic Affairs. Dalton inadvertently solved this problem by telling a journalist on the London *Star* on 12 November details of his Budget just in time to make the 3.15 p.m. stop press. His subsequent resignation left the way clear for Cripps to become Chancellor, taking the machinery of economic planning from Economic Affairs to the Treasury. Britain finally had a politically unified economic directorate.[94]

The changes at the personnel and administrative level were paralleled at the Cabinet committee level. Two committees were set up to coordinate and plan economics, a production committee headed by Cripps concerned with giving 'effect to general economic planning and ... certain questions of internal economic policy' and an economic policy committee chaired by Attlee. It 'dealt with high economic policy and generally supervised economic planning for both external and internal matters'.[95] Morrison chaired the social services committee, the socialization of industries committee and the legislation committee, and Attlee retained chairmanship of both the defence committee and the India and Burma committee.

Naturally this structure by no means eliminated intra-governmental clashes of interest. For example, Shinwell, who went to the War Office after the administrative fiasco in Fuel and Power, found himself battered between Cripps who wished for a reduction in the cost of defence and Bevin who wanted the armed forces strengthened. As usual the matter had to go to the PM.[96] But the more rational structure of 1947–8 did reduce the burden on the PM and it may have had the effect of transferring to the committees discussions which apparently had tended to be held in the Cabinet. Despite Mr Attlee's reputation for maintaining strict relevance in the Cabinet – 'you must stop people talking' – Dalton at least was constantly complaining about the frequency and length of *other* minister's interventions. And with the reduction of the Cabinet from twenty ministers in 1945 to seventeen in 1947 the problem of integrating the larger number of ministers outside the Cabinet was urgent.[97] But if the size of the Cabinet marginally decreased, that of the ministry as a whole increased with the appointment in October 1946 of Hector McNeil to act as Bevin's chief substitute on the defence committee and at the UN.[98] And it increased still more with the appointment of a further Parliamentary Secretary to help at the Treasury with economic policy. During the changes Attlee took the opportunity to include a number of younger men in more responsible positions by elevating Hugh Gaitskell to Minister of Fuel and Power, Harold Wilson to the Presidency of the Board of Trade and Douglas Jay to an Economic Secretaryship in the Treasury.[99]

The new system with its more rational distribution of committees and its distribution of chairmanships among departmental and non-departmental ministers resembled in some respects that suggested by Sir John Anderson.[100] But it was also the outcome of the experience of 1945–7 together with considerations of political expediency.[101] Within the Government as a whole the status system amongst ministers was not greatly changed, although the resignation of Dalton left Cripps more powerful. Having withstood the challenge Attlee was clearly and obviously at the top of the pyramid, still underpinned by Bevin who remained his closest ally. So long as he was in good health Bevin remained something like an equal both in the sense that Attlee had an immense personal admiration for him and because, had he really wished, he might have replaced Attlee. The two ministers were in constant correspondence and there is no record of their having taken opposite political stances on any issue other than that of steel nationalization, where Bevin sided with the 'radicals' in the Cabinet against Attlee and Morrison. It is not very convincing, as most commentators have done, to place Attlee on a lonely pinnacle – there were two people on it.[102]

Below this level, clearly below, were Cripps and Morrison. That they were below is perfectly evident from the way in which power was taken from Morrison and given to Cripps. These four at the ultimate and penultimate levels of power met frequently, consulted frequently (especially Bevin, Cripps and Attlee) and made the major policy decisions.[103] By the end of 1947, however, it is almost certain that, relative to Cripps, Morrison had lost authority since so far as is possible to ascertain he was not a significant figure in the discussions of the 1947 shuffle. His loss would have been a grievous one, but he was as economic coordinator deeply implicated in the near disaster of 1947 and his hold on the PLP might well have slipped since 1945. This is perhaps underlined by the consideration that in 1945 Morrison wanted the leadership dispute settled in the PLP, but in 1947 he made no such suggestion whilst Cripps was willing that the matter go to the PLP. He was, of course, as 'deputy Prime Minister', technically above Bevin who was simply a departmental minister, but in this case plumage was not everything.

Below this level were Alexander, Lord Addison, Chuter Ede, Lord Jowitt, Dalton and Bevan.[104] All had important offices (Defence, Health, Lord Chancellor), a significant body of parliamentary or popular support, a close friendship with Attlee (Lord Addison), or a good departmental reputation. Some combined a number of these assets, Bevan and Chuter Ede, for example, but all could be dropped without too much hesitation, although in 1947-9 this might not have been true of Bevan. The next level of authority was made up of the seven or eight departmental ministers in the Cabinet who did not chair any of the important coordinating committees. This group would have a significant impact on departmental policy through their office and would be relatively powerful on the appropriate coordinating committee, but they could easily be dispensed with. They were not in the situation of the outer ring, those not in the Cabinet, of being sometimes invited to present a particular issue to the Cabinet and then leave, or the situation in which Shinwell claims he was when in charge of the War Office, of simply getting 'Cabinet orders to do this or that on existing resources'.[105] It was through membership of the Cabinet committee or committees appropriate to their department that this group was made to feel not 'neglected'.

Not by any means in the stygian gloom of the back benches, this ultimate layer of the Cabinet system consisted in the main of politicians on the way down, such as Alfred Barnes, Noel-Baker and Shinwell or those about to or considered able to move, such as

Gaitskell, Younger and Marquand. At that stage in their careers they could be dropped at any time without the slightest risk.

There was no parity of power between the Inner Cabinet and the rest and, indeed, between the Attlee-Bevin entente and the rest, although it was clearly prudent to carry the Cabinet. In only one case did the Attlee-Bevin alliance break down, and that was on steel nationalization and the Cabinet was split on the issue.[106] Bevin, Bevan, Dalton, Cripps, Alexander and Ellen Wilkinson all favoured steel nationalization as did Wilmot, the Minister of Supply, who was not in the Cabinet, whilst Morrison, Greenwood and Attlee were against.[107] Sometime in early 1946 a Cabinet committee consisting of Bevin, Wilmot, Jowitt (the Lord Chancellor) and Dalton was appointed to consider iron and steel; it reported to the Cabinet on 12 April 1946 in favour of nationalization; there was a row but the Cabinet accepted the principle and referred the details back to the committee.[108] Since Morrison through his chairmanship of the legislative committees controlled the Government's legislative priorities and Attlee was against it, there was little use in Wilmot's 'repeatedly pressing upon Attlee the view that the nationalization of iron and steel should have a high priority'.[109]

At Attlee's suggestion Morrison negotiated with representatives of the iron and steel industry and there is evidence that Wilmot was present at these negotiations.[110] Apparently no senior minister favouring nationalization was present and the two came to the Cabinet with a scheme falling well short of nationalization. In July 1947 Bevan threatened resignation unless a Bill were introduced and on 7 August 1947 Morrison introduced some proposals, based on talks with the owners, for nationalization which were rejected by the Cabinet.[111] Attlee then appears to have shifted from opposition to support of a Bill for nationalizing steel; that is, he went along with the Cabinet majority.[112]

It is possible, although there is no evidence, that Attlee was also swayed by the fact that the issue had been hotly debated at meetings of the PLP. Whatever the cause, it is clear that this was one of the very few times when Attlee allowed himself to move away from the alliance with Bevin and supported Morrison. It was also one of the very few occasions upon which he found himself committed to a minority line in his own Cabinet.

Normally relations in the Cabinet were a good deal smoother; since there was a great deal to be done by ministers, Attlee kept a firm grip on the agenda and in order to get on the agenda the minister or committee chairman had to consult with him. He would keep some issues confined to a relatively small circle. Such an issue was the decision to produce a British atomic bomb in 1946 upon which the discussion was confined mainly to the Cabinet defence committee; an agreed memorandum was put before the Cabinet, but the *decision* had in fact been made between Attlee and Bevin.[113] It was not challenged in the Cabinet. But unlike the previous situation at least the defence committee discussed the problem and the Cabinet had a chance.[114]

Again, although in most cases the membership of a Cabinet committee *almost* decided itself, e.g. defence, fuel and the Lord President, on others Attlee had considerable discretion. Such a committee was that on India, chaired by Attlee, with Cripps and Dalton (both of whom were on record as favouring Indian independence) as members together with Pethick-Lawrence, who had spoken in favour of colonial independence in the 1920s, and Lord Wavell; the choice was entirely Attlee's and the eventual policy outcome, that Britain would withdraw in June 1948, was Attlee's idea. On most occasions Attlee was in no danger since he made a habit of consultation, but it was also very difficult for a minister not on a Cabinet committee to challenge an agreed memorandum from that committee. At best his objection would have to be one of principle, and Attlee was not one to allow a wide-ranging discussion of party principles to come between him and the end of the agenda.

There is one other important matter at issue here: whether or not the Cabinet had the area of manoeuvre in taking decisions that would allow many serious disputes to arise. Could the Cabinet have refused to nationalize the mines? Had it any alternative but to grant independence to India, Burma and Pakistan? Could it have refused to accept the American loan of 1945 despite the conditions attached? Had it any alternative but to establish some form of popular health service more effective than the old panel system? What was the area of discretion in foreign policy between Russia and America? The mere posing of such questions goes far to explain the conditions underlying the 'harmony' within the Cabinet; given sensitive leadership, during the 1940s, the sheer weight of the problems and the lack of open options, there simply was not the intellectual room for serious dispute. The Cabinet responded, it did not initiate: it drifted in foreign affairs with the American tide and in home affairs from the controlled to the fiscal economy. When the leadership of the Cabinet began to fall apart, in the case of Bevin, Attlee, Morrison and Cripps literally fall apart,[115] the major economic and political decisions had been arrived at and the broad direction of post-war Britain mapped out.

By 1949–50 the initial impetus of 1945, itself a consequence of inter-war policy proposals of immediate responses to pressing problems, and of a broad wartime consensus, had petered out into a meaningless struggle with the Lords over a painfully contrived nationalization of the iron and steel industry. Most of the demands of the inter-war generation of Labour politicians had been translated into political machinery and new social forms; a wide-ranging health service; a universal insurance system; basic industry controlled by the state and a low level of unemployment, all formidable achievements, but they were the intellectual achievements of the 1920s enacted in the 1940s. Labour lacked, and Attlee was not the one to supply, any sort of guidance or intellectual coherence to help it when the most obvious and pressing problems of late industrialism had been overcome. By 1950 the party, and the Cabinet, 'was travelling in a strange country, exposed to climatic rigours it had not anticipated and against which its "traditional" equipment gave little protection'.[116]

When Mr Attlee decided on a general election for February 1950 he did so after a meeting of the NEC where the policy statement *Labour Believes in Britain* was agreed.[117] He probably consulted Cripps who wished for an election,[118] but Bevin was away abroad at the time and hence may not have known. Morrison was against having an election so early in the year.[119] The election was disastrous for the Government since it reduced the PLP to 315, with 298 Conservatives, nine Liberals and three including the Speaker and two Irish Nationalists giving the Government an overall majority of five.[120] Its total vote, 13.3 million, was substantially above the Conservative vote of 12.4, but below the combined Liberal and Conservative vote of 15 million and its share of the votes had marginally decreased to 46.1 per cent. The new administration was sworn in on 2 March. One Cabinet minister,

Creech-Jones, was defeated but Attlee brought three outsiders, Gordon-Walker, Harold Wilson and Hector McNeil into the Cabinet; yet of the eighteen members of the Cabinet no less than twelve were back in their old posts. Both Dalton and Shinwell, who had dropped out of the previous Cabinet, were brought back as Minister of Town and Country Planning and Minister of Defence respectively: the average age of the Cabinet was greater than in 1945 with Cripps at sixty-seven the youngest of the gerontocrats. Bevin, Morrison, Cripps and Attlee were almost cripples and two of them died within the year.

The Government was clearly in a weak position in the House of Commons and the Opposition harassed the PLP to wear it down, but during the period the Government suffered no major defeat; its wounds were a combination of natural and self-inflicted. Two major changes were made as consequences of the resignation of Bevan in April 1951 and Cripps in October 1950 who were replaced by Morrison and Gaitskell respectively.[121] Morrison obtained the Foreign Office although there were various moves by Addison and Jowitt to get it for Hartley Shawcross, and by Dalton and Bevin on behalf of James Griffiths.[122] In appointing Morrison to the Foreign Office Attlee showed no very great enthusiasm, but Morrison wanted it: 'It boils down to the fact that you are the inevitable choice' was his glum explanation to Morrison.[123] The appointment of Gaitskell was by no means inevitable, since Bevan wanted the job and was clearly senior in party and Cabinet and Dalton also had claims, but Cripps had advised that Gaitskell should have it.[124] Morrison's term of office was brief and inglorious whilst that of Gaitskell was marked by the dispute with Bevan over the costs of the NHS.

If Attlee was grooming Gaitskell as his successor, and there is no reason to suppose that he had this in mind, it would have been prudent to have given him a Cabinet job earlier and then to have promoted him further. As it happened he was brought from outside the Cabinet into one of the most senior positions, whilst Bevan had actually been demoted. Attlee had, in so rapidly bringing on Gaitskell, upset the legitimate expectations of more senior men in the Cabinet, expectations based upon the relative immobility of men in the first and second ranks of the Cabinet since 1945.[125] In doing this he made no contribution to intra-Cabinet harmony, nor did he ease the question of his succession.

An obvious consequence of the various illnesses and disputes amongst the senior members of the Cabinet was the breakdown of the inner cohesion which had, on the whole, been the most marked feature of the previous Cabinet. It was clear that the Government could not last long and that a change of leadership was on the agenda. At the same time the impact of the Korean war and Britain's involvement in it had dramatically increased the British defence burden to £3,600 million over three years in August 1950.[126] Whilst the increases were accepted by the Cabinet, there was some unhappiness that re-allocation of resources involved cuts elsewhere, especially in the National Health Service. Although on 17 January 1951 Bevan had become Minister of Labour, almost certainly a consequence of his unwillingness to sanction payment for some items on the NHS, he was still bitter about Gaitskell's insistence that limited payment be introduced.[127] Bevan had long been distressed about the conduct of foreign affairs; he had thought of resignation over Palestine, used the issue as a *casus belli* and in April 1951 he, together with Harold Wilson and John Freeman, resigned from the Government. In his letter of resignation Bevan widened the issue from the £13 million charge to the general conduct of the Government.[128]

At the time of the split Attlee was ill in St Mary's Hospital, London, and Morrison, the deputy Prime Minister, was in charge, neither Cripps nor Bevan being available to the Cabinet. Possibly the issue was mishandled by Morrison and certainly this is the impression given by Attlee who claimed that 'there was no real difference of principle between Nye and the rest of the Cabinet and I was sorry it was allowed to develop into one'.[129] However, this is less than fair. Bevan certainly regarded the service with pride, and he did regard a free service as a matter of principle, both as a point of policy and as an aspect of his concern with socialism as a system of priorities, and the new charge contravened both.[130] He was also growing more despondent with the conduct of the Government, especially in foreign affairs, but also in home politics; it is not unimportant to remember that Jennie Lee, his wife, had been an acknowledged rebel since November 1946 when she had signed the first amendment from the rebel group criticizing Bevin's foreign policy. In addition a Cabinet committee was formed in 1950 specifically to propose economies in a service the cost of which it was felt had got out of control; amongst those sharing this widely held belief was Morrison.[131] Within the Cabinet the issue was a simple one: if his proposed economy was not accepted by the Cabinet, Gaitskell would resign; if it was, Bevan would resign.[132] In this delicate situation Attlee was unable, or unwilling, to provide leadership; he was seen by the feuding ministers and by Morrison who was 'exasperated at his lack of decision or even of opinion'.[133] Yet if it is not quite the case that Morrison 'mishandled' the affair it is certainly true that he saw Bevan's resignation with equanimity having disagreed with Bevan on many issues over the years and it is probably the case that so far from mishandling the incident the actual outcome was as Morrison wished.[134]

Whether or not Attlee, had he been fit and in his accustomed place in the Cabinet, could have healed the breech is for speculation.[135] What is not is that he would have found it more difficult to do so in the absence of Cripps and Bevin.[136] The consequences of the split were important.

The Government was under constant, if unskilful, attack in the Commons having on occasion to wheel invalid MPs fresh from hospital through the lobbies.[137] Its backbench dissidents now had a more formidable leader in Bevan, who immediately assumed the leadership, than it had previously.[138] Under Morrison's leadership it was evident that there would be no dramatic change in foreign policy – nor was there. In fact foreign policy during the second Attlee administration was dominated by the Korean war and from the spring of 1951 by the Persian oil crisis. Attlee clearly dominated the Cabinet scene on the Korean war, having flown to Washington on 3 December 1950 after the possibility of bombing Manchuria had been suggested by General MacArthur.[139] On the oil crisis, Morrison appears to have played a subordinate role since he favoured using force to 'solve' the issue whilst Attlee was against. Stokes, the Lord Privy Seal, on a mission to Teheran, reported back directly to Attlee, not the Foreign Secretary.[140] Attlee's last major act as Prime Minister was to recommend a dissolution of Parliament, and there was certainly no resistance within the Cabinet; neither Shinwell nor Morrison – two very senior ministers – were consulted by Attlee.[141] Dalton pushed for an early election.[142]

In the election Labour won its largest vote ever, 13.9 million to the

Conservative 13.7 million; Labour obtained 48.8 per cent of the total vote to the Conservative 48 per cent and Labour lost the election. Its manifesto, drafted by Dalton, Bevan, Sam Watson and Morgan Phillips, stressed the Government's achievements and in a few rubbery sentences referred to 'concerns which fail the nation' and emphasized that the Government wished for peace but needed to be strong. The manifesto was a dull and enervated document, the product of a stale Government and a stale party. That after two years of stumbling and incompetent rule the electorate still favoured the Labour party was a tribute to Attlee's administration of 1945–9; that Labour had nothing to offer between 1949 and 1951 was no tribute to Attlee who had administered the 'British Revolution' but presented no vision for the 1950s. Victory in 1951 would have left the Cabinet embarrassed; but embarrassed or not, Attlee's administration had left Britain on the edge of economic recovery and poised for the 'affluent society' of the mid 1950s.

Notes

1. It had 393 seats out of 640. On an out-of-date register 73 % of the electorate had voted and Labour had obtained 48 % of the vote, a 12 % swing from the last general election in 1935. For the second time in the twentieth century the British 'left' could reasonably claim it had the support of a majority of the electorate. C. Brand, *The British Labour Party* (Stanford 1964) p. 235.
2. Attlee certainly wished to stay on, as did Dalton, A. V. Alexander and Ernest Bevin; F. Williams, *A Prime Minister Remembers* (London 1961), p. 63, is in error in suggesting that Morrison agreed, see Lord Morrison of Lambeth, *Herbert Morrison, An Autobiography* (London 1960), p. 234.
3. E. Shinwell, *Conflict Without Malice* (London 1955), p. 169 suggests that he and Bevan had heard rumours of a continued coalition and sought Morrison out in order to scotch the idea.
4. In his *Autobiography*, p. 245, Morrison suggests he was not challenging for the leadership, but this is far too naïve.
5. It is characteristic of Morrison that one is much clearer about who were his enemies than who were his friends.
6. F. Williams, *op. cit.*, p. 3. Ellen Wilkinson was effectively muffled by a seat in the Cabinet as Minister of Education, and Webb was to rise high in the Cabinet as Minister of Food.

7. Laski had in a letter to Attlee dated 27 May urged him to resign in order to improve party chances in an election, A.Bullock, *The Life and Times of Ernest Bevin* (London 1967), ii, p. 391.

8. *Ibid.*, pp. 391–2.

9. H.Dalton, *The Fateful Years* (London 1957), p. 467, suggests that Arthur Deakin had approached Bevin to stand against Attlee and was strongly rebuffed.

10. H.Macmillan, memoirs in *The Times*, 24 March 1969, 'These five men constituted a body of Ministers as talented as any in the history of Parliament.'

11. In 1935 Attlee had defeated both Morrison and Arthur Greenwood for the leadership of the PLP after a second ballot.

12. C.R.Attlee, *As It Happened* (New York 1954), pp. 211, 208.

13. Sir Ivor Jennings, *Cabinet Government* (Cambridge 1959), p. 199.

14. H.Fairlie, *The Life of Politics* (New York 1968), p. 48. Attlee returns to the subject frequently, e.g. *op. cit.*, pp. 158, 217; F.Williams, *op. cit.*, p. 84; *Sunday Times*, 15 June 1958. In fact there was considerable movement in and out of the lower reaches of the Cabinet and administration, but amongst the top ten job security was impressive.

15. L.D.Epstein, *Political Parties in Western Democracies* (New York 1967), p. 177. See also the careful analysis in W.L.Guttsman, *The British Political Elite* (New York 1973), pp. 225–277.

16. R.E.Dowse, 'The Entry of Liberals Into The Labour Party', *Yorkshire Bulletin of Economic and Social Research* (1961).

17. F.Williams, *op. cit.*, p. 81.

18. *Ibid.*, p. 84. He also had a rather bizarre idea that George Tomlinson was in the Cabinet as a sort of reference book on the attitudes of the man in the street, a political version of the man on a Clapham omnibus.

19. Attlee, *op. cit.*, p. 216.

20. For further details see J.F.S.Ross, *Parliamentary Representation* (London 1948), part IV.

21. Attlee, *op. cit.*, p. 217, shows himself aware that there was a need to bring the younger men in, but Attlee did 'not like the young except as a general class to be praised', Laski in K. Martin, *Harold Laski* (New York 1953), p. 181.

22. R. Miliband, *Parliamentary Socialism* (London 1961), p. 272. A.A.Rogow, *The Labour Government and British Industry, 1945–51* (London 1955), pp. 2–3, makes a similar point. Asa Briggs, 'The Welfare State in Historical Perspective', *European Archives of Sociology*, (1961), ii, p. 223, sees the legislation of 1945–50 as 'the climax of fifty years of social and political history'.

23. Eldon Barry, *Nationalisation in British Politics* (Stanford 1965), p. 369. See also S.Pollard, *The Development of the British Economy, 1914–1950* (London 1962), p. 388.

24. For a discussion of the previous failures see R.E.Dowse, *Left in the Centre* (London 1966) and R.Skidelsky, *Politicians and the Slump* (London 1967).

25. On the nationalization of the mines W.A.Robson, *Nationalised Industry and Public Ownership* (Toronto 1960), p. 31, claims that the demand from the unions and the public was 'so irresistible that no government . . . could have allowed matters to continue as they were under private ownership'.

26. A.F.Havighurst, *Twentieth Century Britain* (New York 1962), p. 365. Just prior to the poll the *New Chronicle* revealed that a survey it had commissioned showed that 84 % of the electorate had decided how to vote.

27. R.Rose, *Influencing Voters* (New York 1967), p. 61, writes that 'within the Labour Government, many Ministers had no interest in using public relations methods to improve electoral understanding of policies'.

28. Sir John Wheeler-Bennett, *King George VI: His Life and Reign* (London 1958), pp. 636–8. See also Dalton, *op. cit.*, p. 473.

29. *Ibid.*, p. 474; Morrison, *op. cit.*, p. 246.

30. Bullock, *op. cit.*, pp. 393–4.

31. Attlee in *The Observer*, 23 August 1959.

32. Dalton, *High Tide and After* (London 1962), p. 103. That Crossman wanted Bevin in the Foreign Office was ironic in the light of his later comment that 'Seldom can a socialist Foreign Secretary have accepted more conscientiously the advice of the Foreign Office and the Chiefs of Staff, or spurned more roughly all those who suggested that he would best serve the cause of expediency, as well as of honour, by keeping to his promises and sticking to his principles', R.H.S.Crossman, *The Politics of Socialism* (New York 1965), p. 131.

33. D.J.Heasman, 'The Prime Minister and the Cabinet' in R.Benewick and R.E.Dowse, *Readings on British Politics and Government* (London 1968), p. 173, intimates that Churchill might have suggested Bevin to George VI.

34. Thus Bevin is reported to have said of Attlee that he 'never put forward a single constructive idea, but by God he's the only man who could have kept us (the Cabinet) together', L.Hunter, *The Road to Brighton Pier* (London 1959), p. 26. On the relationship between Morrison and Bevin see B.Donoghue and G. Jones, *Herbert Morrison* (London 1973), pp. 345–7.

35. J.P.Mackintosh, *The British Cabinet* (London 1962), p. 385.

36. It is perhaps indicative of Attlee's relative lack of enthusiasm that John Wilmot, Minister of Supply in charge of steel nationalization, at no time had a Cabinet place.

37. E.J.Meehan, *The British Left and Foreign Policy* (New Jersey 1960), p. 71.

38. In August 1945 the Treasury informed the Government that Britain faced economic ruin. Also, by the beginning of 1945 'The Anglo-American

relationship had become that of client and patron', A.J.P.Taylor, *English History, 1914–1945* (Oxford 1965), p. 598.

39. On the intellectual roots of Labour foreign policy see R.E.Dowse, 'The I.L.P. and Foreign Politics, 1918–1923', *International Review of Social History*, 1962.

40. Williams, *op. cit.*, (London 1961), p. 150.

41. Attlee, *op. cit.*, p. 238. But one 'reports' after an event, consultation takes place before, and consultation seems to have taken place only with Attlee.

42. Jennings, *op. cit.*, p. 225, 'it is wise for the P.M. not to intervene except in extreme cases'.

43. Dalton, *High Tide and After*, p. 79. By inference Dalton appears to demote Cripps from the Inner group when he mentions that he cleared his first budget with Attlee, Morrison and Bevin, 'got their broad agreement', but does not name Cripps, at that time President of the Board of Trade.

44. It had little reason to fear the NEC for, as Laski complained in October 1945 of the Palestine policy, 'It is terribly difficult for on the EC are seven Ministers of Cabinet rank, and if you add to them the undersecretaries and the M.Ps. there is a majority with a vested interest in keeping the government out of trouble', K.Martin, *Harold Laski* (New York 1953), p. 203.

45. D.N.Pritt, *The Labour Government, 1945–51* (New York 1963), p. 74, quoting a *New Statesman* leading article.

46. Hoffman, *op. cit.*, p. 236; A.Eden, *Full Circle* (London 1960), p. 5, 'In Parliament I usually followed him (Bevin) in debate and I would publicly have agreed with him more if I had not been anxious to embarrass him less'.

47. R.T.McKenzie, *British Political Parties* (London 1963), p. 446, remarks that 'After the excitement of 1929–31, the history of the inner life of the PLP during 1945–51 seems remarkably placid'. But it should be noted that four left-wing MPs and one right wing MP were expelled from the party in 1947–9 and none were elected in 1950, see A.Ranney, *Pathways to Parliament* (Wisconsin 1965), pp. 155–9.

48. B. Crick, *The Reform of Parliament* (New York 1965), p. 14; see also *Select Committee on Procedure* (1959), p. 194.

49. See Donoghue and Jones, *op. cit.*, ch. 27, for details.

50. Miliband, *op. cit.*, p. 296 asserts that 'this body was much more a watch-dog for the Government than a lever for pressure on it', but does not give evidence.

51. The system was changed in 1947 to emphasize geographical rather than functional considerations.

52. Morrison, *op. cit.*, p. 255.

53. J.M.Burns, 'The Parliamentary Labour Party in Britain', *American Political Science Review* (1950), 44, p. 860.

54. Dalton, *High Tide and After*, p. 22. It was mainly through Dalton's finance group that the next generation of Labour party leaders emerged.
55. *Ibid.*, p. 22.
56. *Ibid.*, pp. 22–3. D.J.Heasman, 'Parliamentary Paths to High Office', *Parliamentary Affairs* (1963), xvi, no. 3, p. 324, states that 'Persons holding important positions on back-bench committees are frequently selected for corresponding posts in the ministry'. But for the 1945–51 period this was not true, McKenzie, *op. cit.*, p. 448.
57. P.G.Richards, *Parliament and Foreign Affairs* (London 1967), p. 135.
58. Burns, *op. cit.*, p. 859. McKenzie, *op. cit.*, p. 448 states that 'Ministers tended to take party feeling into account before attempting to make a case for a particular line of policy at party meetings', and G.Loewenberg, 'The British Constitution and the Structure of the Labour Party', *American Political Science Review*, 52, no. 3, p. 779 concurs in this judgement. This argument is developed at greater length in R.E.Dowse and T.Smith, 'Party Discipline in the House of Commons', *Parliamentary Affairs* (1963), xvi, no. 2.
59. Miliband, *op. cit.*, p. 296. It also lacked serious extra-parliamentary support.
60. Guttsman, *op. cit.*, p. 271.
61. This account is taken from Burns, *op. cit.*, p. 865.
62. A further consequence of the episode was that it was resolved to make greater attempts to discuss controversial issues more fully and privately in the PLP prior to their coming on to the floor of the Commons. P.K.Alderman, 'Discipline in the Parliamentary Labour Party, 1945–1951', *Parliamentary Affairs* (1965), xviii.
63. S.Beer, *British Politics in the Collectivist Age* (New York 1965), p. 187 (my italics).
64. See Williams, *op. cit.*, ch. 12, for the joint Attlee/Bevin handling of the Palestine problem; Dalton, *High Tide*, ch. 16, for the doubts amongst some Cabinet members, and A.H.Birch, *Representative and Responsible Government* (Toronto 1964), pp. 142–3.
65. Cited in *The Guardian*, 21 April 1963. Also Williams, *op. cit.*, p. 81.
66. R.Rose, *Studies in British Politics* (London 1966), p. 324. Morrison, *Government and Parliament* (Oxford 1966), p. 50, 'Mr. Attlee was essentially the good Chairman, giving guidance, maintaining the relevance of discussion and leading (the Cabinet) to a generally acceptable conclusion'. This was also the judgement of Laski, 'an admirable chairman', Martin, *op. cit.*, p. 181. R.H.S.Crossman in his Introduction to Bagehot, *The English Constitution* (London 1963), p. 49, does not agree with the characterization of Attlee as a 'Chairman'.
67. It was not untypical of the way the party developed that during the Cabinet crisis of 1947 the anti-Attlee group objected to his lack of

dynamism but had nothing to suggest other than more of the same, only quicker.

68. C.R.Attlee, *The Labour Party in Perspective* (London 1937); Jennings, *op. cit.,* p. 309; Mackintosh, *op. cit.,* pp. 421–42.

69. Attlee, *As it Happened*, p. 213.

70. *Ibid.,* p. 214.

71. *Ibid.,* p. 161.

72. Williams, *op. cit.,* p. 82.

73. P.Gordon-Walker, 'On Being a Cabinet Minister', *Encounter* (1956), vi, which substantially agrees with Morrison, *op. cit.*

74. Jennings, *op. cit.,* p. 78, 'The experience of Mr. Churchill's War Cabinet . . . enabled Mr. Attlee to change the tradition'.

75. Attlee, apparently, intended from the beginning to reorganize defence, *As it Happened*, p. 214.

76. Morrison, *Government and Parliament*, p. 34. As with other committees the Lord President's produced sub-committees, e.g. on development areas under Dalton.

77. *Ibid.,* pp. 33–4. The Chiefs of Staff were also present.

78. *Ibid.,* p. 36.

79. Thus in November 1945 Attlee flew to Washington to confer with Truman and MacKenzie King on the A-bomb, and again in December 1950 to discuss General MacArthur's command in Korea.

80. Jennings, *Ibid.,* p. 256.

81. Dalton, *High Tide and After*, p. 141.

82. H.Eckstein, *Pressure Group Politics: The Case of the British Medical Association* (Stanford 1960), p. 104. It is also apparently the case that two committees were involved, that of Greenwood on the Social Services and Attlee's *ad hoc* committee on the NHS.

83. Williams, *op. cit.,* pp. 125–7. Attlee supported Bevin.

84. A.J.Youngson, *Britain's Economic Growth, 1920–1966* (New York 1967), p. 167. Pollard, *op. cit.,* p. 373, refers to the crisis of 1947 'shocking the Government out of its complacency'.

85. But it is the case that what he might have called coordination others might describe as interference: 'Morrison . . . must be checked from trying to interfere with everybody and everything. On this Cripps and Bevan strongly agree with me', Dalton, *High Tide*, p. 141 (July 1946). Morrison, as one commentator put it, 'collected chairmanships as other men may collect stamps', M.Foot, *Aneurin Bevan*, (London 1973), 2, p. 259.

86. E.Watkins, *The Cautious Revolution* (New York 1950), pp. 46–7, suggests that there was a Cabinet crisis in late 1946 over the question of whether or not

to publish the full facts of Britain's economic position in the *Economic Survey for 1947*, Attlee and Bevin favouring publishing a full account whilst 'some trade union members of the Cabinet' were against doing so: 'Mr. Attlee . . . threatened resignation if his views were not accepted'.

87. Dalton, *High Tide*, pp. 336–7; Williams, *op. cit.*, pp. 222–3.

88. Morrison, *Autobiography*, p. 260.

89. Dalton, *High Tide*, p. 239 (July 1947). Attlee later stated that Bevin was against the move, Williams, *A Prime Minister Remembers*, pp. 224–5. L. Hunter, *The Road to Brighton Pier* (London 1959), p. 19, denies that Bevin was involved.

90. Morrison, *Autobiography*, p. 260; Williams, *A Prime Minister Remembers*, p. 224 states that Morrison took no part, but it is clear from Dalton, *ibid.*, ch. 19 that he did.

91. Dalton, *High Tide*, p. 245. It was not untypical of Attlee that when political trouble had to be dealt with he was inclined to suggest administrative solutions. He did so again in late 1950 when he mused on the idea of separating the NHS from the Ministry of Health, giving it a separate department and excluding the Minister from the Cabinet.

92. For a useful general analysis on the ability of a Prime Minister to withstand pressure see P. G. Richards, *Patronage in British Government* (Toronto 1963), ch. IV, which concludes 'M.Ps. may select their leaders with great shrewdness, but once established the latter are difficult to replace.'

93. D. N. Chester and F. M. G. Willson, *The Organisation of British Central Government, 1914–1956* (London 1957) p. 328.

94. The Korean war clearly revealed that the planning staff, upon which the minister relied, was totally inadequate to the task of gathering information and collating it.

95. Morrison, *Government and Parliament*, p. 35.

96. Shinwell, *op. cit.*, p. 198.

97. All three Service Ministers were replaced in the Cabinet by the Minister of Defence; the Ministry of Fuel and Power was excluded following the nationalization of mines; the new Ministry of Commonwealth Relations was included and the old one of Secretary of State for India abolished. By 1951 Attlee had twenty-one in the Cabinet, including Dalton in town and country planning, which had not been in under his predecessor.

98. During Attlee's administrations the number of MPs in the Government increased and by 1950 numbered 95 out of 393 in the PLP. By a decision of May 1949 when 5 PPS's voted against a government 3-line whip and were dismissed from office it was evident that the system was a powerful disciplinary weapon; (by 1950 there were 27 PPSs), see B. Crick, *The Reform of Parliament* (New York 1965), p. 30; see also Alderman, *op. cit.*, pp. 302–3.

99. Hilary Marquand was promoted in 1948 to the Ministry of Pensions.

100. In the Romanes Lecture for 1946, reprinted in *Public Administration* (1946).

101. F. Stacey, *The Government of Modern Britain* (Oxford 1968), pp. 266–7, rather over-emphasizes Anderson's influence. As a matter of fact the idea was also mooted in the 1947 *Keep Left* pamphlet which Cripps may have influenced, L. Hunter, *The Road to Brighton Pier* (London 1959), p. 18.

102. *Ibid.*, pp. 267–8. Mackintosh, *op. cit.*, p. 430, and Crossman, *op. cit.*, p. 49.

103. They were, suggest W. J. M. MacKenzie and J. W. Grove, *Central Administration in Britain* (London 1957), p. 345, 'a clearly marked inner group of Ministers'.

104. Mackintosh, *op. cit.*, p. 431, places all except Bevan on this third tier; but his threat in 1946 to resign on the failure to introduce a bill nationalizing steel was not taken lightly, R. K. Alderman and J. A. Cross, *The Tactics of Resignation* (London 1967), p. 17. Further, Bevan was consulted over the 1947 Cabinet changes, L. Smith, Harold Wilson, *The Authentic Portrait* (New York 1964), p. 119.

105. Shinwell, *op. cit.*, p. 197. The Minister of Works was in a similar position 'under frequent pressure from more powerful colleagues who were impatient for results', F. Blackburn, *George Tomlinson*, (London 1954), p. 157. But Gaitskell, as Minister of Fuel and Power and a member of Cripps' Production Committee, was able to withstand pressure even from Cripps himself; W. T. Rodgers, *Hugh Gaitskell, 1906–1963*, pp. 92–3.

106. Attlee, *As it Happened*, p. 216.

107. Morrison had been against including it in the 1945 programme: Dalton,

108. *The Fateful Years*, pp. 432–3. See also Morrison, *Autobiography*, p. 296. Dalton, *High Tide*, p. 138.

109. *Ibid.*, p. 139. Priority was important since there was no reason, technically, why a Bill could not have been introduced earlier, and hence the politically meaningless fight with the Lords avoided.

110. Morrison, *Autobiography*, p. 296; Dalton, *High Tide*, p. 248 (1947). In September 1947 Wilmot left the Government (never to appear again) and was replaced by George Strauss; obviously a new minister, even had he been inclined, would not have been in a strong position to demand nationalization.

111. Dalton, *ibid.*, p. 251. Morrison, *ibid.*, p. 296, suggests that only three were against, but Dalton denies this.

112. Morrison, *ibid.*, p. 296.

113. Mackintosh, *op. cit.*, p. 431; Crossman, *op. cit.*, pp. 54–5 and H. Berkeley, *The Power of the Prime Minister* (London 1968), p. 54, put the matter too sharply. See G. W. Jones, 'The Prime Minister's Power', *Parliamentary Affairs* (1965),

and the correspondence in the *New Statesman* between Crossman and Strauss in May and June 1963, and *The Times*, 26 March 1969.

114. Churchill had not even consulted Attlee, his deputy Prime Minister, on the issue, only Sir John Anderson and Field Marshal Wilson being in on the secret; Taylor, *op. cit.*, p. 598, footnote 1.

115. Donoghue and Jones, *op. cit.*, p. 432, write of this period 'The ministers began to gossip about one another's health rather like old village women.'

116. R.H.S.Crossman, *The Politics of Socialism* (New York 1965), p. 36; see also Miliband, *op. cit.*, and J.Saville, 'Labourism and the Labour Government', *Socialist Register* (London 1967), pp. 43–71.

117. It is not clear from Attlee's account, *As it Happened*, p. 272, whether the NEC knew the date, but by the end of 1949 it was no secret that a general election would soon be necessary.

118. Dalton, *High Tide*, p. 337, Rodgers, *op. cit.*, p. 95, suggest that Cripps' determination to hold an early election was a major factor in Attlee's decision.

119. Morrison, *Autobiography*, p. 268. The Government had in 1949 passed a consolidated Representation of the People Act which amongst other things had redistributed parliamentary seats to Labour's disadvantage, D.Butler, *The Electoral System in Britain Since 1918* (Oxford 1963), p. 163.

120. Labour had not lost a by-election since 1945.

121. Attlee had in the end to request Bevin's resignaion.

122. Dalton, *High Tide*, pp. 360–1; Morrison, *Autobiography*, p. 273.

123. *Ibid.*, p. 273. Williams, *A Prime Minister Remembers*, p. 243, 'Herbert Morrison was anxious for it ... the others one could think of were all too young and inexperienced. It had to be a senior man and Herbert was the most senior'. Shinwell, *op. cit.*, p. 225, denies that Morrison wanted the FO, as does Hunter, *op. cit.*, p. 28, and Rodgers, *op. cit.*, p. 99. Dalton, *High Tide*, p. 359, states that Bevan also wanted the FO.

124. *Ibid.*, p. 245, and Shinwell, *op. cit.*, pp. 224–5. Attlee had thought of Bevan as Chancellor, but Morrison and Bevin were also against it, Hunter, *op. cit.*, p. 27. Foot, *op. cit.*, p. 299, argues that Bevan's objections to Gaitskell as Chancellor of the Exchequer were twofold: Gaitskell represented no considerable segment of the party and his ideas were petty.

125. See D.J.Heasman, 'The Ministerial Hierarchy', *Parliamentary Affairs*, (1962).

126. This was a 49% increase over the 1949–50 estimates and 45% over the budget figures; on 29 January 1951 Attlee announced a further increase to £4,700 million over three years. In September 1950 conscription for a two-year period was accepted.

127. H. Marquand replaced Bevan in the Ministry of Health.

128. It is clear that Bevan was not able to establish the close rapport and personal friendship with Gaitskell that he had with both Dalton and Cripps, M. Krug, *Aneurin Bevan: Cautious Rebel* (New York 1961), p. 113, and Williams, *A Prime Minister Remembers*, p. 249.

129. *Ibid.*, p. 246. According to one report, Attlee actually saw Gaitskell and 'strongly (advised) him to exercise caution', L. Smith, *op. cit.*, p. 149. But Bevan, Wilson and Freeman all thought that had Attlee been well the crisis would not have occurred, pp. 154–5.

130. A. Bevan, *In Place of Fear* (London 1952), chs. 5, 9.

131. Dalton, *High Tide*, pp. 364–5; Morrison, *Autobiography*, p. 266. It was not until 1956, with the report of the Guillebaud committee, that it was found that this belief had no foundation in fact; see also B. Abel-Smith and R. M. Titmuss, *The Cost of the National Health Service* (London 1956), p. 60.

132. Dalton, *ibid.*, p. 365.

133. Morrison, *Autobiography*, p. 267, also says that Attlee 'appeared to agree with all of us in turn'. Shinwell, *op. cit.*, p. 224 also states that neither Bevan nor Gaitskell would compromise on the issue.

134. M. Foot., *op. cit.*, esp. p. 333.

135. Mackintosh, *op. cit.*, p. 432, sees it as 'significant' that the breach occurred when Attlee was absent.

136. Bevin did try to change Gaitskell's mind, but was too ill to persevere; L. Smith, *op. cit.*, p. 149.

137. J. D. Hoffman, *op. cit.*, p. 266, 'Conservatives were fully aware that a full scale attack on the Government united the Labour Party as much as their own'.

138. At the October 1951 annual conference of the Labour party four, including Bevan, left-wingers were elected to the NEC. But due to the small Labour majority the problem of controlling the back bench did not arise.

139. Attlee, *As it Happened*, p. 282. He consulted Bevin prior to flying.

140. Williams, *A Prime Minister Remembers*, pp. 249–54 and Morrison, *Autobiography*, p. 281. And, anyway, Morrison was away from the UK during most of the crisis.

141. It would be more accurate to say that Morrison was not consulted about the actual date – he favoured 1952 – but Attlee had mooted 1951 in a letter to Morrison in May. Donoghue and Jones, *op. cit.*, pp. 501–2.

142. Dalton, *High Tide*, pp. 376–7; Morrison, *Autobiography*, p. 289. Gaitskell, the Chancellor of the Exchequer, was in America with Morrison and was not consulted; Hunter, *op. cit.*, p. 43.

Anthony Eden

Robert Blake

I

Anthony Eden's premiership, apart from those of Bonar Law and Alec Douglas-Home, was the shortest in the twentieth century. He succeeded Churchill in April 1955 and resigned through ill health in January 1957. His brief period in office will inevitably be remembered more for the Suez crisis than for anything else. It seemed at the time a symbolic turning-point in British history and the perspective of over twenty years has not invalidated that judgement, even though some of the direr predictions have not been fulfilled. Whatever may be said about the rights and wrongs of the Suez policy, it cannot possibly be described as a success, for it achieved neither the ostensible nor the covert aims of its authors. The ostensible aims were to safeguard the Suez canal from interruption and re-establish British influence and prestige in the Middle East. The covert aim was to overthrow Nasser and regain physical control of the canal. None of these goals was attained. Inevitably, therefore, Eden's premiership is stamped with the mark of failure.

It is unlucky for a statesman who achieved so much in his long and distinguished public career to go down to history in this way. Unlucky – but in the rough justice of political history is it entirely unfair? The answer depends on many issues not all of which can be settled yet. It is not part of this brief study to draw up a balance sheet of personal praise and blame. The most that can be done is to examine how Eden's conduct of the premiership differed from that of his predecessors and successors and to see what light his brief prime-ministerial career throws upon the working of the British political system.

The experience of office enjoyed by Prime Ministers before they reach the supreme position has greatly varied. Winston Churchill had been head of nearly all the principal departments of state except the Foreign Office. Ramsay MacDonald had never even held an Under-

Secretaryship. Most of them, however, have had some experience of the Cabinet. Eden had had a great deal, but he is unique among twentieth-century Prime Ministers in that his earlier career was wholly confined to foreign, imperial and defence policy. He never headed one of the great departments that deal with internal affairs – Treasury, Board of Trade, Home Office, Health, Education. But he did hold the Foreign Office for over ten years[1] – a record surpassed in the twentieth century only by Sir Edward Grey. His other posts included the Dominions Office (September 1939–May 1940) and the War Office (May–December 1940). No one who tried to guess the area in which disaster was to occur, if it was to occur at all, would have guessed at foreign affairs.

The second unusual feature of Eden's pre-prime-ministerial career was the amount of time he spent as heir apparent to the leadership of the Conservative party. As early as December 1940 Churchill had told him that he must be his successor. It is not normal for a Prime Minister to proffer advice to the Crown on this subject, but in June 1942 when Churchill was about to undertake a perilous flight to America, the King asked him whom he would recommend to succeed him, and Churchill at once named Eden. In theory there could have been a change of mind or, if Churchill had resigned between 1945 and 1951 while the Conservatives were in opposition, the party might have elected someone else. In practice Eden was bound to be his successor. Thus he was what he himself describes as 'crown prince . . . a position not necessarily enviable in politics'[2] far longer than any other twentieth-century Prime Minister.

The period was even longer than it might have been because of Churchill's reluctance to retire. If he had won the election of 1945, it is hard to believe that he would have gone on in politics for another decade. Yet there is nothing surprising in Churchill's determination to avenge that painful defeat and to show that he could win an election, even if only by a narrow margin as he did in 1951. Nevertheless, it is hard to defend his occupation of office for twenty-two months after his severe stroke late in June 1953. It is true that Eden himself was seriously ill at the time and after two unsuccessful gall-bladder operations had gone to Boston for a third at the end of June. Churchill was justifiably anxious not to resign at once, for Eden might have missed his chance entirely, and at that time the premiership would probably have gone to R.A.Butler. But Eden had recovered from his convalescence by the beginning of October and the operation seemed to have been a success. Churchill might reasonably have retired once his successor was restored to health. Eden, though far too loyal to express any complaint even in his memoirs, had some cause to consider that he should have become Prime Minister a good year and a half earlier than in fact he did.

Eventually Churchill saw that the time had come to depart. Loaded with honours and fame, and still highly popular with a public who little knew how grievously his powers had been failing over the last two years, he bowed himself out on 5 April 1955. Eden, his successor designate for nearly fifteen years, moved into his place the next day. He was fifty-eight, at the height of his powers, and, as far as was known, had quite recovered from the illness of two years before. His hour had come at last.

What sort of a person was the new Prime Minister? Tall, slim, good looking, perfectly dressed – perhaps the best looking and the best dressed of all the holders of his high office – Anthony Eden was in many ways the ideal political figure for the television age. Although he was educated at Eton and Christ Church – those traditional nurseries of statesmen – and although he was a younger son of an old landed family in County Durham, there was nothing anachronistic about him. He spoke with clarity and sincerity in the language of the ordinary man. He was no phrase maker. There were no echoes of the eighteenth century as with Churchill, or of the Edwardian era as with Macmillan. If Anthony Eden seemed to belong to any 'period', it was perhaps to the 1920s. In appearance he might well have stepped out of one of the brittle, glittering plays of Noël Coward. His habit of addressing his friends as 'My dear', which annoyed virile, barbecue-loving statesmen across the Atlantic, only confirmed this impression. But it was of course merely superficial. Behind it there lay a seriousness of purpose, a toughness of mind, and a devotion to duty, which were quite alien to the feverish frivolity of the years after the First World War.

Eden drove himself hard, and not only himself but his secretaries and his whole entourage. He could be irritable and, though he usually kept it well under control, he had inherited something of his father's temper. However, he possessed a charm which soon overcame any hurt feelings. He was a highly civilized figure, keenly interested in literature and the visual arts, and his choice of pictures and sculpture reflected his excellent taste. In matters of food and wine he could be described as an abstemious gourmet who ate and drank little himself but provided an admirable table for his guests. He spoke excellent French, the only twentieth-century Prime Minister to do so, apart from Macmillan. Moreover – and this accomplishment is unique among Prime Ministers since the office first came into being – he was an expert on the Persian language and literature, in which subject he had gained first class honours at Oxford.

At Oxford he had shown no particular interest in politics. After a gallant war career as an officer in the King's Royal Rifle Corps, gaining the Military Cross in 1917, he went up to Christ Church and read Oriental languages – an unusual choice of subject even today, and more so then. He took no part in the Union, preferring to be President of the Uffizi Society – a club to discuss painters and pictures, of which he and Lord David Cecil were founding fathers. But in 1922 he surprised his friends by standing as a Conservative candidate for Spennymoor in County Durham – a forlorn hope in that citadel of radicalism. The following year he obtained a more promising nomination for Warwick and Leamington where he defeated both Liberal and Labour candidates. The Labour candidate was the eccentric socialist Countess of Warwick, a former mistress of Edward VII. By an ironical chance she was the mother-in-law of Eden's sister and the step-grandmother of his fiancée, Miss Beatrice Beckett, whom he married on 5 November 1923. Consequently the election was very much a family affair. Eden held the seat for thirty-three years, in fact for the whole of his active parliamentary life.

The first fifteen years of his political career were smooth and highly successful. From 1926 to 1929 he was Parliamentary Private Secretary to the Foreign Secretary, Sir Austen Chamberlain. For the next two years the Conservatives were out of office. From 1931 to the end of 1933 he was Under-Secretary at the Foreign Office. From 1 January 1934 he was Lord Privy Seal attached to the Foreign Office but not in the Cabinet. This was an odd arrangement. What followed was even odder. In the summer of 1935, as a gesture to the 'Leagueomaniacs', Baldwin made him Minister for League of Nations Affairs and a member of the Cabinet. This was tantamount to having two Foreign Secretaries. It is surprising that the new tenant of the Foreign Office, Sir Samuel Hoare, agreed to such a potentially awkward duality. Eden himself had the gravest misgivings and only accepted on a temporary basis. At the end of the year the unfortunate Hoare destroyed himself with the famous Hoare-Laval Pact, and Eden became Foreign Secretary.

There is no need to recount the story of his first period at the Foreign Office. Increasingly at loggerheads with the new Prime Minister, Neville Chamberlain, over the right attitude to take towards Mussolini and Hitler, Eden eventually resigned in February 1938. His critics have tried to belittle his decision and to suggest that it was based on personal *amour propre* rather than real dissent over Chamberlain's policy of appeasement. His cautious line after his resignation and his lack of close cooperation with Churchill have also been attacked. These criticisms are not fair. The Cabinet papers of the period clearly show that there was a real and fundamental difference between Eden and Chamberlain. No doubt Eden must bear a certain responsibility for some of the errors and evasions of British diplomacy in these years, but no one should underestimate the pressure on a man in his position not to 'rock the boat', or the inevitable compromises into which a minister ill at ease with his colleagues is forced before the final breach comes. Ministers are rightly slow to resign, not because they are avid for 'the fruits of office', but because Cabinet government simply cannot be carried on without some element of flexibility and concession.

As for cooperation with Churchill, it is easy to forget how unpopular Churchill was, and how deeply mistrusted by people of all parties. It was far from self-evident that an open alliance with Churchill was the best way of combating appeasement and influencing the Government during the nineteen months between Eden's resignation and the outbreak of war. When he left the Cabinet Eden had good reason to think that he had sacrificed all his prospects of rising to the top. He could not possibly have predicted the turn of events which was to make his resignation one of his greatest assets.

War brought political advancement and, later, personal tragedy.

The vindication of Eden's distrust of the dictators obliged Neville Chamberlain to give him office, though as Dominions Secretary he was not in one of the key posts. Churchill's advent to power elevated him to the more important office of Secretary for War, but he still remained outside the small inner Cabinet which had been established for the conduct of the war. At the end of 1940, Lord Lothian, the British Ambassador in America, died suddenly and unexpectedly. Churchill moved Lord Halifax from the Foreign Office to Washington, making Eden Foreign Secretary in his place and a member of the War Cabinet. Eden's personal wartime tragedy was the death of his elder son, Simon. Little more than a boy, he was killed in June 1945 flying his plane over Burma.

With the possible exception of Ernest Bevin all the members of the Cabinet during the war were overshadowed by Churchill, who wielded a degree of power such as has fallen to no Prime Minister before or since. Eden was far from being a yes-man; he frequently and forcibly represented the longer-term Foreign Office view of the post-war balance of power, which at times diverged from the shorter-term military objectives of Churchill. But inevitably in war it was the latter view which usually prevailed. From 1942 onwards Eden was Leader of the House as well as Foreign Secretary. Ceaseless work, exhausting participation in nearly all the great war conferences, long hours in the House, and even longer hours of talk after midnight with Churchill took their toll on his health. On the eve of the 1945 general election a duodenal ulcer was diagnosed, and his doctors insisted on rest for the whole of June, limiting him to a single broadcast at the end of the campaign. It was in this same month that the sad news came through of his son's death.

By his own account Eden seems to have been uneasy, not only about the result of the election but about his own position as a Conservative. In February that year after seeing some of the troops in Greece he wrote in his diary:

It would be the highest honour to serve and lead such men. But how is one to do it through party politics? Most of these men have none as I believe I have none. And how is this General Election to express any of this, for they could not be further from the men of

Munich in their most extreme form, for whom I have to ask the electors to vote. It is hell.[3]

Eden's own comment on this passage, 'Priggish no doubt', does him less than justice. After all those years of struggle against the common enemy it was natural to feel revulsion at the return to party politics and misgivings about those Conservative colleagues who had borne such a heavy responsibility for the failures of the 1930s. But 'England does not love coalitions' – at least not in peace time. The party system soon reasserts itself. For all its imperfections it is less bad than most other systems. Eden does not appear to have entertained any further doubts about the political company which he kept, and as deputy Leader of the Opposition played a vigorous part in the revival of the party's fortunes. His reasonableness, his sincerity, his distinguished appearance and his impeccable record all contributed to make him one of the party's principal assets. Indeed there was a good deal of privately expressed opinion that the Conservatives would fare better under him, electorally, than under Churchill. This, however, could only be a matter of surmise. In 1950 Labour just scraped home. In 1951 the Conservatives were returned with a majority of seventeen, though with a marginal minority of the votes cast. Eden became Foreign Secretary for the third time.

A few months later an important event took place in his personal life. After the end of the war he and his first wife had drifted apart and in 1950 he obtained a divorce. In August 1952 he married Clarissa Churchill, a niece of the Prime Minister. All who knew them can attest that the marriage was a most happy one. Lady Avon, as she now is, supported her husband through all the vicissitudes of fortune with unfailing loyalty and devotion.

Eden's third tenure of the Foreign Office constitutes a record of unbroken success: a triumph of pacification, resulting from persistence, patience, immense attention to detail and a determination to explore every possible method of securing agreement. By the early months of 1955 the general diplomatic situation was in almost every field less menacing and more peaceful than it had been in the autumn of 1951. The Persian oil crisis had vanished. A treaty had been signed with Egypt, criticized only by the extreme right of the Tory party. A cease fire had been secured in Korea. The problem of Trieste had been solved. More important than any of these, a major confrontation between America and China as a result of the French defeat in Vietnam had been averted. Finally, the problem of European military cooperation, which had seemed insoluble after the collapse of the European Defence Community, had been settled, thanks to Eden's resourcefulness, by the creation of the Western European Union. It was very appropriate that, at the end of these negotiations in 1954 Eden, like his former chief Austen Chamberlain, was made a Knight of the Garter.

II

Eden kissed hands as First Lord of the Treasury on 6 April 1954. He was at once confronted with a difficult decision. Should he call for an immediate election? The Government had been in office for three and a half years. There was no constitutional need to dissolve Parliament until it had run its full five years, that is until October 1956. No doubt Prime Ministers seldom leave the decision quite as late as that, though Sir Alec Douglas-Home did so in 1964, but Eden had plenty of time in hand. He could have dissolved in the autumn rather than the early summer of 1955; in fact he would have left himself some room for manoeuvre even if he had waited another year and gone to the country in May or June 1956.

On the other hand, the Conservative majority was slender and a new Prime Minister was fully entitled, though not obliged, to seek a fresh mandate. Moreover, recent by-elections had not shown the usual swing against the Government and the opinion polls, though rightly not accepted by party managers as other than an uncertain guide, pointed in the same direction. A sense of material well-being was widespread in the country, and employment was high. Finally a mandate from the people would strengthen Eden's hand in the high-level negotiations expected in the summer. Yet, despite these considerations, an election was a risk. Eden must have been sorely tempted to give the country a chance to judge him on his own merits rather than as Churchill's dutiful second-in-command. And after all those years of waiting it would indeed have been a sad blow to find the highest office snatched away after a few weeks by the adverse verdict of the polls. Before, but perhaps in anticipation of, the announcement of a dissolution, Attlee, still Leader of the Opposition, half ironically congratulated the new Prime Minister, quoting the words said to have been addressed by his private secretary to Melbourne when the latter hesitated whether or not to accept the premiership. 'Why, damn it, such a position never was occupied by any Greek or Roman, and, if it only lasts two months, it is well worth while to have been Prime Minister of England.'

There were two further considerations to make Eden pause. The summer, according to a somewhat dubious piece of party managerial folklore, was supposed to be a bad time of year for the Conservatives to fight an election.[4] More serious perhaps, no party had actually increased its majority at two successive general elections since the Liberals under Gladstone in 1868 – and the Conservatives in 1955 had very little to spare.

Nevertheless Eden took the plunge and on 15 April announced in a broadcast to the nation that Parliament would be dissolved on 6 May and that the country would go to the polls on 26 May. In between the dissolution and the election came the Budget, which lowered the standard rate of income tax from 9s. to 8s. 6d. and was of course attacked by the Opposition as an 'electioneering budget'. Its effects are hard to gauge. On 21 April the Gallup poll gave the Conservatives a four-point lead. A week later, to the consternation of Government supporters, Gallup made the parties almost equal. But on 5 May there was a swing back to the Conservatives, who had a lead of one point. Thereafter Gallup showed them steadily widening their lead till it was back to four on the eve of the poll. But, in the light of the 1970 fiasco, who can know what these surveys mean?

Everyone agreed that it was a quiet election, the most outstanding feature being Anthony Eden's masterly television appearance. The Conservative campaign was managed by Lord Woolton whose principal aide in propaganda was Mark Chapman Walker, a most able practitioner of the art. Eden was anxious to do a direct face-to-face talk for fifteen minutes without a script. This was a bold step at the time and contravened the received wisdom of the 'experts'. Chapman Walker strongly supported Eden, and the resultant broadcast was a brilliant success. Throughout the campaign Eden remained calm, reasonable, persuasive and convincing. He naturally spoke a great deal about foreign affairs, but he did not neglect the home front. His appeal for a 'property-owning democracy' made good sense at the time and elicited a genuine response from the electorate. He deserved to win, and he did win. The Conservative majority rose from seventeen to over sixty. The prospect for the party and for the Prime Minister, whose personal efforts had done so much to achieve this result, seemed rosy.

Thus far Eden's debut as Prime Minister had been a notable success. There were, it is true, those who criticized him for not making bigger changes in his Cabinet. Of Churchill's ministers only Lords Swinton and De La Warr failed to find a place in the new Government. The vacancy in the Foreign Office created by Eden's own elevation was filled by Harold Macmillan. In his memoirs Eden describes how he would have preferred Lord Salisbury, who had been his Under-Secretary during his first spell at the Foreign Office and the only minister to have resigned with him in 1938. He goes on to explain that he felt it constitutionally impracticable to have a member of the House of Lords as Foreign Secretary. No doubt the pundits who write about the British constitution would have regarded this decision as an incontrovertible precedent but for the subsequent action of Macmillan himself who may not have entirely relished Eden's candour. In July 1960 he calmly bestowed the Foreign Office on the Earl of Home, as he then was. Apart from one or two mild yaps from the Opposition, scarcely a dog barked, and the appointment turned out to be highly satisfactory.

Public attention during the rest of the summer was largely concentrated on the first Four Power (summit) Conference held at Geneva in July which at first seemed promising but whose promise petered out in the sands of the Foreign Ministers' Conference during the early weeks of November. A by-product of the earlier conference was Eden's invitation to Khrushchev and Bulganin to visit London the following year. But there was also an ominous development in the field of foreign affairs; Russia decided to make a major arms deal with Egypt via Czechoslovakia which altered the whole balance of power in the Middle East, and profoundly alarmed the Israeli Government. Eden's first impulse was to conciliate Nasser. In his Guildhall speech on 9 November he suggested that if Israel and her Arab neighbours could reach an agreement on frontiers, Britain might guarantee them, possibly with American cooperation. Israel interpreted this as a hint at concession on her part. In December Eden went even further. The World Bank, the USA and Britain offered in principle to pay the foreign exchange costs of the new proposed Aswan dam, subject to negotiation about details. The object was to forestall a Russian offer. There the matter rested for the time being.

Meanwhile the Government had fared badly on the domestic front. After four years of prosperous growth the economy ran into the first of the many crises over inflation and the balance of payments which have plagued Britain ever since. The Treasury insisted on an autumn budget with higher taxes to 'mop up inflation'. The charge that the April Budget had been a bribe to the electorate was made more loudly than ever. R.A.Butler was deemed to have lost some of his credibility as Chancellor of the Exchequer. Eden made a major reshuffle in the Cabinet. Butler became Lord Privy Seal and Leader of the House. Crookshank and Woolton retired. Macmillan, much against his will, was transferred from the Foreign Office to the Treasury. He informed Eden that a condition of his reluctant acceptance was 'a position in the Government not inferior to that of the present Chancellor', and he insisted that Butler should not be 'deputy Prime Minister', adding in parenthesis, 'Incidentally this post does not exist constitutionally'. Eden agreed to these conditions but insisted that Butler should preside over the Cabinet in Eden's absence – a point which Macmillan apparently disputed, though he withdrew on the argument that Butler had already been doing this since the formation of the Government.[5] Macmillan was replaced at the Foreign Office by Selwyn Lloyd, the Minister of Defence. It has been suggested that Eden made the change in order to secure a less experienced, more pliant figure in that key post. It is fair to say that if there had to be a new Chancellor Macmillan was the obvious choice – a strong man in an area of policy in which the Prime Minister was himself inexperienced. What seems less convincing is the need to move Butler at all. Lloyd was succeeded by Walter Monckton. Iain Macleod became Minister of Labour *vice* Monckton.

Changes of personnel in December were not confined to the Government. Attlee resigned as Leader of the Labour party. Eden hoped that his successor would be Herbert Morrison. The vote, however, gave Gaitskell first place, Bevan second, Morrison third. 'I had no doubt,' wrote Eden, 'that this was a national misfortune. I was unable to establish with Mr Gaitskell the political and personal relations which I had enjoyed with all his predecessors. This was one of my failures but curiously enough in all my years of political life I had not met anyone with his cast of mind and approach to problems. We never seemed able to get on terms.'[6]

This incompatibility felt by Eden, which was not reciprocated by Gaitskell, is at first sight surprising. It is probably explained by the profound difference, not always sufficiently recognized, between the 'intellectual' and the 'man of the world'. Eden, highly intelligent, quick-witted, cosmopolitan, was not an intellectual; that is to say he was not in the least interested in general ideas about society. In fact, like most Conservatives, he operated within a closed world of assumptions seldom queried or if at all, only on highly pragmatic grounds. The exponents of change, Liberal or Labour, are by their very nature bound to question these assumptions. Gaitskell, though slightly donnish, was far from being an extreme example of the intellectual in politics, but he was nearer to it than his predecessor. There was a further cause of incompatibility. Eden differentiated sharply between those who had or had not served in the fighting forces during one or both of the two World Wars. Attlee had. Gaitskell had not.

The start of the new year was marked by a press campaign waged by the *Daily Telegraph* against Eden and his supposedly weak Government. Much gossip was spread about the personal animus against the Edens, which may or may not have lain behind it. The *Daily Mail* also began to attack him. Eden himself seemed curiously affected. Rumours circulated that he intended to resign. An unprecedented official denial was issued from Downing Street. In a speech at Bradford he referred to 'one or two of these cantankerous newspapers' in London. 'Yorkshire,' he said, 'will never forget that the first duty of a citizen of a free country is to think for his or her self.'

The first half of 1956 was an uneasy period. On 1 March General Glubb, Chief of Staff of the Arab Legion, was summarily dismissed by the twenty-year-old King Hussein of Jordan. Eden ran into further trouble with his speech in the House on this occasion. It was criticized as weak, inconclusive and ambiguous. In fact this was intentional. He was trying to mend relations with Jordan and avoid an open breach.

> The speech which I made in the debate was regarded as one of the worst in my career. I have no doubt that it was from the parliamentary point of view. I got well lectured in the House of Commons. My friends were embarrassed, my critics exultant ... But as diplomacy, the speech served its purpose. It broke no bridges with Jordan.[7]

In April the celebrated visit of Bulganin and Khrushchev took place. Whether any lasting results could have emerged from it no one can say. The Suez crisis and the Hungarian revolt, which followed so soon afterwards, swept away any chance of a détente for many years to come. One episode occurred, which still remains slightly mysterious. This was the affair of the frogman, Commander Crabb, who was killed in Portsmouth harbour during an unauthorized attempt to inspect the hull of the cruiser *Ordzhonikidze* which had conveyed the Russian party to England. When the Russians protested several days after their return, Eden took the very unusual, but in the circumstances fully justifiable, step of formally dissociating the Government from Commander Crabb's ill-fated venture. 'What was done was done without the authority or knowledge of Her Majesty's Ministers. Appropriate disciplinary steps are being taken.'[8] This last sentence, though correct, scarcely did justice to the convulsions which followed in the Secret Intelligence Service. The Prime Minister was understandably furious at what had happened. If 'C' (Sir John Sinclair) had not been due to retire within a week or so he would have certainly been dismissed. But Eden was determined to shake up violently the complacent department which by luck rather than good judgement had survived unreformed since the 1930s. Many heads rolled. He rejected Sinclair's official pre-selected successor, and horrified the mandarins of the service by not only appointing a civilian – the first ever – but by appointing the man who was head of MI5, the department which had always been SIS's deadly rival. Sir Dick White, the new 'C', brought a much needed breath of efficiency and common sense into his new empire. The reform of Britain's secret intelligence services is a by no means unimportant achievement of Eden's premiership.[9]

III

From the summer of 1956 to his resignation in January 1957 Eden's premiership was dominated by the Suez crisis. All other issues faded into the background. Lady Eden had good cause when she said that at times the Suez canal seemed to be flowing through her drawing-room. It is impossible in a brief essay to give a considered judgement on a matter so complicated and still highly controversial. Discussion must be confined to those aspects of the affair which are relevant to the working of the premiership.

The crisis began with the decision of the US and Britain to withdraw their offer of lending money to finance the Aswan dam. Many considerations contributed to this decision, including the removal of Glubb (attributed to Egyptian intrigues), Nasser's hostility all over the Middle East, his broken promise to Selwyn Lloyd in March to drop anti-British propaganda, his intrigues with Russia, as well as increasing doubts about Egypt's capacity to repay the loan. Apparently, though the exact facts are not quite clear, the British took the initiative, but the American Secretary of State, Foster Dulles, had independently come to the same conclusion. It was one of the few things on which he and Eden saw eye to eye, though even here they differed about the timing of the announcement. Dulles had considerable ability and was very knowledgeable about foreign affairs. But his knowledge tended to be more academic than practical, since his actual experience was limited. Most of his career had been in the law and he tended to take a rather legalistic attitude to problems. He was also extremely devious. These characteristics, together with a fondness for the high moral line on 'colonialism' and a remarkable capacity for thinking aloud in a slow voice at interminable length, were not calculated to endear him to Eden, any more than Eden's superior expertise, long experience and fashionable upper-class English mannerisms endeared him to Dulles. Though scrupulously polite, the two men disliked each other from the start. Eden, if Eisenhower's account is correct, had even gone so far as to ask the President not to appoint Dulles.[10] These personal antipathies may have contributed to the troubles that followed.

Eden says in his memoirs that he would have preferred to delay an announcement of the decision to withdraw from the Aswan dam project, but that Dulles on 19 July felt obliged to act without consultation for reasons connected with the timing of the American financial year. Nasser heard the news while he was at a meeting of leaders of the Third World at Brioni in Yugoslavia. It is unlikely to have been a shock to him. The evidence suggests that he himself was less than enthusiastic about the loan, and was using the negotiations chiefly to push up a Russian offer. But on 22 July Shepilov, the Russian Foreign Minister, disclaimed any promise by Russia to build the dam. Professor Hugh Thomas suggests that this may have finally tipped the scales in Nasser's mind in favour of nationalizing the Suez Canal Company, and using its revenues to finance the dam. However, Nasser said in retrospect that he would anyway have done something of this sort in the end.

Even if this is so, the timing and style of a political act are often as important as its content. On 26 July Nasser proclaimed the nationalization of the company in the most violent and offensive manner possible. He declared martial law in the canal zone, forbade employees of the company (including foreigners) to leave their posts, denounced Britain as a US satellite, poured scorn on Eden's cherished diplomatic achievement – the Baghdad Pact – and linked national-ization of the company with the financing of the dam, thus raising by implication the question whether it would only be built at the cost of running down the canal. His only concession was to promise compensation to shareholders at current prices, but this brought a liability of £70 million in addition to the cost of the dam in foreign exchange – at least £100 million – and seemed to put the general solvency of Egypt in jeopardy.

The news of Nasser's decision arrived while Eden was entertaining the King of Iraq and his Prime Minister Nuri es-Said to dinner at Downing Street. It could scarcely have come at a more provocative moment. Iraq was the corner-stone of Brtain's Middle Eastern policy. Nuri had been a loyal ally of Britain and the effective governor of his country for many years past. He was bitterly opposed to Nasser and all his works, rightly sensing the menace of pan-Arabism which was to bring barbaric slaughter to himself and his young master two years later. Eden regarded Nasser's action as the last straw. He had long abandoned any hope of conciliation. According to Anthony Nutting he had in his own mind declared war on Nasser immediately after the dismissal of Glubb in March. Nutting, Minister of State at the Foreign Office, had at that time, in conjunction with other officials, made suggestions (which sound singularly futile even by his own account) for neutralizing Nasser and isolating him from his Arab allies. Eden rang up in a rage, 'What's all this nonsense about isolating Nasser or "neutralizing" him as you call it? I want him destroyed, can't you understand?'[11] People say such things without necessarily meaning them, but an outburst of this kind may at least indicate the direction of the speaker's thoughts. Anyway it is clear enough that, whatever Eden believed in March after the fall of Glubb, he had finally made up his mind after Nasser's declaration on 26 July.

It was not merely a matter of the canal. Britain's whole position in the Middle East seemed in danger if Nasser was allowed to remain and consolidate his position as the secular caliph of the modern Arab world. Eden continually recalled the analogy of Hitler and the Rhineland. He made it clear in confidential communications, though not in public speeches, that the British Government had two objectives from then on, not only the safeguarding of transit through the canal but also the overthrow, or at any rate the open submission, of Nasser. These purposes might be achieved, Eden hoped, by the same policy but they remained distinct; it was quite practicable to devise a course of action which would attain the first without necessarily attaining the second.

Eden's commitment to this dual aim was spelled out unambiguously both in a telegram to Eisenhower on 5 August and in his directive to the Chiefs of Staff issued immediately after the Cabinet meeting of 27 July. That meeting, held on the day after Nasser's coup, was crucial and conditioned everything that followed.[12] It was agreed that failure of the Western powers to reassert their control over the canal would be fatal; if international pressure failed, Britain must be ready to use force – and if necessary, alone. Thereafter anyone who had doubts about later developments could be referred to this decision. Did he accept it at the time? If so, did he really wish to re-open the question? Had he not already consented to a whole series of diplomatic, military, logistic steps which as time passed became ever less easy to reverse?

The difficulty of backtracking was compounded by the creation of a committee to deal with the day-to-day handling of the crisis. The Egypt committee which was set up on 27 July consisted of the following: the Prime Minister, Anthony Eden; the Lord President, Lord Salisbury; the Chancellor of the Exchequer, Harold Macmillan; the Foreign Secretary, Selwyn Lloyd; the Commonwealth Secretary, Lord Home; the Minister of Defence, Sir Walter Monckton. Others attended as and when needed. It is perhaps significant that the person whom most people would have regarded as Eden's second-in-command, R.A.Butler, was not a member of the committee. There were precedents for devolving the day-to-day work in a crisis on to a small ministerial group. Indeed Neville Chamberlain had adopted a similar method of consultation during the summer of 1938. But inevitably the committee tends to make the running in such circumstances. However carefully the authority of the Cabinet is safeguarded in theory, it becomes extremely difficult in practice to overrule the advice of the group of ministers intimately involved in all the details of the affair.

It is right, however, to emphasize that no charge of unconstitutionality can be levelled at any of these proceedings. The crucial decisions which started the train of events – the withdrawal of support from the Aswan dam project, and the determination that Britain would in the last resort use force to re-establish international control over the canal – were taken in full accord with the usages of the British constitution. This does not necessarily make them right, but no minister is entitled to say that he did not have his chance to protest. In particular the charge made by Lord Kilmuir that the Cabinet had not been properly consulted about the decision to withdraw support from the Aswan dam seems to have no substance.[13]

There is no need to go into detail about the complicated international negotiations which took place between the beginning of August and the end of October when the decision in favour of Anglo-French intervention was finally taken. The later developments were all implicit in the events of the first few days following Nasser's announcement on the nationalization of the Suez Canal Company.

Eden informed the American Government the very next day that Britain would use force if necessary, and he repeated this declaration again and again in the ensuing weeks. Two days later on 29 July Herbert Hoover Jr, speaking on behalf of the State Department in the absence of Dulles, told the British Ambassador in Washington, Sir Roger Makins, that, 'in default of further overt action by Egypt, military action could not be justified'. Robert Murphy, sent as an emissary to see Selwyn Lloyd in London as soon as the crisis broke, said the same thing; and Dulles, arriving on 1 August with a letter from Eisenhower which emphasized American disapproval of force, confirmed that, although Nasser's action was intolerable, no justification existed yet for armed intervention. But Dulles used a phrase which long lingered in Eden's mind: 'a way had to be found to make Nasser disgorge what he was attempting to swallow'.[14] The Prime Minister undoubtedly took his observation too seriously. Murphy was nearer the mark when he said that it should be 'taken with a warehouse full of salt'.[15] In fact the American opposition to force, reinforced by the prospect of the presidential election in November, remained consistent throughout.

The French attitude was equally consistent. M.Pineau, the Foreign Minister, arrived to join the talks with Murphy and Selwyn Lloyd. He made it clear that the French Government which was headed by M.Guy Mollet, a socialist, was fully prepared to use force, would prefer to do so as soon as possible, and was ready to contribute substantially to Anglo-French military intervention.

Neither the Americans, British nor French looked at the problem in quite the same light, although the last two were much closer to each other than either was to the first. The Americans had far less at stake. The canal was not vital to them, and they did not depend on the Middle East for oil. They regarded European influence in that areas as something that was on its way out. They were anxious to be on reasonably good terms with the new nations which were replacing the old empires.

The American attitude tended to be legalistic and to dwell on the difficulty of establishing that Nasser had actually committed any breach of international law. The Suez Canal Company was arguably Egyptian. Its ninety-nine-year concession came to an end anyway twelve years later, and Nasser had offered full compensation to the shareholders. The American Government preferred to rely on the Maritime Convention of 1888 as a basis for any international action. In effect this meant that the only justification for force would be an actual blockage of the canal. The Americans would endeavour to secure international control, though this was asking for something which had not existed even before Nasser's 'grab' but only by economic and political pressure. Armed intervention would not be warranted until, whether through incompetence or malice, the Egyptians allowed the traffic in the canal to be obstructed.

The British and French Governments were as one in regarding this attitude with contempt. They believed that Nasser should be 'made to disgorge' by the threat and if necessary the use of force as soon as possible. Their motives were not quite the same. The French had no friends at all in the Arab world. They had a nationalist rebellion on their hands in Algeria, which they believed to be fed and supplied from Egypt. The rulers of the Fourth Republic regarded Cairo rather as the Hapsburg monarchy regarded Belgrade in 1914 – a hostile magnet for all the subversive nationalist forces in their own empire. They were quite prepared to enlist Israeli aid. They had, or believed they had, nothing to lose.

The British position was different. Eden too wished not only to assert international control over the canal but to topple Nasser, whom he regarded as a menace to the oil supplies and prestige of Britain in the Middle East. But he was far from having burned his boats with the rest of the Arab world. There was the Baghdad Pact signed early in 1955 to which Britain, Turkey, Pakistan, Iran and Iraq all adhered. Efforts to persuade Jordan to join had not been successful, but the Anglo-Jordanian treaty of 1948 was still in force. It is true that Britain was on bad terms with Syria, where Egyptian influence increasingly prevailed, and with Saudi Arabia which was using her immense oil revenues derived from the Arabian American Oil Company (ARAMCO) to stir up trouble in Jordan and Iraq. The role of ARAMCO was indeed a contributory factor to the uneasy relations between Eden and Dulles. Nevertheless Egypt, Syria and Saudi Arabia did not constitute the whole of the Middle East. The British Government still hoped to retain the goodwill of important Arab countries and Eden was certainly not regarded as a friend by the Israelis.

These differences between Britain and France were relevant as far as their attitude to Israel was concerned but did not affect their joint determination to use force at the earliest opportunity. There was only one snag which became apparent as soon as the issue had been referred to the Chiefs of Staff. Neither country was in a position to intervene, singly or jointly, for at least six weeks, unless it was prepared to risk the use of airborne troops unsupported by land forces.

Ever since Arnhem it had been an article of military faith that airborne troops must be supported within twenty-four hours. At the beginning of August, however, no such support could have come in less than ten days. It is said that the British Chiefs of Staff would have resigned if the Cabinet had insisted on sending in the Parachute Brigade immediately. No Prime Minister could have overruled them in such circumstances. Nevertheless in retrospect one cannot but wonder whether an immediate airborne landing might not, for all its risks, have been the only hope of achieving Eden's short-term objective. The old British bases in the canal zone might have been seized. They were still intact under the provisions of the 1954 treaty with Egypt, and contained stores and equipment for 80,000 men. Alternatively an immediate drop on Cairo might have brought down Nasser's regime. In spite of frequent comparisons made between Nasser and Hitler, the Egyptian army could hardly be equated with the sort of opposition which the airborne troops received at Arnhem. However, it would no doubt have been a risk and might have been a disaster.

What is certain is that inability to act at once immensely weakened the Anglo-French position. Negotiation could not now be avoided. But when negotiations begin they tend to go on and on; it becomes ever more difficult to break them off unless one's adversary provides a further *casus belli*. This was precisely what Nasser was determined to avoid. There were hopes that he might seize a ship as compensation for non-payment to Egypt of canal dues, alternatively that Egyptian technicians would be too incompetent to keep the canal open for traffic. Neither these, nor similar hopes were realised. Ships continued to pass through the canal, as easily as they always had, right up to the Anglo-French intervention. Then it was blocked for several months, but Nasser's most ardent enemy could hardly put the blame for that exclusively on him.

Before considering the course of negotiations it is necessary to glance briefly at public opinion in Britain. The immediate reaction to the nationalization of the Suez Canal Company had been strong and largely bi-partisan. Nasser's action was unanimously condemned in the House of Commons and in the press. Even *The Times* was hot for action:

> If Nasser is allowed to get away with his coup all the British and other Western interests in the Middle East will crumble. The modern world has suffered many acts like Hitler's march into the Rhineland or the Stalinist overthrow of freedom in Czechoslovakia which were claimed to be assertions of domestic sovereignty. They were, in fact, hinges of history. Nasser's seizure of the Canal Company was another such turning point. Quibbling over whether or not he was 'legally entitled' to make the grab will delight the finicky and comfort the fainthearted, but entirely misses the main issue.[16]

The Conservatives rallied to the Prime Minister's support with fervour. After the doubts and misgivings of the last few months Eden could feel that he now headed a loyal, united and determined party at last.

The Opposition took a strong line too. Herbert Morrison adjured the Government 'not to be too nervous'. On 2 August Hugh Gaitskell said: 'It is all very familiar. It is exactly the same as that we encountered from Mussolini and Hitler in the years before the war.' It is true that in the last few minutes of his speech, while supporting military preparations, he went on to say that Nasser had not so far done anything to warrant the use of force, which should only be employed in accordance with the UN Charter. But the weight of his words was in his condemnation of Nasser, not in the proviso at the end which sounded – and reads – like a postscript written in very small print. Later he tried to redress the balance and twice saw Eden in order to emphasize the point about force and the Charter. Eden regarded these reservations with contempt as another way of saying 'force never'; the Russians would always veto its use against a client state. He seems to have treated Gaitskell's démarche as 'a simple dissociation by the Opposition from his policy, which entitled him henceforth to ignore them'.[17]

The upshot of Eden's attitude was one of the few breaches of prime-ministerial convention that can be attributed to him. He told Gaitskell nothing at all until half an hour before the announcement of the Anglo-French ultimatum on 30 October. Never in modern times has a leader of the Opposition been kept so much in the dark about an impending military operation. Absence of official warning was probably a factor in the bitterness with which Gaitskell attacked the Suez intervention. Ironically that bitterness proved to be largely self-defeating. If Labour had not so palpably appeared to be the 'unpatriotic party' over Suez, they might not have fared so badly in the election of 1959.

The press, the parties and public opinion are not the only elements which matter when a country faces a grave crisis. What about 'the establishment' – that shadowy, indefinable but nonetheless real entity comprising Whitehall, the embassies, the City, the mandarins of academe, the episcopal bench? It is hard to be precise about their attitude. Perhaps the most that can be said is that it was quieter, less fervent, less excited. Certainly there was no serious dissent from the line taken by the Government but, in the Foreign Office at least, there were some misgivings lest the iniquities of Nasser should lead the Cabinet to abandon Britain's traditionally pro-Arab stance, or, worse still, sever 'the special relationship' with Washington. No one knew the personalities, prejudices and presuppositions of 'the Office' better than Eden. The extreme secrecy with which he surrounded his plans and his keeping of even the most closely concerned embassies in the dark can be partly explained by his knowledge that the permanent officials would deeply disapprove.

IV

Military preparations were complete by the beginning of September, and D-Day for operation 'Musketeer', as it was called, was fixed for the 26th, which meant that the Anglo-French armada would sail from Malta ten days earlier, on the 16th. The original plan was to bombard and land at Alexandria, proceeding thence to Cairo. It was later decided to make Port Said the point of attack instead. The hope was that occupation of the canal zone would automatically result in the fall of Nasser. If it did not the Anglo-French forces 'would turn right to Cairo'.

Meanwhile negotiations had been proceeding in London and Cairo. How seriously these were taken by Britain and France it is hard to say. No doubt a complete climb down by Nasser would have been welcome, but it cannot have been seriously expected. The Americans perhaps hoped for some results, but to most members of both British and French Governments diplomacy was a convenient sop to public opinion and a way of filling in time until military preparations were complete. At the beginning of September Sir Robert Menzies, the Prime Minister of Australia, took the proposals of the Twenty-two Power Conference, which had been sitting in London, to Nasser in Cairo. These proposals backed by eighteen of the countries concerned involved the creation of an international board of user nations of the canal. Nasser refused the proposals on 7 September, and three days later Menzies returned to London to confer with Eden and the French ministers, Mollet and Pineau, who had flown over for discussions. The critical decision now had to be taken whether or not to launch the expeditionary force from Malta. It was agreed that an essential preliminary would be to try to secure a mandatory resolution by the UN against Nasser. This would not take long. The resolution would certainly be vetoed by Russia and in that event force would be morally justified.

Sensing that hostilities were imminent Dulles came up with an elaborate proposal for the creation of a Suez Canal Users' Association. This body was to have its headquarters in Rome with an executive committee elected by the eighteen user powers. It would have ships stationed at each end of the canal and would deal with dues, maintenance and general administration. The French rightly regarded the plan as a means of prevarication. Eden, still reluctant to break with America, and almost certainly befogged by Dulles' obscure language, decided to give it a chance. The Cabinet agreed on 11 September. Selwyn Lloyd, after a sleepless night, came to the conclusion that the decision was wrong and that it was better to go straight to the Security Council. Eden dissuaded both him and the French from this course of action, and the die was cast on 12 September when Eden announced the news to Parliament, which had been specially reconvened at the request of the Opposition.

The ensuing debate was a splendid example of ignorance and cross purposes. Labour, now much more hostile to force than when the news of the 'grab' first burst, denounced the Government for not going to the UN. This was precisely what Eden and his colleagues had wanted to do – though for very different reasons – and would have done but for American pressure. Gaitskell attacked the SCUA as a means of by-passing the UN and of introducing force, which indeed Eden had clearly implied in his speech. But Eden might well have thought in the light of what followed 'If only Gaitskell had been right . . . !', for it soon became clear that Dulles intended to water the plan down till it meant virtually nothing. At an early stage he declared to a press conference that there was no question of shooting our way through the canal. This was to give away all the best cards in advance. Eden was understandably furious. On 22 September he and Mollet riposted by announcing without prior notice to Dulles that they intended to go to the Security Council. It was now Dulles' turn to feel that he had been double-crossed.

Relations between the two men could hardly have been worse. The last straw was Dulles' remark on 2 October to another press conference: 'There is talk of teeth being pulled out of the plan, but I know of no teeth; there were no teeth in it.' Nutting, who was with Eden when the report of this remark arrived and had been trying to persuade the Prime Minister not to abandon efforts at Anglo-American cooperation, vividly recalls his master's reaction as he contemptuously flung the piece of paper across the table: 'And now what you have to say for your American friends?' Nutting continues:

I had no answer. For I knew instinctively that this was for Eden the final let-down. We had reached breaking point. Up to now several ministers had been clearly concerned about the Prime Minister's go-it-alone policy so long as there was the slightest hope of getting the Americans to form a firm front with us . . . I knew that henceforth Eden would be able to count on the overwhelming majority of his Government for settling the issue by force irrespective of what the Americans might say. Dulles had provided him with an alibi [sic]* which none of his colleagues would be able to challenge.[18]

* The word 'alibi' is all too often used by writers who mean 'excuse'.

The Anglo-French recourse to the United Nations predictably ended in an impasse. Selwyn Lloyd and Pineau put a resolution in two parts to the Security Council. The first part contained six principles for the future status of the canal. They included free and open passage, insulation from the politics of one country, allocation of a fair percentage of tolls to development, and respect for Egyptian sovereignty. They were carried unanimously. The second stated that the principles were embodied in the proposals of the London Conference and the SCUA, and called on Egypt to implement them. It was vetoed by the Russians on 13 October. To the Prime Minister this was the end of the road. True, there was a suggestion that further discussions might take place between Egypt, France and Britain later at Geneva, but Eden with ample reason regarded this as a mere excuse for procrastination.

V

Precisely when the idea of acting in conjunction with Israel began remains obscure. The first record of its appearance is in a discussion at Chequers on Sunday 14 October, described by Anthony Nutting, who was there himself.[19] Since it has never been repudiated, this account must on the present state of the evidence be regarded as substantially correct. If so it settles the vexed question of 'collusion' for, according to Nutting, after luncheon the Prime Minister, his private secretary and Nutting discussed this very question with two emissaries from Guy Mollet – Albert Gazier, acting Foreign Minister in Pineau's absence, and General Maurice Challe, deputy Chief of Staff of the French air force. They outlined a plan which broadly corresponded to what eventually occurred: the Israelis should be invited to attack Egypt across the Sinai peninsula after which France and Britain would intervene to 'separate the combatants' and save the canal from damage by sending a joint expeditionary force to occupy its two terminal ports and control the passage of shipping. Neither the exact timing nor the extent of Israel's commitment was defined, but Nutting infers that the French wanted action as soon as possible and that the Israeli Government had given some measure of encouragement to the plan. Eden said that he would consider the matter carefully and give his reply after suitable consultation.

There is no doubt that the French Government had been in close contact with the Israelis from the very beginning of the crisis, and that the idea was not new to Eden. It seems clear that the possibility of some manoeuvre involving Israel had been floated by Eden to the Cabinet by 3 October at the latest. Nutting, who was not a member, evidently did not know this; nor did he know that the Cabinet, if Professor Thomas is correct, had agreed in principle to the plan, albeit half-heartedly in the case of some ministers.[20] Probably Dulles' inept remark about 'teeth' was the turning-point in the minds of many waverers. The news of it came through on the very morning of the Cabinet meeting. That afternoon Pineau on his way to New York is said to have seen Eden. It is not certain whether a definite decision was then taken in favour of joint action with Israel. Pineau subsequently said that it was; but he also said on another occasion that he simply told Eden of Israel's firm intention to wage a preventive war in the Sinai, and asked him to consider the next step.

The precise extent of the British commitment at this stage is far from clear. What does seem certain is that an ever-increasing degree of secrecy began to envelop ministerial discussions – so much so that when the Cabinet papers become available in 1987 they are unlikely to shed any more light on the transactions which ensued. Much was not documented and some documents did not survive. Although there was agreement in the Cabinet to take advantage of a preventive war which Israel was correctly believed to intend anyway, the detailed knowledge of individual ministers probably varied – particularly concerning the degree of cooperation between France and Israel, and the extent to which British plans would have to be aligned, by however indirect methods, with those of the Israeli General Staff.

On 5 October Eden was suddenly taken ill with a fever and a very high temperature. It was connected with the operation on his bile duct in 1953 and was an ominous sign that he was far from cured. But he recovered quickly. He was back at Downing Street on 8 October, and five days later, on the last day of the Conservative Conference at Llandudno, he made a highly successful speech. It clearly confirmed his ascendancy over the party re-established by him during the early days of August.

Although it is likely that the decision of principle had been taken before General Challe's visit on 14 October, the importance of that visit should not be underestimated. Principle is one thing, details another. Here was a definite proposal needing a definite answer. Selwyn Lloyd was summoned back from New York. On 16 October he and Eden flew to Paris to collogue with Mollet and Pineau without the presence of any advisers or officials, much to the consternation of the ambassador, Sir Gladwyn Jebb. On 18 October the Cabinet discussed the whole situation in the light of the latest information about Israeli plans.

It was certainly true that Israel intended to strike against Egypt. For nearly a year Ben Gurion had been determined to destroy the *fedayeen* bases in Gaza and to secure the gulf of Akaba for Israeli shipping. There had been continuous Franco-Israeli military discussions about the matter from the beginning of the crisis. Eden had at first regarded any sort of cooperation with Israel as out of the question and had repulsed French hints in that direction, but at least one minister – Selwyn Lloyd – apparently told Lester Pearson, the Canadian Foreign Minister, on 7 September that he would not be surprised if, in the event of further delay by Britain and France, Israel acted on her own. Professor Thomas suggests that this possibility, though not the only reason, may have had something to do with the switch from Alexandria to Port Said as the landing point of the Anglo-French expeditionary force. That decision was taken on 10 September. The Israeli attacks on Jordan, which we now know to have been a diversionary smoke screen for preparations against Egypt, began on the same day.

It was one thing for Eden to be aware of the possibility of an unsolicited Israeli attack on Egypt and to know off the record a good deal about Franco-Israeli military talks; it was quite another to engage in a joint operation coordinated in advance with the Israeli Government. Ideally any British Cabinet would have preferred to intervene without consulting Israel at all. The snag was a military one. The original Israeli plan of campaign simply involved the elimination of the Gaza bases and the opening of the gulf of Akaba. Such limited objectives were no use for Anglo-French policy since they could not conceivably raise the bogey of a battle anywhere near the Suez canal and thus constitute an excuse for intervention. What was needed, if intervention was to be at all plausible, was an Israeli advance across the Sinai desert. But the Israelis required for that a degree of air support which could only be supplied by Britain – i.e. a continuous watch over Egyptian air fields from the moment the Israeli forces crossed the frontier and the elimination of the Egyptian air force before they committed themselves to the desert. Ben Gurion was going to take no risks on this. It is the key to the whole question of 'collusion'. If the French air force had possessed the necessary striking power, Britain could have preserved a seeming innocence till war actually began. As it was, however, the Israeli Government had to be certain in advance of what Britain would do.

The meetings of the four ministers in Paris on 16 October and of the British Cabinet two days later were decisive. According to Eden's own account, his primary concern in Paris was the danger of Israel attacking Jordan; King Hussein would then invoke the Anglo-Jordanian treaty of 1948 – clearly a most embarrassing possibility given the close relations between France and Israel and the likelihood of Nasser coming in on Jordan's side. 'For this reason if there were to be a break-out it was better from our point of view that it should be against Egypt.'[21] The possibility of an Israeli attack on Jordan had been genuinely feared in Britain during the first fortnight of October. There was no means of knowing that Israeli raids into Jordan were intended as a diversion; even if they were the diversion could easily have grown into a real crisis. But it is hard to believe that this fear could have been quite so serious after General Challe's visit on 14 October, although perhaps it could not yet be wholly dismissed. According to Nutting, whose source was Selwyn Lloyd himself, Eden at the Paris meeting on the 16th definitely endorsed the French plan, though he hoped to keep direct contact with Israel to the minimum.[22] Eden's own account of the subsequent Cabinet meeting does not refer to the possibility of an Israeli-Jordanian war, but merely to discussion of 'the growing danger that Israel, under provocation from Egypt, would make some military move'.

In the light of later events it must be assumed that Eden also informed the Cabinet, at least in broad outline, of the French plan which at once put paid to any danger of an Israeli attack on Jordan. How far the full military details were passed on to the Cabinet it is impossible to say, but the course on which the Government was embarking must have been clear enough by now, and anyone who had real doubts could have challenged the helmsman. It is significant that 18 October was the date of Walter Monckton's resignation as Minister of Defence. He was replaced by Anthony Head, Secretary for War – the substitution of a 'hawk' for a 'dove'. Monckton rather feebly remained in the Cabinet as Paymaster General. There is plenty of evidence to show that from 14 –18 October onwards the decision to go in with the Israelis was almost irrevocable. The Americans noticed a sudden cessation of the usual inter-Military Attaché exchanges. There was a curious gap in ambassadorial links; Sir Roger Makins left Washington on 11 October, Sir Harold Caccia arrived by boat on 8 November. The British Government became far more cautious with the press. Extreme secrecy enveloped all British diplomatic dealings. It is said that the only civil servants to be fully informed were Lord Normanbrook, Secretary to the Cabinet, Sir Ivone Kirkpatrick, the Permanent Under-Secretary at the Foreign Office, and Sir Patrick Dean, deputy Under-Secretary dealing with the coordination of political and military intelligence. None of the ambassadors was told of what impended.

There were the usual last-minute hitches to be expected in a clandestine and ill-thought-out plan of this nature. Ben Gurion had misgivings about Britain's role. It is alleged on evidence, anonymous but claimed to be reliable, that he insisted on a signed tripartite declaration of intent, and that after secret flights by various high personages between Tel Aviv and Paris, and London and Paris, such a document was drawn up. At first Sir Patrick Dean signed on behalf of Britain, but Ben Gurion insisted on a more weighty signature and got it. The participants in this episode are supposed to have sworn never to reveal their knowledge in the lifetimes of any of the others.[23] These events apparently occurred on 23 and 24 October at Sèvres.

Sir Patrick Dean acted as a loyal Government servant throughout. His conduct, which was entirely correct, was ill-requited. He had every expectation of becoming head of the Foreign Office. He was passed over, and the real reason, whatever justification may have been found, was his involvement in an episode of which the newly returned Labour Government had deeply disapproved.[24] Such treatment of a civil servant who simply obeyed orders can only be termed shabby. It could be a bad precedent if followed, and it could damage the whole nature of the relationship between politicians and those who serve them.

The Cabinet took its final decision on 25 October. Any misgivings must have been diminished by the announcement two days earlier of a united Arab command between Egypt, Syria and Jordan, with Egypt in the lead. There is no reason to believe that the Cabinet was other than fully informed about the discussions at Sèvres and the measures which were about to be taken. No doubt some ministers were more *au fait* than others with exact details and precise timing; this is usually the case in operations of war and implies no departure from constitutional propriety. The Israeli Cabinet did not finally ratify the plans of Ben Gurion and his Chief of Staff, General Dayan, until 28 October, but the French, and through them the British, had already been informed that the attack would go in on the 29th. The joint Anglo-French command had been planning on this basis for several days past. On the 27th aircraft carriers moved east from Malta, and on the next day the slower transport ships began to sail for Port Said.

At 4 p.m. on 29 October Israeli troops crossed the Egyptian frontier, and the RAF began its watch over Egyptian airfields that evening. The next day Eden informed the Cabinet that an Israeli force 'was reported to be striking towards Suez'. At 4.15 p.m. the ultimatum agreed by the Cabinet on the 25th was presented to the Egyptian and Israeli ambassadors. It called on both sides to withdraw ten miles from the canal. If they did not comply within twelve hours, British and French forces would occupy the canal zone temporarily in order to stop hostilities and safeguard shipping. The Israelis promptly accepted – not surprisingly since they were nowhere near to being within ten miles of the canal. The Egyptians naturally refused. The ultimatum expired at dawn on 31 October, and the allied air offensive began that evening, but the rigid planning of the seaborne invasion meant that no landing could take place till 6 November. This delay was to be fatal to whatever chances of success the operation might have had. Among other things it gave the Egyptians ample time to sink over thirty block-ships in the canal.

Meanwhile Eden had informed Gaitskell of the Government's note to Egypt and Israel only ten minutes before it was delivered, and the House of Commons a quarter of an hour after. In the circumstances the reaction of the Opposition could hardly fail to be hostile – and it was. The Americans and the Commonwealth countries learned the news on the ticker tape. If it was any consolation British embassies all over the world were similarly treated. That most sober of ambassadors, Sir William Hayter, reading the news on his return from a party at the Kremlin, could not believe his eyes and thought that he must have drunk too much vodka. This secrecy even extended to the man on the spot, Sir Humphrey Trevelyan in Cairo. His account in his memoirs, though a masterpiece of self-restraint, leaves no doubt about his opinion of his treatment.

The events which followed need only be recapitulated in outline. Eisenhower, Dulles and the American administration felt themselves duped, as indeed they had been – though one can well see why Eden and Mollet chose that course. The whole American weight was thrown behind various moves to condemn Britain and France in UNO, and the two countries were twice forced to use their veto in the Security Council. On 2 November the General Assembly passed a resolution tabled by Dulles by sixty-four votes to five, calling for an immediate cease-fire in the Middle East. The next day Eden replied on behalf of France as well as Britain. The two Governments would stop military action if a UN peace force were created, if it were accepted by Israel and Egypt pending a settlement, and if both sides meanwhile agreed to the stationing of limited detachments of Anglo-French troops between the combatants. A resolution in favour of a peace force was proposed by Lester Pearson, Canadian Foreign Minister, and duly carried.

By 5 November Israel had obtained all her objectives and had nothing to gain by resisting the UN call for a cease-fire, but Ben Gurion agreed to prevaricate for the sake of his allies. The Anglo-French armada of over a hundred ships and 100,000 men was at last approaching Port Said – slowly, but strictly according to schedule. All efforts to expedite it, or to put in parachute troops earlier and take a risk on the lack of immediate support, had foundered. The Anglo-French parachute troops were dropped near Port Said at dawn on 5 November. The operation was a complete success and a further wave arrived at 1.45 p.m. Shortly afterwards the local Egyptian commander agreed to discuss terms for a cease-fire. This was ordered at 3.30 p.m. and when the news came through to London in a slightly garbled form there were scenes of wild excitement on the Conservative side of the

House, contrasting sharply with a glum silence on the Opposition benches, which made Labour seem more than ever like the 'unpatriotic' party. But Nasser quickly countermanded the surrender. A note of a most menacing and offensive nature was sent to Eden by Bulganin on behalf of the Russian Government which, having been immersed for several days in the brutal suppression of the Hungarian nationalist revolution headed by Imre Nagy,[25] had only just come to appreciate that the Americans really were as hostile as they said they were to the whole Suez operation.

At dawn on 6 November a carefully selective naval bombardment of Port Said began. Commandos followed by tanks landed soon after. Late that afternoon the Egyptian governor surrendered, and an armoured column under Brigadier Butler set out along the road to Suez. He had gone some twenty-five miles and was a little beyond the village of El Cap by midnight when the news came through that the British Government had ordered a cease-fire.

Why did Eden call off the troops just when the occupation of the whole canal zone was within easy reach? This has always been the most curious feature of the whole story. It is easier to say what did not influence the decision than what did. Parliamentary opposition, whether from Labour or from within the Conservative party, appears to have had little effect. True, there were scenes and uproar in the House, the apogee being reached on 1 November when the Speaker had to suspend the debate for half an hour. But the Conservative front bench was too tough to be shaken by that sort of thing. Gaitskell played his cards badly. Aware of the existence of a dissentient group of Conservatives, he appealed to them in a television broadcast to overthrow the Government. Anything more certain to be counter-productive is hard to imagine. As for the dissident Conservatives there is no way to be sure how strong a force they constituted. When the crisis was all over they had every reason to keep quiet. The reputation of being 'unsound on Suez' was something which for many years to come did a politician no good at the grass roots of the party.

There seems to have been a group of about fifteen MPs who made their misgivings known to the Chief Whip, Edward Heath. They were led by Alec Spearman, and included the ex-Attorney-General, Sir Lionel Heald, Walter Elliott, Robert Boothby, Keith Joseph, Peter Kirk,

Nigel Nicolson, J.J.Astor and John Foster.[26] They might well have come out into open opposition if the cease-fire had not been announced on 6 November. But as it was they probably had little effect on Eden. Certainly he claims this in his memoirs, referring to them rather slightingly as 'weak sisters'.[27]

No one resigned from the Cabinet, though, as we have seen, Walter Monckton came near to doing so. Two junior ministers resigned – Anthony Nutting, Minister of State at the Foreign Office, and Edward Boyle, Financial Secretary to the Treasury. The Solicitor General, Sir Harry Hylton-Foster, is said to have penned a letter of resignation which he did not send.[28] There may well have been other ministers who viewed the Suez policy with misgiving but found their dilemma solved by the rapidity with which it was put into reverse.

The press was on the whole hostile, *The Times* making a complete volte-face and thus giving credibility to the notion that, when the crunch came, it would always be on the side of appeasement. The *Express* was almost the only wholehearted supporter of Eden's policy. The BBC was strongly opposed to Suez, or at any rate was believed to be by the Government. As for other influences, the churches were highly critical, and the universities, always citadels of belief in the high left-wing moral line, bombinated against the Prime Minister. There was much discontent too, though private rather than public, in the corridors of power at Whitehall. Had the crisis continued there might have been resignations high up in the Foreign Office which tended to be pro-Arab and pro-American. In the event only a few junior members of the service felt obliged to leave.

It is safe to say that none of the internal manifestations of dissent shook the Government which had some reason to think that public opinion as a whole was on its side. The Gallup poll on 11 November showed fifty-three per cent satisfied with Eden's conduct of affairs in the Middle East as against thirty-two per cent dissatisfied and fifteen per cent 'don't knows'.[29] Eden quotes the *Daily Express* poll which showed support of the Government rising from forty-eight and a half per cent to fifty-one and a half per cent between 30 October and 5 November while opposition fell from thirty-nine per cent to thirty per cent.[30] He says too that the proportion of hostile letters which he received fell from eight to one at the beginning of the week to one in four just before the cease-fire.[31] The only Labour leader to be aware of this widespread working-class support for Eden was Aneurin Bevan whose attacks were far more skilful than Gaitskell's, concentrating on ineptitude, rather than immorality which cut little ice with the masses, however much it distressed some middle-class consciences.

If internal protest had no effect, we must look abroad for the cause. The pressure of world opinion, for which the cease-fire has sometimes been claimed as a triumph, can be dismissed. Eden and Mollet must have expected an uproar from the UN. They certainly got it, but there is no reason to believe that it swayed them. Nor can Bulganin's note have been taken seriously. Although he hinted at a threat to fire rockets into London, the best evidence today shows that the Russians could not have done it. In any case the American Government, however much annoyed with Britain and France, at once made it clear that they would retaliate with their far greater nuclear capacity, if Russia attacked London or Paris.

There seem to have been two major reasons in the decision to stop. The first – and it is the one Eden himself gives – is that as soon as the Israelis accepted the UN demand and fighting between Israel and Egypt ceased, 'the justification for further intervention ceased with it'. This may seem odd when one remembers what the British Government of course never admitted, viz. that the real object was to occupy the canal and 'topple Nasser'. 'Separation of the combatants' was an excuse, and a cover for another purpose altogether; the timing of our intervention and the many revelations which have subsequently appeared without being denied leave no doubt on this score. But the Government by 6 November was caught in a web of its own weaving. What reason could it give in public for going on after the fighting had ended? The French, realists to the end, were quite ready to continue hostilities without giving any reason but the British were not, and Mollet was unwilling to go on alone.

The other reason for stopping was financial – the run on the pound. The details are still slightly puzzling, and not least of the puzzles is the role of the Chancellor of the Exchequer. All accounts agree that Harold Macmillan was one of the most vigorous supporters of the Suez intervention and one of the most influential members of the Egypt Committee of the Cabinet. As Chancellor he presumably regarded it as his special duty to attend to the economic aspects of the operation, but he seems to have foreseen neither the likelihood of heavy selling of sterling nor the unlikelihood of any help from the US Treasury except on conditions of a very unpalatable nature.

Exactly what happened is still obscure and the exchanges between the monetary authorities in London and Washington have never been published. According to Randolph Churchill,[32] Macmillan was advised on 6 November that only a loan of 1000 million dollars from the International Monetary Fund could prevent the devaluation of the pound. The Americans had an effective veto on any loan by the IMF and Macmillan was told from Washington that he could not have it unless the British Government ordered a cease-fire at midnight. Macmillan, according to another version, went so far as to say that he could not remain responsible for the Exchequer unless there were a cease-fire.[33] Other accounts suggest that the situation was by no means as desperate as this and that Britain could have continued for another six or eight weeks before being obliged to devalue.[34] It is no doubt true that financial difficulties would, in the absence of American aid, have forced the devaluation of sterling at a fairly early date. The question is, how early? It is hard to believe that there was not enough time for the Anglo-French forces to establish themselves the whole length of the canal[35] – which would at least have given Eden and Mollet a better bargaining position, not to mention the opportunity of removing the sunken blockships.

It was probably not so much the immediate threat to the pound which influenced the Cabinet as the final realization that the Americans meant business, that they were not putting up a mere front and that Britain could not sustain her policy in the long run against strong American opposition. One of the strangest features of the whole Suez crisis is the way in which British ministers persuaded themselves that they had been somehow let down by Washington. Yet none of the documents and memoirs so far published suggest the slightest possibility that the American Government would condone the action taken. One can only surmise that Eden and his colleagues simply did not believe what was said to them, that they regarded it as a form of words made necessary by the impending elections, and expected the Americans to accept, no doubt with disapproval, a *fait accompli.* If this was really the case, it is difficult to see what Eisenhower and Dulles could have done to show that they meant what they said except by actions; and these could only be taken after the beginning of the very crisis which words were powerless to avert.

Eden says in his memoirs that there was no dissent in the Cabinet at the decision to cease hostilities. Other versions suggest that three ministers, Thorneycroft, Lennox-Boyd and Head, pressed for continuing the advance to Suez.[36] It would be incredible if no one had at least argued this case, which in retrospect seems overwhelming. Head was the only one to give his opinion in public. To the House of Commons on 18 December he said in defence of the military planners:

> The operation is now regarded as a failure. Why? (Hon. members: 'Because it failed'). Because of its execution? Because of its planning? No – because it stopped. When we ask why it stopped, Hon. and Right Hon. Gentlemen opposite have not, I think, an entirely clean sheet.
>
> In my view the tragedy is that the operation stopped....'

Head was also the only Cabinet minister who dropped the pretence of 'separating the combatants', declaring to the House on 8 November that the canal must not be solely the concern of the Egyptian Government. 'That is what all this has been about.' Evidently the dissentients were overruled and accepted the majority view. One would like to know more of the deliberations of this unhappy Cabinet, but it will be many years before the truth emerges, if it ever does.

Eden's premiership did not last long beyond the cease-fire, though it would be wrong to see in this a case of cause and effect. The strain of the crisis coming on top of his feverish attack in October resulted in medical advice that he must at all costs take a respite from work. On 23 November he flew to Jamaica to recover, leaving Butler in charge of the Cabinet. He returned on 14 December. By then the humiliating obsequies of the Suez expedition were well advanced. A UN peace force of a sort had been assembled after much haggling with Nasser and its advance guard was in the canal zone. The canal remained blocked – likewise all offers to clear it under Anglo-French auspices. Relations between London and Washington had reached the nadir of the post-war era. The French for opposite reasons were scarcely on better terms with Britain. On 22 December the great armada began its departure. As was often said at the time, there had been nothing like it since the days of the Grand Old Duke of York.

Soon after Christmas Eden suffered from signs of a recurrence of the fever which had laid him low in October. He consulted his doctor, Lord Evans, who gave a gloomy verdict, but advised him to obtain further opinions. In the light of these Eden decided that he had no option but to retire. He formally tendered his resignation to the Queen on 9 January. It is often stated that he was not asked to advise who should succeed him. This is not true. He was consulted, but very properly never revealed what his advice was. In any case it could not be binding, and many others were consulted too. The press and public expected R.A.Butler to be the choice, but on 10 January the Queen sent for Harold Macmillan who accepted her offer to form a Government.

VI

Anthony Eden's premiership does not raise any notable constitutional questions as far as the office is concerned. Suez, writes Professor Thomas, 'showed the almost limitless power of a Prime Minister in present circumstances, particularly when supported by a powerful group of Ministers'. This is true enough, but the same could be said of Munich, of Chanak, of the outbreak of the 1914–18 war, and of Disraeli's Near East policy in 1876–8. It is hard to find in Eden's conduct any breach of the principle of collective responsibility, although hints to that effect have sometimes been given. No doubt some ministers knew more than others. Eden like many of his predecessors preferred to take counsel with those who sympathized rather than with those who did not. In an undated note written some time afterwards Walter Monckton, after describing his own misgivings when 'I discovered the way in which it was proposed to carry out the enterprise', goes on to say:

I did not like the idea of allying ourselves with the French and the Jews in an attack on Egypt. . . . One of the curious features of the whole affair as far as the Cabinet was concerned was that owing to the not unnatural habit on the Prime Minister's part of preferring to take into complete confidence, when things were moving fast, only those with whom he agreed, many of us in the Cabinet knew little of the decisive talks with the French until after they happened and sometimes not even then. . . .

I ought to add for the guidance of those who may read this, that I was the only member of the Cabinet who openly advised against invasion though it was plain that Mr Butler had doubts and that Mr Heathcoat Amory was troubled by it.[36]

This is the only first-hand account by any member of the Cabinet, apart from memoirs written with the Official Secrets Act in mind and doctored accordingly by the Cabinet Office. It therefore has a particular value as historical evidence, but it does not amount to an indictment of the Prime Minister on constitutional grounds. Eden's relationship with his Cabinet did not differ from that of many of his predecessors. One gains a strong impression that, if some ministers knew less than others, it was because they preferred to do so, not because they were deliberately kept in the dark.

Anthony Eden had a comfortable parliamentary majority and on the general question of taking a tough line towards Nasser public opinion was behind him from the beginning. Moreover he was under very strong pressure from his own party to reverse the Egyptian dictator's coup. It would have been difficult for any Prime Minister to swallow the insult and wait in the hope that economic and other forces would induce Nasser to negotiate a satisfactory settlement. One could go so far as to say that the political climate in Britain in 1956 was such that a passive reaction was simply not possible. The same applied even more strongly in France.

The alternatives were either Anglo-French force openly applied to make Nasser 'disgorge', or exploitation of the quite separate quarrel between Israel and Egypt. In retrospect it is clear that the first of these courses would have been much the better. In fact the best of all would have been instant action within a day or so of the nationalization of the Suez Canal Company. The unprepared state of the armed forces made this impossible, but an invasion could have been launched any time after the middle of September. It was a major error to be diverted by Dulles' SCUA proposals. Britain would have done better to follow French advice, go straight to the United Nations, and, after the inevitable Russian veto, claim the freedom to act in defence of her vital interests. No doubt American opposition to such a policy would have been strong and the Labour party would have been highly critical, but there would not have been the sense of moral outrage provoked by the duplicity which 'collusion' with Israel made necessary. Nor would the British and French Governments have been prisoners of their own public reasons for intervention; they could legitimately have continued at least till the canal was in their hands, if not till Nasser was 'toppled'.

The Israeli plan to wage a preventative war that autumn, together with the delay caused by SCUA, made it inevitable that Anglo-French intervention would be tangled with Israeli action. In the immediate aftermath of Suez the question was often asked why Britain and France intervened at all. Why was it not left to the Israelis to do the work for them? As we have already seen the answer which could not be made at the time was that the Israelis' original intention had been too limited. Occupation of Gaza and the gulf of Akaba did not help the canal situation in the least, and Ben Gurion made it quite clear that he would not commit his forces to cross the Sinai desert without a guarantee, which only Britain could give, that the Egyptian air force would be eliminated first.

Perhaps it would have been better, as Professor Kedourie has suggested,[37] to have intervened on publicly stated grounds that the quarrel was with Egypt, not with the other Arab States, and that in such a quarrel Israel was a natural ally. The French, left to themselves, would have been quite happy to do this, but they were aware of Eden's anxiety to avoid overt identification with Israel lest he should lose all his Arab allies. Hence their suggestion of the subterfuge that was adopted. In the event it deceived scarcely anyone who mattered, and Britain's subsequent relations with the other Arab states would have been no worse if cooperation with Israel had been unconcealed. Indeed they might have been better, since the charges of hypocrisy and dishonesty would not have been added to that of being on the wrong side.

Moreover, the clandestine nature of the operation resulted in a breach of one of those usages of the constitution which are nonetheless real for being hard to define. Never before in moden

British history has so little been revealed not only to our allies and to the Commonwealth but to civil servants, the military planners and the other executive figures upon whom the execution of policy depends. The need to avoid any leak about the true nature of the relationship with Israel was the primary reason, but it is difficult to avoid the impression that there was a subsidiary reason too. Civil servants advise as well as execute. The majority of Foreign Office opinion, especially that of its legal department, would have been against the Suez venture; and so too would have been the principal ambassadors. Once Eden and Selwyn Lloyd had made up their minds and carried the Cabinet with them they may well not have wished to hear adverse counsel from their officials any more than they wished to hear it from Dulles, or Lester Pearson, or Nehru. This was natural enough but it meant that the administrators knew virtually nothing till the ultimatum was presented, which is hardly the most efficient way of conducting an operation of war. The British system of government is not geared to conspiratorial methods, and, whatever the justification may have been for adopting them in this case, such secrecy must have been detrimental.

In addition it led to another breach of convention. A Government contemplating the use of armed force would normally do all it could to 'square' the Opposition. Gaitskell's side of the story has yet to be told, but it is clear that he was informed about the ultimatum only a few minutes before it was delivered and that he had never expected the Government to use force without consulting him. Whatever hope there was of national unity disappeared. Perhaps there was not much anyway, but some of the bitterness might have been mitigated.

The clandestine nature of the affair made it impossible for ministers to deal candidly with the House of Commons. Actual falsehoods were rare, though it is possible to identify one or two, but unless we discount entirely the evidence in Walter Monckton's papers, together with the revelations of Anthony Nutting and of the numerous unnamed ministers whom Professor Hugh Thomas consulted when writing his book, there must have been a great deal of *suppressio veri* – principally of course in connection with the charge of 'collusion'. No one of sense will regard such falsehoods in a particularly serious light. The motive was the honourable one of averting further trouble in the Middle East, and this was a serious consideration for many years after the event. The conferment in 1971 upon Selwyn Lloyd of the Speakership, the greatest honour which the House of Commons can give, showed that politicians on both sides recognized the dilemma in which he found himself, and did not in retrospect count his conduct against him.

Two points were often made at the time about the Prime Minister himself. One concerned his health. It was alleged that but for illness clouding his judgement Eden would not have made the miscalculations which he undoubtedly did make during the Suez crisis. This is an issue on which it is impossible to be certain, but as far as present evidence goes, there is no reason to believe that affairs would have gone differently if the Prime Minister had been in the best of health. After all he was not a dictator and he carried with him not only the whole Cabinet, some of whom may have been dubious and hesitant, but a substantial group of ministers headed by Macmillan, who were enthusiastically in favour of his policy and of whose good health there has never been any question. The miscalculations over Suez are not to be explained by one man's illness. They stem from much wider causes: a failure to appreciate the changed status of Britain and France as world powers and the changed attitude of Washington toward 'the special relationship', and above all perhaps a failure to think out clearly what would follow if the Anglo-French intervention succeeded and Nasser actually was toppled. These were collective errors of judgement which influenced almost the whole of the Conservative party and a large section, probably a majority, of the nation. ·

The second point made about Eden was that, whatever his health had been like, he would have been ousted from the premiership sometime in 1957 as a result of the failure of his policy. Here again one is in a realm of uncertainty. All that can be said is that no evidence for this proposition has been produced. No doubt the breakdown that obliged him to recuperate in Jamaica at the height of the crisis shook the confidence of his colleagues; it may be that an effort would have been made to persuade him to retire, and that it was anticipated by the illness which early in January finally made him decide to resign. His departure to Jamaica was itself necessitated by bad health. What would have happened, if he had remained fit and well in London throughout, is quite another matter. Prime Ministers are not toppled so easily. Eden was highly popular even after the cease-fire. But for his illness he probably could have survived.

Suez was a turning-point, 'a hinge of history', in the words of *The Times*. But the consequences were not as sensational as many people predicted. Britain's relations with the Arab countries of the Middle East were deteriorating anyway. It is hard to discern particular developments which would not otherwise have occurred, apart from short-term embarrassments like petrol rationing caused by the blocking of the canal. The importance of the canal itself has much diminished since the discovery of new oil deposits and the construction of the gigantic tankers which take the route round Africa. The Six Days War in 1967 blocked it yet again, but the Western world scarcely noticed this minor inconvenience. To say this is not to belittle the fears of those who in 1956 foresaw a stranglehold by Nasser on the economies of Britain and the other West European countries. The events of 1973 show how vulnerable the Western world can be. Technological changes are difficult to predict. But this very fact is perhaps a reason for not reacting too suddenly when 'vital lifelines' are allegedly threatened. There is something to be said for playing it long and cool, and waiting for time's revenge. In the aftermath of Suez a book was published with the title *The Most Important Country*, a reference to Egypt. It was an exaggeration even then. Who would even think of describing Egypt like that now?

At the time of Eden's resignation the Suez fiasco was generally expected to ruin the Conservative party. People talked of its being wrecked for twenty years and of a set-back comparable only to the crisis over the repeal of the corn laws in 1846. No one would have dared to predict that less than three years later the party would win its third successive general election – and with a substantially increased majority. This recovery owed much to the personal sang-froid of Macmillan, to the high level of national economic prosperity, and perhaps something to a feeling that, even if Suez was a blunder, it was not the crime which the Opposition had accused it of being. The Labour party, conscious of being tarred with the 'unpatriotic' brush, signally failed to profit from the Conservative disarray.

On a longer-term view Suez did the Conservatives harm. The

relationship between the Tory party and the intellectual classes has always been an uneasy one, and, although right-wing intellectuals exist, it is a safe guess that they are usually outnumbered by those who are Labour, Liberal or simply non-political. The party can live with this situation and can still continue to win general elections, as long as strong passions are not stirred and as long as it does not seem positively disreputable in the eyes of the professors, writers, commentators and publicists. But if its intellectual support falls below a certain point, its electoral fortunes will fall too. The process takes time. Suez shocked the intelligentsia but Macmillan won the 1959 election. A few years later, however, the moral censure of that class was contributing to the general anti-establishment mood which led to the narrow defeat of 1964 and to the decisive defeat of 1966. 'Suez,' the late Mr Iain Macleod once said to the author, 'that was when we lost the intellectual vote.'

On the national level Suez will always be remembered as a moment of truth, a decisive revelation that Britain was no longer a great power. Whatever tactics had been employed and even if 'collusion' had been avoided, the expedition could not have succeeded in re-establishing for any length of time Britain's ascendancy in the Middle East. The world had changed. In the days of the Rhineland crisis of 1936 to which Eden so often harked back, Britain and France could have checked Hitler whatever the attitude of the other powers. Twenty years later they could not overthrow Nasser without a degree of American support which there was no possibility of obtaining. If Eden had taken no action at all, the lesson would still have been the same, though perhaps less expensive. The Egyptian dictator would have got away with it. There is something deeply tragic in the unhappy dilemma confronting a Prime Minister who in his long and honourable service to the state had done so much to forward the cause of peace, the sanctity of treaties and the interests of Britain. Eden deserved a happier ending to his political career.

Notes

1. December 1935–February 1938; December 1940–July 1945; October 1951–April 1955.
2. Anthony Eden, *Full Circle* (London 1960), p. 266.
3. Anthony Eden, Earl of Avon, *The Reckoning* (London 1965), p. 522.
4. Since the Reform Act of 1885 there had been five general elections held in the summer months – those of 1886, 1892, 1895, 1929 and 1945. The Conservatives won two (1886 and 1895) and lost the other three. After 1955 there has been only one (1970) which the Conservatives won.
5. Harold Macmillan, *Tides of Fortune* (London 1969), pp. 692–4. Macmillan was quite correct about the post of deputy Prime Minister – a wartime invention of Churchill which had no real validity. To preside over the Cabinet in the Prime Minister's absence is no guarantee of the succession. Crewe deputized for Asquith, Curzon for Bonar Law, Attlee for Churchill in the War coalition, Butler for both Eden and Macmillan.
6. Eden, *Full Circle*, p. 320.
7. *Ibid.*, pp. 352–3.
8. *Ibid.*, p. 365.
9. See Hugh Trevor-Roper, *The Philby Affair* (London 1968), pp. 54–5, for a fuller account. The book makes fascinating reading for all who wish to understand the nature of SIS during and after the War.
10. Dwight Eisenhower, *Mandate for a Change* (London 1963), p. 142.
11. Anthony Nutting, *No End of a Lesson* (London 1967), p. 34. The shrill and petulant tone in which so much of the book is written does not deprive it of evidential value.
12. Professor Hugh Thomas, whose account of the crisis, *The Suez Affair* (London 1970), is by far the best so far dates the crucial Cabinet meeting on 2 August (p. 55). Although the point is of no great importance there is reason to believe that 27 July was the critical day: it may well be that the decision taken then was confirmed on 2 August, though probably modified in detail, in the light of intervening information about the state of Britain's armed forces.
13. David Patrick Maxwell Fyfe, Earl of Kilmuir, *Political Adventure* (London 1964), p. 267. See Thomas, *op. cit.*, p. 23 for a refutation based on private information.
14. Eden, *Full Circle*, p. 437.
15. Quoted in Thomas, *op. cit.*, p. 54.
16. *The Times*, 1 August 1956.
17. Thomas, *op. cit.*, p. 58, based on evidence of an unnamed Cabinet minister.

18. Nutting, *op. cit.*, p. 70.
19. *Ibid.*, pp. 90–4.
20. Thomas, *op. cit.*, p. 96.
21. Eden, *Full Circle*, p. 513.
22. Nutting, *op. cit.*, p. 98.
23. Thomas, *op. cit.*, pp. 113–15.
24. Private and reliable information.
25. It was one of the charges against Eden that the Suez operation made it possible for the Russians to destroy the Hungarian revolt. The dates, however, show that this is baseless. The vital Russian decisions were taken before the Israeli attack on Egypt. No doubt the Suez affair distracted the UN and weakened its condemnation of Russian action, but only the most naïve fellow-traveller will believe that anything said or done by UNO would have made the smallest difference to the fate of Hungary.
26. Thomas, *op. cit.*, p. 138.
27. Eden, *Full Circle*, p. 557.
28. Thomas, *op. cit.*, p. 139.
29. *Ibid.*, p. 133.
30. *Ibid.*
31. Eden, *Full Circle*, p. 546.
32. Randolph Churchill, *The Rise and Fall of Sir Anthony Eden* (London 1959), pp. 288–9.
33. Thomas, *op. cit.*, p. 146.
34. Paul Bareau, then Editor of the *News Chronicle* in a broadcast, 5 July 1966. See *Suez ten years after* (BBC 1966), pp. 24–7.
35. Opinions differ as to how long this would have taken. Eden (*Full Circle*, p. 558) says that his military advisers 'reckoned on five days more'. Head in the House of Commons said 'about seven days'. The men on the spot, however, considered that forty-eight hours would have been ample.
36. Lord Birkenhead, *Walter Monckton* (London 1969), p. 308.
37. In *Suez Ten Years After* (London 1967), p. 89.

Harold Macmillan

Keith Sainsbury

There is a very good chance that the ultimate judgement of history will put Harold Macmillan at the head of the list of post-war Prime Ministers, and near the top of all those who have held the post in this century. Churchill and Lloyd George stand alone, since the special problems of wartime leadership make comparisons inapt. But among peacetime Prime Ministers Macmillan left a mark equalled by few of his contemporaries.

This was due not simply to the fact that he held the office for one of the longest continuous periods – nearly seven years – but to qualities of leadership, character and creative ability. His style of leadership was positive, sometimes impulsive, sometimes more cautious, but never negative. As one of his contemporaries has put it, Macmillan led his Government from the front, Attlee from the middle and another contemporary premier, who shall be nameless, from the rear. The role of Duke of Plaza-Toro, who 'led his regiment from behind, he found it less exciting', would never have appealed to Macmillan. He had pretty clear ideas of what he wanted to do, recognized that considerable efforts of persuasion, argument and sometimes manoeuvre might be necessary to achieve it, and would, one suspects, have found comparatively little pleasure in holding office, if the price of power had been masterly inactivity.

He came to office at a particularly difficult period. No post-war Prime Minister, of course, has had an 'easy ride'. All have had to contend to a greater or lesser extent with the fact of Britain's declining power in the world, which has posed continuous problems of foreign policy. Similarly, the recurrent economic and balance of payments crises, the problems of 'stop-go', of reconciling economic growth and a reasonable level of unemployment with the control of inflation – these difficulties have confronted all who have had to lead this country since 1945. Macmillan, however, had initially to deal with a pressing problem of a different kind – that of restoring the morale of a party which was trebly divided and very much shaken and a country which was bewildered and outraged. At Suez, this country had embarked on an enterprise which had apparently proved a disastrous failure; and which had led to most of our friends deserting us, with Britain put in the dock as an international criminal. That there were elements of unfairness and hypocrisy in that judgement of the Suez operation does not alter the fact that it was so. Macmillan had to repair Britain's friendships, restore our reputation in the world and instil a fresh sense of confidence in the nation. But first he had to reunite and reinvigorate the Conservative parliamentary party, since all else depended, as it always must in British politics, on the ability to stay in office by maintaining a reliable majority in the House of Commons. It is indicative of the situation as he saw it at that time, that he hesitated to ask an old friend like John Wyndham to rejoin his staff, because he could not be sure at first that the Government would not fall in a few months.[1] It is equally clear that he succeeded in achieving the various objectives mentioned above to a considerable degree.

How did he do it? At the time it was fashionable to talk of Macmillan's 'unflappability'. No one who knows Harold Macmillan well, however, is likely to accept that as an adequate description of a much more complex and effortful quality. In the sense of a natural calmness, an innately unemotional approach to affairs, the word could be more sensibly applied to his successor, Lord Home. Macmillan himself was and is both an emotional and a sensitive man, capable of explosive outbursts and quite colourful language in private. What he did have was the ability to *project* an image of calmness and self-assurance, so far as the public role was concerned. This was what mattered. He also had the ability, because he took a long-term view conditioned both by a sense of history and a forward-looking judgement, to see the minor difficulties and upsets of political life in perspective – in one of his more celebrated phrases as 'little local difficulties' – and not to be deflected from his course and ultimate goals by them. Therefore the negligent pose, the languid manner, the pinning of 'Quiet calm deliberation disentangles every knot' to the door of the Cabinet office, was part of a necessary act. Every successful politician, every leader, must be in this sense a good actor, as Macmillan himself recognized when he wrote of his refusal to continue any form of political activity after retirement, that one should not 'hang around the greenroom too much after final retirement from the stage'.[2]

As with most men of his temperament, the maintenance of the role was not achieved without an effort of self-control and a certain strain. That had its price. On one or two critical occasions – in Moscow in 1959, at the time of the abortive summit meeting in Paris 1960, and again before the large-scale Cabinet changes of 1962 – he became physically ill. The cause was probably at least partly accumulated nervous tension, or in the fashionable language of the present moment, it was 'psychosomatic'; a piece of jargon which has this much value, that it recognizes at any rate that such illnesses are as real as any other kind.

Macmillan, in short, was not a Prime Minister who was naturally phlegmatic, but a man of sensitivity, intelligence and humanity who was able nonetheless to project an image of calm and positive leadership. By these personal qualities he was able to restore Conservative morale, in the Government, in the House and in the country, to give the feeling of a fresh wind blowing through affairs.[3] He was fortunate in having most of the qualities and abilities which were required for his task.

Lord Swinton, a colleague and friend of many years, has said that he was the greatest all-rounder of the Prime Ministers of this century.[4] Swinton mentions particularly his scholarship and sense of history, his ability as a party manager and his instinct for timing and for the trend of public opinion. There is much truth in this, but it is not an exhaustive list. A successful Prime Minister must firstly, since our system is a parliamentary one, be an able parliamentarian. That Macmillan could, and usually did, dominate the House, and make the most powerful speech in a debate, that he was quick and resourceful in answering questions and dealing with interruptions, was a prime reason for his early and continued success in restoring his party's morale. He was not, like both his predecessor Eden and his successor Home, one of those debaters who gains acceptance by a conscious courtesy towards the Opposition. It was his natural temperament to be aggressive, to take the offensive, and he probably also judged correctly that it was the right policy for the times. It was more important to spur on his own side than to conciliate the parliamentary foe. His tactics generally succeeded, for there were relatively few of his opponents who were a match for him – Bevan and Harold Wilson occasionally, Gaitskell more rarely. The other leading Labour figures of the next decade – Brown, Callaghan, Jenkins, Healey – had either not yet developed full maturity as debaters or lacked the right combination of prestige, quickness and panache to deal with him. As has been mentioned, he generally thrived on heckling and interjections. Indeed, one of the relatively few occasions when the Opposition was able to take the wind out of his sails was during a debate when, by prior agreement, the Labour benches remained absolutely silent during the Prime Minister's winding-up speech. Disconcerted by the absence of interruptions, for which he was well prepared, Macmillan, as he admits, made a relatively lame and unsuccessful speech.

It is also important from the viewpoint of party leadership and party management in the House that a Prime Minister should be what is usually called 'a good House of Commons man', that is to say approachable and to some extent sociable within the purlieus of the House. Macmillan was in many ways a shy man and certainly by general testimony not easy to know intimately.[5] Few of his Cabinet colleagues, for example, would have claimed to do so. But like Attlee, and unlike Chamberlain, he was not aloof or completely remote from the rank and file, little though he had in common in tastes or 'life style' with the rising generation of young middle-class Conservatives such as Maudling, Heath and Macleod. Like Attlee he knew the importance of dropping in occasionally to the smoking-room or the tea-room, and in such social intervals he was not handicapped by Attlee's formidable taciturnity.

A Prime Minister must also be able to dominate and lead his Cabinet. Here again Macmillan was successful, partly because of his aura of confidence and poise and partly because he possessed the particular skills required. He was a good manager of men, as most of his colleagues agree. He understood the necessity for a leader to concentrate on the broad essentials and not be unduly fussy, or interfere unnecessarily in the details of departmental administration, in short, to let people get on with their jobs, and by so doing give them the feeling that they had the confidence and support of their leader. He was fond of saying with characteristic exaggeration that a Prime Minister had 'nothing to do', (i.e. that he had no department to run), and should not behave as though he did. It is the difference, as Harold Wilson has put it, between playing an instrument and conducting the orchestra.[6] On occasion, when he felt a sense of urgency or attached special importance to a particular matter, he might deal directly with a department or concern himself specially with a departmental minister's responsibility – as with incomes policy in 1961-2[7] – but not to a degree which made his colleagues feel that they were being constantly supervised. Sometimes too, with matters of major importance, he would convoke a small meeting of the leading ministers – the unofficial 'Inner Cabinet' without which no modern Cabinet can really function effectively. In such a case, if agreement were reached between the Prime Minister, the Foreign Secretary, the Chancellor, the Leaders of both Houses and so forth, then the full Cabinet might be presented with an effective *fait accompli*, since it was unlikely that the decision would be reversed. It is probably this which led one of his colleagues to feel that 'the Cabinet was sometimes consulted at too late a stage in the evolution of policy'.[8] Some outside observers who dealt with Macmillan, notably Sir Roy Welensky, have made the same point.[9] The nature of the modern Cabinet probably makes this inevitable, since most Cabinets are well above the optimum size for really effective decision-making, and moreover many departmental ministers become immersed in the details of their work and have relatively little to contribute to general policy, whether domestic or foreign.[10]

But again, it is a matter of degree, and the evidence is that Macmillan's Cabinet colleagues did not in general feel themselves side-tracked or inadequately consulted. Within their own sphere in particular he would ask them to come and see him from time to time to discuss their special problems. He knew, too, the importance of encouragement to a minister under attack, and how 'the morale of a minister could be boosted by a comforting note'.[11]

Nor was it the case that serious discussion did not take place in Cabinet; here also Macmillan had, as a successful premier must have, the qualities of a good chairman. That is to say, he could present a problem in a balanced way, refrain from interfering too much, or at too early a stage in the discussion, and then give as a rule a reasonable and fair-minded summary of what he felt the general conclusion was: and he would accept with a good grace that he was in a minority. He was in fact businesslike in this regard, after the fashion of an Attlee rather than a Churchill, though his summings-up would often be characteristically expansive and philosophical rather than dry and clipped.

In one other important aspect of man-management he showed in general the necessary talent; that is in the field of selection. Certainly he was not always the best of judges of the suitability of a man for a particular office. Nevertheless, looking at the whole record of Cabinet selection, one can see that he had a firm grasp of essentials, particularly of the necessity of including a representative selection from every wing of the party in his Government and maintaining a balance between them. Part of the exercise of 'healing the wounds' after the trauma of Suez lay in the inclusion in his Government of representatives of the right-wing 'pro-Suez' group such as Julian Amery, and his retention of Selwyn Lloyd at the Foreign Office. While, on the other hand, Sir Edward Boyle, who had courageously resigned over the issue, was recalled and promoted. At a later stage in his Government he recalled to office two of the three Treasury ministers who had resigned at a particularly awkward moment in January 1958 – an example of magnanimity and good sense. As against the occasional mistakes in selection, too, must be set some notable successes, the most striking being the appointment of Heathcote Amory to the Treasury and the controversial appointment of Lord Home to the Foreign Office in 1960.

In another respect, that of bringing on younger men with an eye to the future – an important part of a party leader's job – Macmillan generally showed considered judgement in his choice. The names not only of Maudling, Heath and Macleod, but also of Enoch Powell, Boyle and Keith Joseph come to mind. At the same time he gave the men of the middle generation – Butler, Hailsham, Thorneycroft, Sandys – ample opportunity to display their talents in a variety of posts. The question of the famous 'purge' of 1962 needs separate consideration. It was an uncharacteristic episode in Macmillan's career, not so much because of its apparent impulsiveness – Macmillan was capable at times of acting on impulse – but because it was one of the few occasions in his career when he seemed to be acting in a somewhat panicky fashion, showing a lack of his usual judgement in estimating the probable consequences of his actions. On the first count, it would seem that he allowed himself to be unduly worried by a number of by-election reverses and by the possibility that the proposed Government changes had been leaked to the press (by a Cabinet minister, according to some reports). He is even reported to have said 'If I don't finish this now, the Government will fall.'[12] But this was clearly a gross exaggeration. A Government with an ample majority in the House and two years to go before the next election need not fear a few by-election reverses, or the minor embarrassment of well-informed press forecasts. The succeeding Wilson Government indeed survived repeated by-election losses without damage, save to its morale. Moreover the reshuffle was probably too early, as well as unnecessarily drastic.

On the second count, it is clear that the 'purge' did the Government and Macmillan personally more harm than good. It shook the party, exposed Macmillan to the charge of disloyalty to old friends and left him more isolated, as a much older man among youngish colleagues: and of course it added to the number of powerful backbench critics among his own party. It is ironical that Macmillan normally set considerable store by personal loyalty and usually displayed it. But in the last resort a Prime Minister cannot, and should not, allow personal loyalty to be the overriding consideration. The particular case of the Chancellor of the Exchequer, Selwyn Lloyd, is an example of this. There is no doubt that Macmillan felt, rightly or wrongly, that Lloyd had temporarily lost his zest and creative ability and in particular was failing to come to grips with the problems of the 'pay pause' and incomes policy.[13] Having decided to ask for the Chancellor's resignation, it would have been difficult to fit him into the Government in any other way. There are, after all, not many posts that one can offer to a former Foreign Secretary and Chancellor. It may be, as has been suggested, that he felt it kinder to Lloyd to include his departure in a wide-ranging reconstruction of the Government, but this too was a misjudgement. It did not soften the blow. It is also true that some of those who departed had indicated their willingness to do so when it was convenient. Humanly, they did not always take it well when the time came, but there is some justice in Lord Hill's remark that they were entitled to a little more notice and a little more dignity in their going.[14] It remains true, as Gladstone put it, that 'a Prime Minister must be a good butcher'. But the episode is oddly uncharacteristic nonetheless. Possibly it was the result of tiredness and accumulated strain. Possibly too, Macmillan may have been already feeling the first effects of the illness which brought about his retirement from office a year or so later.

Be that as it may, Macmillan was usually an effective manager of his Cabinet and highly regarded by his colleagues. He was also effective in communicating with the wider circle of the party organizers and workers in the constituencies and with the country as a whole – an equally necessary quality in a party leader and Prime Minister. Both, of course, played an important part in his revival of Conservative and national morale after Suez, and were successfully sustained thereafter. He was usually able to produce the right note of inspiration and guidance on the big set-piece occasions at the end of Conservative party conferences and in local meetings for the heartening of the faithful up and down the country. On the wider national scale he made himself one of the ablest masters in modern times of the relatively new medium of television, particularly in the interview or 'conversation piece' kind of broadcast. The most celebrated examples were the notable interview with Edward Murrow in 1958 and the equally successful conversation with President Eisenhower in 1959. The first undoubtedly conveyed to the nation, more fully than before, Macmillan's original qualities, and the second probably helped to win the 1959 election. But there were many others. It can be said that in using television Macmillan succeeded in converting what should have been liabilities – the old-fashioned, Edwardian style, appearance and manner – into assets. It was no mean achievement.

On the other side of the ledger there were undoubtedly debits – his somewhat eighteenth-century attitude to patronage and party politics, the occasionally unnecessary rudeness and discourtesy to the Opposition, the occasions when impulsiveness overruled judgement. He was sometimes lacking too in appreciation of the divisiveness of some Conservative policies. But taking the picture of the whole man, it is difficult not to conclude that Macmillan possessed in larger measure than most of those who have held the office of Prime Minister the varied qualities and abilities that make for success in that role; and that because of this he did in fact achieve much success. If one is looking for the major reason for this – for the positive achievement that is, as opposed to the mere success of remaining in office and generally master of the situation – the answer lies surely in his creative and imaginative qualities. In foreign policy, particularly, the comparison with Attlee, another masterful and able Prime Minister, is favourable to Macmillan. For whereas much of the creative impulse in foreign affairs in Attlee's Government came from the Foreign Secretary, Ernest Bevin, in Macmillan's Government much of it came from the Prime Minister.

In another sense Macmillan was an all-rounder in a way that some of his predecessors were not. That is to say he equally cared about, was interested in and had ideas on both domestic and foreign policy. It has been rightly said that Baldwin was disinterested in and therefore weak on foreign policy, while Lord Avon, whose entire administrative experience had been in external affairs, was inadequately informed on domestic matters, a defect of which he himself seems to have been conscious. One of Macmillan's biographers, Anthony Sampson, has asserted of Macmillan too that 'his real passion was foreign affairs'.[15] This is an oversimplification, and in some ways quite misleading, though it might seem to be given some colour by some of Macmillan's own remarks in his memoirs on the extent to which foreign problems can dominate the horizon. Yet these can be matched by similar quotations on the periods when major domestic issues must occupy most of a Prime Minister's attention.[16]

In fact Macmillan, as both his own memoirs and those of his contemporaries show, gave a great deal of attention during his premiership to domestic issues, equally for temperamental and intellectual as well as practical reasons. As he himself implies, it may be that temperamentally and emotionally too much has been made of his memories of the depression years, when he represented a northern industrial constituency which bore the full weight of large-scale unemployment. Nevertheless most of those who worked with him seem to have felt that these memories were an important part of the varied elements and impulses in his character. He himself says, 'I was constantly accused of being too much concerned about the personal tragedy of unemployed families', and many of his colleagues felt that he was at various times too concerned about the possibility of future recession and too anxious to 'reflate'. He was in any case an expansionist by nature.[17] Caution was not the dominating feature of his character, and he was rightly sceptical of the accuracy of economic forecasts on which the advice towards cautious and restrictionist policies were often based. If in addition he was concerned about the human misery caused by large-scale unemployment, it is certainly not to his discredit. Whatever the cause, on successive occasions, with successive Chancellors – Thorneycroft, Amory, Lloyd – he found himself pleading the cause of expansion and reflation of the economy, at times when 'official' advice was generally still in favour of a more cautious and limited approach. The resignations of Thorneycroft and his two junior ministers from the Treasury in January 1958 were occasioned by this difference of approach. A year or so later, Amory allowed himself to be persuaded that an 'expansionist' policy was justified by the favourable economic climate of the time. Selwyn Lloyd's departure from the Government in 1962, however, was not directly occasioned by this difference of view, though his resignation letter makes it clear that he was concerned about this issue.[18]

Domestic issues of course are not simply questions of economic policy. But Macmillan recognized that at all times, but particularly when a country's economy is as shaky as Britain's has been since the war, all other problems of domestic policy become entangled with the central economic problem – a problem which he sums up as that of achieving and maintaining four desirable objectives, namely stable prices, full employment, a secure balance of payments position and economic growth. As Macmillan concedes, his Government did not succeed in solving this particularly malign and complex conundrum. But in the second half of his term of office he successfully identified what all future Governments have recognized as the key to a solution – a system of voluntary economic planning and direction, involving the cooperation of both sides of industry and applying particularly in the field of incomes policy. It is clear too, that he was well aware of some of the major stumbling-blocks, in the shape of trades unions and shop floor organizations which were often either conservative or irresponsible, sometimes both; and economic advisers who were apt to be too attached to orthodox methods and insufficiently imaginative and creative in their approach to changing and worsening problems. Looking across the Atlantic he saw the same attitude, often of an even more fiercely orthodox and rigid kind, reflected in the views of the US Treasury, which often prevented measures of international monetary reform which would have helped not only this country but world trading prospects as a whole.[19]

If one can criticize Macmillan on this score, it is perhaps on the ground that he did not realize – or at any rate does not make it clear that he realized – that the problem was and is as much one of obstructiveness, timidity and unoriginality on the part of management and the financial institutions of the City of London; and there were occasions too when he showed a certain lack of imaginative insight into the probable effects of budgetary concessions which seemed to be overtly designed to favour the well-to-do and to increase inequality. But as against that, it can be said that his Governments took the first major steps along the necessary road to voluntary cooperative regulation of the economy, through the creation of the National Economic Development Council and its offshoots, the 'little Neddys'; the National Incomes Commission; and such tentative essays in incomes policy as the 'pay pause', the 'guiding light' etc. which foreshadowed later 'social contracts', in the same way as the NIC foreshadowed Labour's Prices and Incomes Board and similar bodies. In these developments both Macmillan and his third Chancellor, Selwyn Lloyd, played a part. Macmillan recognized too that in all these matters the first essential was the cooperation of the trades unions, if that could be achieved; and while his Government, like all post-war Governments, had to weather many industrial disputes, he was able to avoid or bring to an end those that were likely to prove really damaging and to maintain reasonably good relations with the more moderate and responsible trades union leaders. In his attitude towards industrial disputes one can see a pragmatic appreciation of the importance of such factors as public sympathy and the economic power of unions in key sectors of industry. On the threatened railway strike of 1958 he remarks 'Above all, we must not "challenge" the trades unions as some . . . would like. We must appeal to the unions and try to take ourselves some constructive initiative.'[20] It is advice that could well have been heeded by at least one of his successors. So then, if it were a choice of confronting the railwaymen or the electricity supply workers on the one hand, or the busmen on the other, it was as well to measure the respective strengths of each and the damage they could inflict. A little Machiavellian? Perhaps. Macmillan himself hints at the thought.[21] But a successful democratic leader must take such considerations into account. The dividing line between practical realism and cynicism is sometimes thinly drawn, but so too is that between high-minded adherence to principle and obstinate rigidity or fanaticism. It is at least arguable that those who err in the latter direction do a great deal more harm than those who tend to the former.

At all events Macmillan's genuine interest and concern, not only with the broad issues of economic policy but also with specific domestic issues such as industrial relations, social welfare and immigration emerge clearly from the numerous diary references, memoranda and accounts of ministerial meetings which occur throughout his memoirs. The problems of foreign policy might be more glamorous and exciting, and in a nuclear era even more fundamental, but there was clearly a considerable intellectual interest in domestic policy as well as an emotional force; and this, as has often been pointed out, is not particularly surprising in a man who had been much preoccupied with social and economic issues for at least a decade or more of his early political career; and who had served as Chancellor of the Exchequer and as a successful Minister of Housing before becoming Prime Minister.

To some extent indeed, Macmillan's career is merely an illustration of the point that a successful Prime Minister must devote much attention to both domestic and foreign problems, and appreciate the interrelationship of the two. Particularly for a country like Britain, external forces often impinge on internal policy, as when pressure on the balance of payments or speculation against sterling enforces internal measures which from a purely domestic point of view may be both unpopular and even damaging. But so too does our capacity to solve our own internal problems affect the impact of British foreign policy. In the wider context Macmillan felt that this applied to the

Western world as a whole. In the conflict of ideas which the relationship with the communist world must always reflect, whatever the extent of 'co-existence' or 'détente', the Western way of life would prevail or at any rate survive, as much because of its practical superiority in providing the good things of life for its people as for its superior ideals. It was a view he often urged upon his American friends. Indeed it is striking that, when he wrote to President Kennedy on the latter's assumption of office in 1961, the first and longest part of the letter was devoted to the need for a radical rethinking of 'the policies and institutions of the Free World ... particularly in the economic field' and the necessity of demonstrating 'that our modern free society can run in a way that makes the fullest use of our resources and results in a steady expansion of our economic strength'.[22] It is only after this that he turns to questions of foreign policy – to disarmament for example, and relations with Russia.

The two themes of the necessity for international monetary reform, in order to increase the credit basis of international trade, and the necessity of sustaining international commodity prices in order to help the underdeveloped as well as the developed world are both argued in this letter. Macmillan was often to return to the former theme, in particular, in his dealings both with his own ministers and with the Americans. But success here depended on first the acceptance of a high priority for this matter by the Americans (as well as other countries) and secondly on their acceptance of those reforms Britain might have preferred. It is not very surprising that he was unsuccessful, in view of the plethora of other urgent matters at Anglo-American meetings and the difficulty for an American Treasury minister to accept that the 'Almighty Dollar' might itself be vulnerable. In fact, as we now know, President Kennedy was concerned by the first signs of America's over-commitment externally producing too great a strain on the dollar. But neither Kennedy nor Macmillan could foresee the immense strains which would fall on the dollar as well as the pound in the next decade. Macmillan at least recognized that the problem was there and might become urgent, and tried to get some action in this direction. He did achieve a limited measure of success in increasing international credit, though this did not go nearly as far as Macmillan wanted.[23]

International monetary reform represents *par excellence* the kind of area where domestic and foreign problems meet and interconnect; and enough has been said to show that Macmillan's interests were at least as much directed to domestic policies as towards foreign affairs; and to demonstrate his claim to be in that sense an all-rounder. He would not indeed have been anything like so successful as party leader and politician if it had not been so. Foreign triumphs are gratifying to those concerned and sometimes to domestic public opinion, but seldom win elections. Undoubtedly, however, Macmillan's place in history will rest to a considerable degree on the extent of his successes and failures in the field of international diplomacy; and no commentator has seriously questioned his deep concern for certain aspects of foreign policy, nor that he had some marked achievements to his credit.

As with most politicians of his generation, the experience of the First World War had left its mark on Macmillan, and meant that he could never be simply disinterested in that field. But it was the growing menace of Naziism in the late 1930s which first led him as a politician to focus more deeply on these problems. He then served a considerable apprenticeship in diplomacy during the Second World War as Minister Resident in North Africa and later Italy. In these posts he negotiated with, among others, Eisenhower, de Gaulle and Tito, and revealed, in the judgement of a close colleague of the period, 'superb diplomatic skill'. Confidence came with success, and no doubt partly explained his later taste for international high diplomacy. He later added to his experience in the field with a brief period at the Foreign Office.

That Macmillan was a skilful negotiator need not be questioned simply because he had his setbacks, and in particular found the task of negotiating with the Russians and with de Gaulle a singularly difficult one. A man is no less an able mountaineer because he has not quite succeeded in climbing Everest. So far as Macmillan's success in this field as Prime Minister is concerned there is not much doubt about the basis on which his record, and that of his two Foreign Secretaries, Lloyd and Home, wil be judged. It will rest on the one hand on his attitude to the interlocking relationships which bound us to America, the Commonwealth and Europe; and on the other hand on his contribution to the lessening of tension in the East–West 'cold war' – in other words, détente. In each case it is necessary to consider the objectives he had in view, the skill with which he pursued them, and the extent to which he succeeded or failed in his objectives. It is right to single out these two broad fields, because all other specific issues which arose, whether in Europe (for example the problem of German reunification), in the Middle East, as in the 1958 Lebanon–Jordan crisis, or such Far Eastern problems as Indo-China and Formosa, have to be seen in relation to those two broad issues.

It is generally accepted, and rightly, that one of Macmillan's major achievements was the restoration of Anglo-American relations after the breach over Suez; and his subsequent maintenance of a close and cordial relationship with America over the next seven years and with two Presidents of totally different views, personalities and indeed generations. He took exactly the right line in the first reconciliation meetings with President Eisenhower and his Secretary of State, Foster Dulles, in the first half of 1957. Taking full but not unfair advantage of the genuine concern of the Americans over the rift with their old allies and the dangers it had created of Soviet advantage in Europe, and even more in the Middle East, Macmillan adopted the simple posture of 'no excuses and no recriminations'; that the right course for both Britain and America was to look forward, not back, and concentrate on repairing the damage, rather than arguing about who was responsible for it.

This approach was welcomed by the Americans and within a surprisingly short time the 'special relationship' was to a large extent restored. It continued to function effectively for the remainder of Eisenhower's presidency. It functioned in the Middle East with the American enunciation of the 'Eisenhower doctrine' which involved America in the maintenance of peace and security in that area in a far more positive sense than before, and formed the basis for the effective and successful intervention in the Middle Eastern crisis of 1958. Indeed it is now quite often said that the immediate effects of the Suez fiasco on British interests and influence in the Middle East were much less than anyone expected or had a right to expect. But if this was so it was due to an important extent to the skilful repair job Macmillan and Lloyd had achieved in Anglo-American relations.

Equally the Anglo-American alliance continued to function in

Europe, and it weathered for example the long drawn out and potentially very dangerous crisis over Berlin, which dragged on for almost four years between 1958 and 1962. It also functioned effectively in South-East Asia and the Far East, in the Formosa Straits crisis of 1958 and the Laotian crisis of 1960–2. In all these matters the detailed conduct of negotiations rested naturally in the hands of Lloyd and then Home. But there was always the sustained support and 'thrust' from the Prime Minister for the main overriding objectives – namely to maintain unbroken the Anglo-American alliance and the unity of the West, while at the same time restraining America from over-reacting or unnecessarily escalating these disputes; and at the same time keeping negotiations going, however intractable and difficult the other side seemed to be; and losing no opportunity to 'defuse' the crisis. It is not necessary to exaggeratè the role Macmillan played, or to underrate that of others, to recognize that he made a significant contribution to the maintenance of these objectives in each successive crisis.

It can be said of course that in one respect Macmillan was fortunate, in that he had the advantage of a long-standing friendship with Eisenhower, dating back to their wartime association in Algiers, and that there was therefore a strong basis of mutual trust and confidence between them. With Kennedy on the other hand there was the advantage of a President who knew this country well and had family connections with it and indeed with Macmillan himself[24] – a President, moreover, who shared certain attributes with Macmillan, in particular a sense of style, an intellectual fascination with the problems of politics and diplomacy, and a dry sense of humour. By the general testimony of those who observed them together, both American and British, there was a genuine concordance or empathy between them which made unimportant the difference in age, except in so far as Kennedy perhaps felt the greater respect for Macmillan's judgement because of the latter's long and varied political experience.[25]

The point should be made that an advantage may exist, but may still be unrecognized or not utilized. Eisenhower's trust and Kennedy's responsiveness could easily have been damaged or destroyed by clumsy handling. Macmillan therefore deserves the credit which he has usually been given for the way in which he nursed both relationships.

His approach to both was based on the same realistic view, that Britain, being much the weaker, must accept the plain fact of American leadership of the Western alliance and support it loyally; but within that general context it would, indeed should, be possible to exert some influence over American policy if tact, reason and common sense were properly applied. As it happened the new administration which came to power in America in 1961 was both, at first, a little unsure of itself and open to reason. In this situation the special advantages of a common language and a long-standing alliance could be used to advantage. In such crises as that over Laos, and to a degree over Berlin and Cuba they *were* used; and in the broader sense in the gradual progress towards détente with Russia, where the Test-Ban treaty of 1963 was the outstanding achievement. Again one need not exaggerate the extent of British influence on American policy, to recognize that at times it existed and was constructively used; and that Macmillan deserves some credit for this.

That Macmillan regarded the Anglo-American relationship at this period as still the overriding and essential feature of our diplomatic policy is clear. He has sometimes been censured for this. In the extreme case this takes the form of the argument that it should have been clearly recognized, even at this early stage, that useful though the Anglo-American relationship might be at times, Suez had clearly shown its limitations where British and American interests conflicted. This was certainly the conclusion which was drawn by the French. It was also true that the process of imperial emancipation was clearly going to continue (and in fact gathered speed under Macmillan) and that the new Commonwealth showed few signs of becoming a coherent political or economic bloc. Therefore the British choice lay between continued and increasing dependence on America or effective and full participation in the newly emerging European Community. Macmillan is to be faulted for not grasping this sooner, and pursuing this objective more vigorously.

This, however, is one of those cases where the critics not only make use of a hindsight denied to those who must actually take decisions, but also ignore some of the relevant factors in the situation and, to some extent, even the sequence of events involved. Macmillan himself was, and had been for a long time, a committed European in a significant sense of the expression. There is more than one road to Damascus and more than one way of pursuing the European ideal. Macmillan certainly favoured (like de Gaulle) a confederal rather than a federal approach. It was precisely for this reason that he thought a great opportunity had been missed at the time of the creation of the European coal and steel community in 1950, when Britain should, he felt, have entered and joined in shaping the community, rather than stood aside. Similarly he favoured a more positive British approach to the problems of Western European defence in 1953–4, and indeed contemplated resignation on the issue.[26] After the collapse of the European defence community in 1954 and the patched-up solution of the European defence problem the following year, the prospects for a further positive movement towards European unity did not appear very bright. Indeed even so enthusiastic a European as the Belgian Paul-Henri Spaak did not at first display any optimism about the negotiations for a European economic community which began at Messina in 1955 and culminated in the treaty of Rome in June 1957.[27]

By this time Macmillan had become Prime Minister, but was still mainly preoccupied with restoring the situation, both domestically and internationally, after Suez. Moreover he had been given some reason to think that the Europeans felt it would be easier for the 'Six' to complete their own negotiations first and then come to some arrangement for a wider free trade area with Britain and the Scandinavian countries; an arrangement which would take account of Britain's special obligations to the Commonwealth. Also it seemed at that time that the 'Six', including the French, would be willing to enter into such an arrangement. Such hopes proved nugatory, largely because of de Gaulle's return to power in France soon after the European Community began to operate in January 1958. Whether things would have been otherwise if de Gaulle had not come to power then we shall never know, but one cannot blame Macmillan for not foreseeing that this event would happen when it did. France had weathered a good many Algerian crises before 1958 without de Gaulle. After he had been kept waiting in the wings for thirteen years, there seemed no special reason in 1957 to think that within a year he would at last be called to power.

After it became clear that there could be no wider European free trade area including the EEC countries, British policy turned to the creation of a more limited European free trade association – Britain and the so-called 'outer seven'. Here again Macmillan and his Government have been blamed for embarking upon what some Europeans regarded as a divisive, even a wrecking exercise. It does not seem to have been intended as such, but rather as a defensive measure, and to some extent perhaps a negotiating basis for future arrangements with the EEC. The EFTA, with its market of 90 millions, was after all hardly in a position to wreck the EEC with its market of 250 millions. In any case Macmillan fairly soon came to the conclusion – by 1961 in fact – that the right course for Britain was to apply for membership. Although British hesitation may have postponed full membership of the Community by four or five years, it was the French veto which postponed it for a further ten years.

All of these events have to be judged within the context of the time, and Britain's position in the world as it actually was in 1957, not as it is now nearly twenty years later. In 1957 the British empire was still largely intact, and we had commitments and obligations all over the world – in the Middle East, in Africa, in the Far East. In relation to these American goodwill was vital, and far more important than that of the western European countries, whose interest in these areas was often minimal. This was how the situation seemed to Macmillan in 1957, and is how it actually was, as future crises in Jordan, Kuwait, the Persian Gulf, the Congo and Malaysia were to demonstrate throughout his premiership. In all of these it was important that Britain should have the support, or at any rate the neutrality, of America. In addition, sterling was still one of the two reserve currencies, bearing heavy burdens then as now. In meeting the recurrent attacks on sterling also it was essential to have American cooperation.

Therefore the American tie could not simply be cast off at a moment's notice. Nor could our obligations to Commonwealth countries, whose trade had become closely enmeshed with ours, be honourably ignored. Moreover, even if these considerations could have been ignored in a sudden 'dash for Europe', it is doubtful if British public opinion was ready for it. For that opinion was slow to come to terms with the facts of Britain's altered position in the world. The Conservative party was to require a great deal of persuasion, the

Labour party and Labour movement even more, before the great change could be accepted. Perhaps Macmillan could have given a bolder lead to public opinion earlier and perhaps it might have worked. Perhaps Sampson is half right when he says that Macmillan made the mistake of 'edging backwards into Europe' and that by 'playing it too low' he failed to convince either his own people that the matter was urgent, or the Europeans that we were really serious.[28] It is difficult not to feel, however, that if there was a moment when Britain lost the opportunity of assuming the leadership of a movement towards European unity, that moment happened in the decade before Macmillan's premiership rather than during it; and if there is to be blame for a missed opportunity it ought to fall more on the shoulders of Attlee, Bevin, Churchill and Eden, than on his; and perhaps on Macmillan qua Cabinet minister from 1951 to 1957 rather than qua Prime Minister.

Whatever view may be taken on this point, the brute fact must be faced that in this matter Macmillan failed to achieve his immediate objective of EEC membership, even if he did succeed in laying useful foundations for the future. In his other great foreign policy objective – détente between the West and Russia – there were also many setbacks but some successes. In this field Macmillan's patient and skilful cultivation of the American relationship was of particular importance. In the negative sense Macmillan and his Foreign Secretaries aimed to moderate and restrain American policies, whenever East–West tension showed signs of reaching dangerous levels or blowing up to crisis point. In the more positive sense he aimed to reduce these tensions and bring the two great powers together in regular meetings of heads of Government; and to make progress towards the resolution of specifically dangerous problems such as disarmament and those relating to Germany.

It was a difficult business. In the first part of his administration Macmillan had to deal with Eisenhower and Dulles, neither of whom had any enthusiasm for negotiating with the Russians, and whose reluctance was encouraged by the Pentagon. Moreover the West German leader Adenauer and his French counterpart de Gaulle were of much the same mind. It is more remarkable in the circumstances that Macmillan had any success, than that his success was limited, particularly since the long-drawn-out Berlin crisis of 1958–62 made the atmosphere for East–West negotiations not very favourable.

Macmillan recognized of course that any marked progress towards a general disarmament agreement, particularly in the nuclear field, would be difficult to achieve so long as the Russians regarded any form of inspection and control as a cloak for Western espionage. Nevertheless some progress could be made perhaps towards an agreement to suspend nuclear tests, where the danger of atmospheric pollution gave an additional urgency to the problem. With Lloyd's persistent help he was able to persuade the Americans to open negotiations and keep them going through some very sticky patches. In Kennedy he found a more responsive American leader than Eisenhower, which gave an additional stimulus to the negotiations. Kennedy generously acknowledged the part Macmillan had played, when the Test-Ban treaty was finally signed in 1963.[29] Macmillan stayed in office just long enough to see this objective realized.

He was less successful in his policy of 'summitry'. There are of course two views about the value of such meetings. In general Foreign Offices and Foreign ministers are less than enthusiastic about them, and certainly too much can be expected of such occasions. Certainly they can also, if unsuccessful, do more harm than good. But that is true of almost all difficult negotiations, indeed of most positive ventures in life. It was Macmillan's misfortune that after three years' patiently coaxing his allies to the Summit he saw it wrecked before it had begun, almost certainly by design. The excuse used by the Russians was the capture of an American 'spy plane'. But whatever one may think of American handling of the U2 incident, or indeed of the use of 'spy planes' generally, it is clear that the Russians could have shrugged the incident off or even concealed it, had they wished.

On the difficult problem of Germany, Macmillan, and Kennedy also, would have been prepared to go farther and faster towards achieving some form of *modus vivendi* than the rock-like figure of Chancellor Adenauer would permit. The essence of the problem was that the rearmament of West Germany in the 1950s had made it very unlikely that Russia would agree to the reunification of Germany on any terms that would be acceptable to the West. Therefore it looked as though one would have to come to terms with the fact of East

Germany, at any rate in the short or medium term. But any suggestion that East Germany might be recognized, even *de facto*, was liable at this period to arouse Adenauer's deepest suspicions of a Western sell-out to the Russians; and the abandonment of reunification as the main objective of Western policy was also liable to inflict grave damage on German morale.

There is no doubt that Macmillan was at any rate prepared to consider such concessions to Soviet views as the *de facto* recognition of East Germany, at any rate so far as it was involved in the settlement of the perennially troublesome problem of access to Berlin. He was also prepared to consider acceptance of the Oder–Neisse line as the Polish–German border, in return of course for Soviet concessions of equal value and as part of a movement towards genuine détente and a general German and European settlement. In all this some form of disengagement from Germany by East and West might have played a part. In the event Macmillan's theories were never really put to the test, since neither the Russians nor Adenauer could be induced to move sufficiently from the postures in which they had become frozen over a considerable period. Détente in this area had to wait for Brandt and his *Ostpolitik*, by which time Macmillan had passed from the scene.

There are differing views on the value of pursuing détente with Russia, just as there are differing views as to the value of 'summitry'. It is too soon after the event to say whether Macmillan was right, or those whose suspicions of Russia were greater. All that can be said with certainty is that Macmillan in many respects anticipated the way in which events were destined to move, and that, if subsequent history has not necessarily proved him right, it has not yet proved him wrong.

Little more needs to be said. It remains only to sum up, as far as one can do so only a decade or so after a man's departure from power. It can only be an interim judgement. Something was said, at the beginning of this study, of Macmillan's qualities and talents. On this score the verdict of history is not likely to be very different from that of his contemporaries. It is easier indeed to agree on a man's quality than it is to agree on his achievements. Macmillan was intelligent, knowledgeable and imaginative. He was capable of understanding the principal phenomena of his time and coming to terms with them, to a greater degree than many of his contemporaries. Unlike some who had played a major part in the war, when Britain still ranked as an equal with Russia and America, he appreciated the extent of Britain's rapid decline in power. On the whole he drew the correct conclusions from this, namely that in the short run Britain must continue to uphold the American alliance, while seeking to make use of the 'special relationship', so long as it existed, to try to modify American policy whenever it seemed to us misconceived; and to some extent to act as a mediator and link between the two super powers when the opportunity arose. In the long run, however, he also saw the necessity for Britain to move closer to Europe. His real dedication to the European idea has been questioned by some critics, but the criticism does not seem well founded. He was in fact one of the most convinced of the early workers in the European movement with Winston Churchill. He did not certainly foresee precisely the direction in which events would move on the Continent, and he can be faulted perhaps for not bringing more pressure to bear on Churchill and Eden in the early 1950s to cooperate more fully in these developments. In relation to the coal and steel community as well as west European defence he himself seems to have felt, like some other Conservative 'Europeans', that this was so.

Equally he did not regard an effective form of European unity as necessarily incompatible with a close and fruitful European relationship with America. Nor indeed need it have been, if French policy had not been pushed into a particularly inflexible posture towards America by the iron hand of de Gaulle. Some people believe that if Macmillan had shown a greater willingness to break completely with America and to shrug off our obligations to the Commonwealth, Britain would have entered the EEC in 1962. It seems at least as likely, however, that de Gaulle decided fairly early in the negotiations that French interests were best served by keeping Britain out, at least for the time being. If it was so, the veto would have been imposed whatever line Macmillan had adopted.

It would be strange indeed if Macmillan were criticized for attaching too much importance to imperial ties, whether in the old Empire or new Commonwealth form. On the contrary he recognized as clearly as anyone, and more clearly than many members of his party, that the rise of Asian and African nationalism was steadily making it more and more difficult to maintain European imperialism in its old form, even if Britain's declining power had not ruled that out as a practical possibility. He certainly restored relations with the new Asian Commonwealth countries after the shock they had sustained from the Suez crisis, but he recognized that the peaceful liquidation of empire must go on, and actively encouraged the process.

Equally in internal affairs he was aware of the major facts of the situation – of the growing power of the unions, of the necessity for developing some effective form of voluntary economic planning suitable for a mixed economy, and of the 'revolution of rising expectations' among the mass of the people. In this field he has been accused of too materialistic an approach, and the phrase 'our people have never had it so good' has been used against him. Perhaps there is something in the criticism. To some extent it was a pragmatic recognition that governments are apt to be judged by the electorate in precisely those terms – that is on their success in maintaining and improving the national standard of living. In that same speech, however, Macmillan warned against the belief that the prosperity of the 1950s would automatically continue, and of the dangers of unrestricted inflation – warnings which were to prove all too well justified in later years.

On balance then the claim that Macmillan was the most successful all-rounder among post-war premiers seems justified. As an effective and businesslike organizer of Cabinet and Government he was comparable to Attlee; in the arts of political management and parliamentary debate he compares favourably with Harold Wilson; in creative imagination and the ability to provide positive leadership he comes nearer to Churchill than any other post-war Prime Minister. In addition he possessed a sense of judgement and timing which generally served him well.

No Prime Minister of course can have a hundred-per-cent record of success. Towards the end of his administration things began to go wrong, and his touch became less certain. The ministerial 'purge' was probably a mistake; the Profumo affair, unimportant though it in essence was, cast doubt on his judgement and control of events; nor was his handling of the succession entirely happy, though in retrospect his judgement of the situation, namely that neither Butler nor

Hailsham commanded quite enough support in the party and that the younger contenders – Maudling, Heath, Macleod – were not ready for it, does not look so wildly wrong. In this period, too, the major setbacks he encountered – the collapse of the 1960 Summit and the Common Market veto – seemed more to catch him unawares and temporarily knock him off balance than had been the case before.

Even so, history will probably judge the overall attainment to be considerable. The rehabilitation of his government's and party's morale and the restoration of national confidence and self-respect after Suez was a notable achievement. So too was the restoration of British ties with America and other estranged friends and allies. His gradual education of the Conservative party, particularly the right wing, in the realities of the contemporary world, was a necessary task in which he achieved considerable success. Most strikingly this applied to the conversion of the party to European membership, but it applied also to the gradual retreat from empire. In particular Macmillan, with skilful assistance from R.A.Butler, was able to extricate Britain from the Central African imbroglio without accepting any unsupportable commitment to the white minority and in the face of strong and persistent opposition from the right wing.[30]

In home affairs too the record was on the whole one of success. He presided over a period of continuous and increasing prosperity. He was lucky, certainly, in that world conditions were generally favourable and he did not have to withstand the hammer blows that fell on his successors. But a man must be judged in relation to the circumstances of his time, and in relation to those circumstances his Government did in fact steer the right course in economic management, and maintain about the right balance between inflation and deflation. He did not solve Britain's basic economic problems (no post-war premier has done so) but he at least identified some of the fundamental elements of a solution and helped to lay some of the first foundations of a system of economic planning which must form part of the solution – if solution there is. In economic matters, however, perhaps his greatest disappointment was the failure to achieve any real progress towards international monetary reform. If he had succeeded in this, Britain's internal economic problems would certainly have been less critical in the era that followed.

Finally it must be said, and conceded, that he did not succeed in obtaining British membership of the European Community, nor did he make as much progress along the road to détente as he would have liked. But in these two fields also he laid the foundations – psychologically, both at home and in Europe in relation to the EEC; more practically in relation to détente in the form of the Test-Ban treaty. That there is a case for and against détente – or at any rate against a needless pursuit of détente and the too ready acceptance of the Soviet word for the deed – is not questioned. But the Test-Ban treaty was at least a constructive achievement in its own right, the merits of which do not depend on other aspects of détente. It is perhaps the achievement from which Macmillan can take, in retrospect, the most satisfaction.

Notes

1. Lord Egremont, *Wyndham and Children First* (London 1968), p. 161.
2. H.Macmillan, *At the end of the Day* (London 1973), p. 520.
3. c.f. Lord Kilmuir, *Political Adventure* (London 1964), p. 308. A similar phrase was used by Lord Duncan-Sandys, one of Macmillan's Cabinet, to the author.
4. Lord Swinton, *Sixty Years of Power* (London 1966), p. 172.
5. See Kilmuir, *op. cit.,* p. 309: Hill, Lord, *Both Sides of the Hill* (London 1964), pp. 235, 238.
6. Harris,K., *Conversations* (London 1967), p. 271. Wilson was talking of leading the Opposition, but the principle is the same.
7. Macmillan, *op. cit.,* chs II and III, contains a detailed account of the Prime Minister's intervention in the field of incomes policy. c.f. also Egremont, *op. cit.,* p. 168.
8. Hill, *op. cit.,* p. 235.
9. Sir Roy Welensky was Prime Minister of the Central African Federation in the late 1950s and early 1960s. He was highly critical of some aspects of Macmillan's handling of this problem and has written his own account of the matter under the title 'Welensky's Three Thousand Days'.
10. The recently published diaries of Richard Crossman provide new evidence of this feature of contemporary Cabinet government.

11. Hill, *op. cit.*, p. 238. It is Hill also who makes the point that Macmillan would accept the fact that he was in a minority 'with good grace', though in general he thought Macmillan 'dominated his Cabinet'.

12. *Ibid.*, p. 247: c.f. Kilmuir, *op. cit.*, p. 323, also J.R.Bevins, *The Greasy Pole* (London 1965), pp. 133–7.

13. See note 7 above, for the relevant chapters of Macmillan's memoirs.

14. Hill, *op. cit.*, p. 248.

15. A.Sampson, *Macmillan: A Study in Ambiguity* (London 1968), p. 142.

16. See H.Macmillan, *Riding the Storm* (London 1971), pp. 703–4, 731.

17. H.Macmillan, *Pointing the Way* (London 1972), p. 218, *Riding the Storm*, p. 351.

18. On Macmillan's disagreements with his Chancellors, see *Riding the Storm*, pp. 351, 708, 723–8: *Pointing the Way*, p. 218: *At the End of the Day*, p. 35ff.

19. See Macmillan, *Riding the Storm*, p. 708: *At the End of the Day*, ch. XII.

20. Macmillan, *Riding the Storm*, p. 711.

21. *Ibid.*, p. 713.

22. Macmillan, *Pointing the Way*, p. 310.

23. Macmillan, *At the End of the Day*, ch. XII contains an account of some of Macmillan's efforts in this direction. See A.M.Schlesinger, *A Thousand Days* (London 1967), pp. 515–8, for an American account of Kennedy's concern for these problems.

24. Kennedy's sister, Kathleen, had married Macmillan's nephew by marriage.

25. All Macmillan's British colleagues whom the author has consulted agree on the genuine sympathy between the two men. On the American side, Mr Averell Harriman expressed a similar view in a letter to the author, as does Schlesinger (p. 316). Mr Harriman was a member of the Kennedy administration. See T.C.Sorensen, *Kennedy* (London 1965), p. 617.

26. H.Macmillan, *Tides of Fortune* (London 1969), p. 472.

27. Spaak, at different times Belgian Prime Minister and Foreign Secretary, presided over the Messina negotiations, His role and views are commented on by Macmillan in *Riding the Storm*, pp. 62, 69, 72–7.

28. See Sampson, pp. 208–10.

29. Lord Harlech to the author. Lord Harlech was HM ambassador to Washington at the time the treaty was signed.

30. Macmillan's account of the later and most difficult stages of this problem are in *Pointing the Way*, pp. 295–331.

EDWARD HEATH

Lucille Iremonger

In 1965 a new name was added to the roll of honour which includes Peel, Disraeli, Salisbury and Churchill. Edward Richard George Heath became Leader of the Conservative party, and made history by being the first to be elected to that office. In 1970 he became Prime Minister. In February 1974 he lost a general election. In October he lost another. In February 1975 he again made history by becoming the first Leader of his party to be publicly and decisively rejected by the same elective process which had brought him to the top.

Beneath these bald facts, and behind the figure of stolid reserve, lies a story of private tragedy and public concern. It might be claimed that in the rise and fall of Edward Heath the personality of a Leader affected as never before the fortunes of his party, and consequently of the nation.

The story cannot all be told now. Of all the Prime Ministers in this volume Edward Heath is perhaps the one most difficult to assess with accuracy and in perspective. The thirty years rule governing the revelations of Cabinet proceedings during the four years from 1970 to 1974 will keep inviolate important secrets until the years 2000 to 2004. Civil servants, even when retired, are somewhat inhibited by a native discretion – if admittedly less so than I had imagined at the outset of my enquiries. Harold Wilson, when still in office, was more revealed to us in his memoirs, to say nothing of Richard Crossman's. Edward Heath, for whom words more easily conceal than elucidate, may possibly never embark on his. The story is unfinished, in any case. All in all, these are early days in which to attempt a balanced assessment of the man and his period of office.

Nonetheless there may be something to be gained by an attempt to do just that, and particularly so if it is made by one who has been close to all the major events of that unique career without being personally involved in them – close enough too, to have felt the pulse of the party and the public. As the wife of a backbench MP, as a councillor on London's county council, and as a member of one of those groups which influenced the formation of policy in the 1960s, I was able to feel, to sense and to sound out reactions as the purely academic or journalistic observer could not. It may well be that recollections of such matters, and the conclusions reached about them, are best set down while they are still fresh.

Edward Heath, then, was elected Leader of the Conservative party in July 1965. Before that Conservative leaders had either 'emerged', as it was engagingly phrased, or, as Iain Macleod put it more ill-temperedly in his famous outburst in the *Spectator*, been elected by the machinations of the 'magic circle'.

On the face of it this should have been an inestimable advantage to the new Leader. In fact he was at once confronted with a problem from which none of his predecessors had suffered – public knowledge that he did not command satisfactory support in his party in Parliament. It was only too obvious, not only to him, to the parliamentary party and to his political opponents, but to the world, that he had not secured over his nearest rival Reginald Maudling even the minimum fifteen per cent of votes required for him to be elected on the first ballot. Leading by a mere seventeen votes, instead of the forty-five required to dispense with a second ballot, he owed his election at that stage only to the fact that Maudling conceded victory. There was no concealing the fact that although 150 Tory MPs wanted him as their Leader, the 133 who had voted for Maudling, and the fifteen who had voted for the outsider Powell, emphatically did not, and that he was in by an overall majority of only two votes. (Apparently there were no abstainers among the 304 MPs in the party, the six non-voters being either ill or abroad.) For a leader such a factor is one of overwhelming importance, necessarily affecting his outlook and his every action. That is not to say that Edward Heath did not have a loyal party behind him in 1965. In the Conservative party the division between those who voted for him and those who voted against him never represented a deep ideological split, such as divides the 'Marxist' and the 'Methodist' (to use Morgan Phillips's terminology) wings of the Labour party.

What was the Tory party looking at in Edward Heath, and what was it hoping for from him?

At the time the party looked back on several troubled years. When Churchill retired in April 1955 the Conservatives were governing with a narrow majority. When, the following May, his successor Anthony Eden went to the country and increased it to sixty-eight over Labour at the polls, the tide of fortune seemed to be flowing once again. By the following winter and spring, however, the Government was under constant fire because of rising inflation; and by July 1956 Nasser had seized the Suez canal. The story of the Premier's misfortunes, ranging from the Americans' abandonment of him to bad luck with surgical operations, are well known. On 9 January 1957 he resigned, and Harold Macmillan 'emerged' to general astonishment. By the end of January 1958 his Chancellor Peter Thorneycroft and Treasury ministers Enoch Powell and Nigel Birch had resigned, causing Macmillan rather more than the 'little local difficulty' of his elegantly dismissive phrase. The general election of October 1959 seemed to restore matters, with a majority of a hundred for the Conservatives. A time of tranquillity and prosperity supervened.

Inevitably then the disease of inflation began to erode the life of the whole nation, and the Conservatives' confidence in themselves. The Chancellor, Selwyn Lloyd, made the first of continued attempts to limit the growth of demand in the shape of increased incomes by his 'pay pause'. Unfortunately the first victims of this were the nurses. At this juncture came the dramatic loss of the safe Conservative seat of Orpington. After that the Conservative leadership never recovered its nerve. The most startling symptom of this came with the 'night of the long knives', when Macmillan sacked a third of his Cabinet and a host of experienced junior ministers. The Tory party would be deprived of a generation of its giants armed with wisdom, experience and deep understanding of what Conservatives stood for. Its roots would not be watered for a decade.

Those were the days of persistent efforts to gain entrance to the European Community, halted by de Gaulle's resounding 'Non' of 29 January 1963. Even that was regarded by the pro-marketeers as merely a temporary setback. Everyone else in the Community welcomed Britain, and de Gaulle, they consoled themselves, could not live for ever.

Then in early June 1963 came the Profumo scandal, culminating with the famous lie to the House and his confession, which brought Conservative morale even lower.

Finally came Macmillan's resignation on 10 October 1963, and the public struggle for the leadership between the five candidates, Hailsham, Butler, Maudling, Macleod and Home. Butler's hereditary 'crown' was snatched from his head, hovered over that of Macmillan's first choice, Hailsham, and then rested, a little shakily, on that of his second choice, Home. Macleod and Powell at once refused to serve under him. By October of the next year, 1964, Sir Alec had lost the general election to Labour, which had an overall majority of five seats, and the Tory party had entered a period of severe self-criticism. Perhaps the great British public was tired of Conservatives with a 'grouse moor' or aristocratic image? Perhaps the nation was demanding 'a man of the people', a technocrat, or businessman, with whom it identified more easily, and who could lead a new Britain into the modern world? The fourteenth earl had been unable to cope with the fourteenth Mr Wilson. Perhaps what the Tories needed was a Wilson of their own with the right ideas?

Edward Heath seemed to fill the bill in several important respects. He was no technocrat, though he passed for one, and his business experience was scanty, to say the least. But he was certainly a man of the people – the son of a small builder, who had begun as a carpenter, and an ex-parlourmaid, the grandson of a dairyman who became a luggage-porter, with farm labourers, tailors, fishermen, coastguards and merchant seamen for ancestors – not a duke or even a knight to embarrass him. Indeed his mother's father had not been able to read or write. As far as his own education went, his background was equally impeccable. He was a grammar-school boy, not brilliant but hardworking, who had failed to get a scholarship to Balliol, but had gone up on a local authority loan and help from his parents, and had then won an organ scholarship. With no money behind him, he could never have entered the Commons had it not been for the Maxwell-Fyffe reforms which eliminated the need for candidates to have private means. He was competent at digesting official material. He was a man of industry and robust health. At forty-nine he was not too young and not too old.

Heath had a distinguished military record too, unlike his nearest contender, Maudling, and the valiant soldier has always been dear t. the Tory heart. In the war he had become an artillery major, and after the war a territorial lieutenant-colonel in the Honourable Artillery Company. He was not, of course, a brigadier like Powell, but then Powell was not seriously in the running.

Heath's political career had taken him through the stages of deputy Chief Whip under Churchill, Chief Whip under Eden and Macmillan, Minister of Labour for nine months, and then negotiator for Common Market entry under Macmillan. Sir Alec Douglas-Home had made him Secretary of State for Industry, Trade and Regional Development and President of the Board of Trade, where his enthusiasm for regional development and administration had been given free rein. In July 1964 had come his personal triumph – some say a pyrrhic victory party-wise – in the form of the abolition of retail price maintenance, stubbornly hammered through by him despite opposition from the nation's traditionally Tory small shopkeepers. It was after the general election of the following October that he had stepped into Butler's shoes as chairman of the Advisory Committee on Policy, and set up study groups to form new 'policies' for a refurbished party in a modern world.

True, he was not married. True, he was not a 'brain'. True, he was no orator. But Pitt and Balfour had been bachelors, and, as A.P. Herbert said, it wasn't brains, but character, that counted, especially in getting across to the people. Oratory could boomerang in the pedestrian and disenchanted late twentieth century. Sincerity was all.

Those were the arguments used to answer such doubters as felt that a man who sought to appeal to a nation largely consisting of married people with children should share such experiences, and that oratory was one thing, but a blatant insensitivity to words, and an inability to strike chords in others, implied a dangerous lack of warmth and human feeling.

He was, it was admitted, honest, resolute, sincere, high-principled, and, of course, untiringly industrious. But was it enough? There were even those who were widely read enough to recall Clausewitz's classification of leaders: the stupid and lazy, who make useful regimental officers; the stupid and industrious, who make useful staff officers; the intelligent and industrious, who are dangerous, and unfitted for high responsibility; and the intelligent and lazy, who are the natural leaders, and who alone are fitted for the highest command. (They did not misunderstand Clausewitz's concept of laziness, by which he meant the refusal to give way to the exhausting demands of busy-ness, seductively fulfilling but unproductive, as opposed to the opening of the imagination to unperceived potentialities.) They were apt to equate Heath with the third class, and look with mistrust on the prospect of having him as Leader.

There were those, too, who felt and said, with various degrees of emphasis, that one who had had no more than eight sitting months as a back-bencher in his fifteen years in the Commons – and those his first eight months, in days when new Members did not make speeches – had not served the necessary time to feel with the heart of the House. (It has been said that his maiden speech was his last serious speech in the House for over eight years.) Moreover, a man who had spent those eight years in the Whips' Office, and who had himself been Chief Whip, should, they felt, be disqualified. The qualities which make a Whip were antithetical to what was required of a leader. No Chief Whip had ever before been given the opportunity in the Tory party of leading it. Some went so far as to describe the functions of the Whips' Office as being as distasteful, if as necessary, as those of a sewage system, leaving its operators cynical, domineering and all too conscious of how much could be achieved by bullying, bribery and even blackmail. Heath had been an implacable Chief Whip, notoriously unforgiving to those who crossed him. Magnanimity was a must in a Conservative leader. Others, less extreme in their hostility, still doubted whether the necessary qualities for inspiring leadership were engendered from such experience.

More deeply disturbing to some was the question whether Heath was a 'gut Conservative'. They feared that he might fall prey to the soft centre, to the cultivation of the amorphous 'middle ground' of politics, which they were convinced would be pandering to the enemy, and bound to alienate the party's best supporters.

Those who asked such questions and disliked the answers were the people who voted against Heath, and who were out-voted, however unimpressively. They were loyal and silent, hoping that they were wrong and that he would prove to have the three most important qualities for a leader and potential Prime Minister – political vision, an instinct for choosing the right men, and resourcefulness when the unexpected occurred, as it always does in politics.

Before there had ever been any question of Heath's becoming Leader, just after the Conservative Government's narrow defeat in 1964, when Sir Alec Douglas-Home had appointed him chairman of his Advisory Committee on Policy, he had set to work at once – or rather, had set others to work – formulating what he has significantly always called 'policies' and not 'a policy' for the future. Within a month of his appointment he was assembling a number of policy 'study groups' (on one of which I served myself) which were to total more than thirty, covering the whole range of national affairs, and consisting of MPs, a few peers and outside specialists. Each study group was nominally a sub-committee of the national Advisory Committee on Policy. Heath was breaking new ground in his party by enlisting so many outsiders from many fields in order to help form party policy.

The subjects to which the groups were to devote their attention ranged from defence, foreign affairs, crime and future economic policy (with Heath as chairman and fourteen outsiders) to public service pensions, consumer problems and leisure. The fruits of this collaboration duly appeared in the form of papers which had been sent to Heath for absorption. He was obviously pleased with the results, since he later increased the number of policy groups and almost doubled their scope. He also set up several high-powered committees to advise him personally. Edward Heath could never be accused of failing to take cognisance of the ideas of others. Indeed, that is not a charge his severest critics have ever levelled at him. They have consistently accused him of having none of his own.

This work of policy-formation had barely been completed when Heath became Leader. He went off immediately, ostensibly on holiday, but taking with him all the reports of all the policy groups to prepare for the party conference at Brighton only a few weeks later. The resulting pamphlet, bearing his signature, was summarized as follows:

'We believe that new policies and energetic action are needed in particular at five points:

(1) We must open up new opportunities for merit, talent and individual enterprise, and we must change the tax system to provide new incentives.

(2) We need fresh policies to create a more competitive climate in industry and commerce, to speed up the reform of management at all levels and to readjust our agricultural support system.

(3) We need an entirely new approach to manpower problems. In the years ahead we face an increasing demand for labour. Employment prospects must be transformed, the trade unions' responsibilities redefined and restrictive labour practices eliminated.

(4) We must make our social and community services more humane, more efficient, and better geared to people's real needs.

(5) We must pursue a policy which will enable Britain to become a member of an enlarged European Community. Technological advance is making nonsense of national boundaries. Britain's future lies in a larger grouping and that grouping should be the Europe of which the Common Market is already the nucleus.'

Over the years those 'policies' grew in number and scope, but they were the ones which would take him into the election which was only eight months away. Heath worked hard, hoping to turn the slight defeat of 1964 into a Tory majority. The sensational Labour defeat in the Leyton by-election had raised Conservative hopes; but in March 1966 the greatest Labour landslide since 1945 produced a socialist majority of 97 overall. Dishearteningly, Heath faced a long stretch in opposition after a thumping defeat.

The next few years were hard for Heath. As Ian Trethowan has pointed out in a masterly summary, Heath saw himself proved right again and again. Labour called him alarmist in prophesying national bankruptcy; and then, four months afterwards, came the crisis, and in due course, devaluation. Labour rejected his call to accept the Treaty of Rome, then recommended acceptance. Labour refused to talk to Ian Smith, then did so. Labour exploded with rage at his demand for the return of prescription charges, then brought them back. Labour scoffed at his warning that higher unemployment must come, then deliberately increased it.

No matter how right he was proved, and how often, there were three aspects of leadership in which he failed. First, he was bested time and again at the dispatch-box by Harold Wilson, and frequently showed his irritation. Second, he never succeeded in coming to terms with a substantial and important minority in his party in Parliament, which represented a much wider section of the party outside it, and of the public generally, over Rhodesia. Third, he did not seem to be capturing the heart of the people. Even when the Greater London Council elections of April 1967 encouraged the Tories, and the public opinion polls reflected their increasing popularity in the country, Heath himself dragged depressingly behind.

Then Enoch Powell reared his fateful head. Never fitting neatly into any box, he refused to content himself with his prescribed Shadow Cabinet special subject of Defence, and made his so-called 'rivers of blood' speech on immigration which has never ceased to reverberate. It was on Saturday 20 April 1968 that he addressed the annual general meeting of the West Midlands Area Conservative Political Centre at the Midland Hotel in Birmingham in colourful terms without giving notice to the Shadow Cabinet: 'As I look ahead I am filled with foreboding. Like the Roman I seem to see "the River Tiber foaming with much blood".' At 9 p.m. on Sunday his dismissal was announced.

For Heath, however, it was but the beginning of years of trouble stirred up by one who not only commanded a wide popular following, but was the only politician of any party to do so. Despite his making no concessions to supposed public taste, and giving full rein to his academic and even pedagogic predilections, Powell was universally lauded as an orator of consummate demagogic appeal, while Heath, 'the man of the people', was dismissed as tongue-tied or clumsy in expression and apparently unfeeling and egotistical. The climax of Powell's popular appeal came three days after his speech when the dockers, those Labour stalwarts, marched in their thousands into New Palace Yard to support the Tory bogeyman. The nadir of his fortunes would come five years later, when in February 1974 he advised the electorate, because of his antagonism to the Common Market, to vote Labour. Until then he might have been forgiven, and in 1975 he might well have been elected Leader of the party. Even in 1974, and after his defection, there were some to recall that Churchill had twice crossed the floor.

Before the next election there were two resignations which would affect Heath's future. In January 1966 Angus Maude criticized the party for having completely lost effective political initiative because of its handling of the Rhodesia crisis – 'For the Tories simply to talk like technocrats will get them nowhere' – and his resignation from the Shadow Cabinet followed shortly. Edward du Cann also resigned from his chairmanship of the party.

After the election of 1970, however, Heath was Prime Minister at last, and able to ignore Powell's claim that it was he who had won the election for him. (It was certainly a feature of that election that canvassers met again and again with the answer from hitherto loyal supporters, 'Of course I'd vote for you if Enoch were Leader, but I'll have to think about it.')

When Heath formed his administration that June, we have it on the most impressive authority that he had a clear idea of how he wished to change society, and a precise strategy for implementing the necessary policies. So says Brendon Sewill, director of the Conservative Research Department from January 1965 until October 1970, and Special Assistant to the Chancellor of the Exchequer, Anthony Barber, until March 1974. No one was better placed to know the intentions of the Conservative Government which took office in June 1970, and then to see from his temporary vantage point inside the civil service the effect of the pressures of office and of events.

According to Sewill, Heath and his men, alarmed by Britain's state in the 1960s with its slow rate of economic growth as compared with other European countries (leading to relative poverty, and progressively sluggish management and restrictive labour attitudes, constant pressure for higher wages, uncontrollable inflation, and the aggravation of all the social problems of poor housing and education, deprivation, racial tension, violence and crime), intended to try to change the whole attitude of mind of the British people and to create a more dynamic, thrusting, go-getting economy on the American or German model, with new material wealth and new pride in achievement.

The main planks in Heath's programme were to be: entry into the European Economic Community, in order to create a new challenge to industrial management, a new scale of operations, and new inspiration; the reduction, reform and simplification of taxation, in order to create new incentives; and legislation on industrial relations, in order to create strong but responsible unions. Lesser planks were to be the change from agricultural subsidies to levies (which in any case would be called for on joining the EEC), and the attachment of housing subsidies to families instead of to housing, so as to give aid exclusively to those in need, as well as to economize on public spending, and help labour which was tied to council housing to become more mobile.

At the famous Selsdon Park Hotel conference held at Croydon just before the 1970 election, Heath reviewed his policies, many of which were the product of the study groups which had originally been set up by him in 1964. Sewill, reflecting on this period in 1975, suggests that the strategic aim of achieving dynamic growth had been conceived and settled too early, in 1965, and that by 1969 it was clear that 'price stability should be the main priority'. He agrees with those who later criticized the strategy as 'too materialistic – too much efficiency and not enough idealism or principle'. He believes that 'an abrasive image was projected and antagonisms built up, so that in the end when an appeal had to be made to the people the necessary support was not forth-coming'.[1]

After Selsdon, Heath seemed at any rate to be offering an alternative Government with a distinctive character of its own. It did not, however, appear to be gaining ground. Despite loud dissatisfaction at rising prices Labour was surging ahead in the opinion polls and threatening to overwhelm him once again. It is a matter of history how much in error those polls were, up to the general election of June 1970 itself, and how Heath was returned, almost certainly to his own surprise, as Prime Minister.

With the Queen's speech of 2 July Heath went straight for EEC membership. He proclaimed that his first concern was to strengthen the economy and curb inflation. He proposed to introduce an Industrial Relations Bill as a framework of law within which improved industrial relations could develop. He gave support to the Northern Ireland government at Stormont in the crisis of an Ulster rent by conflict and violence.

Eighteen days later Iain Macleod, his Chancellor of the Exchequer, was dead, and Heath had lost the greatest asset — and, incidentally, his most dangerous rival – in his Cabinet. No other obvious rival was to settle for long on Heath's front bench. Over the years, for one reason or another, Peter Thorneycroft, Christopher Soames, Quintin Hogg, Reginald Maudling, Duncan Sandys, Ernest Marples and John Boyd-Carpenter would have disappeared. Fate, which had eliminated Lord Randolph Churchill, Sir Charles Dilke and Joseph Chamberlain by syphilis, adultery and a stroke respectively, had taken a hand once again to help one man hold the reins of power unchallenged.

On 1 December the Industrial Relations Bill was introduced and by 5 August 1971 it had obtained the Royal Assent. On 28 October 356 MPs voted in effect for going into the Common Market (69 of them Labour members who had defied their Whips, for by that time Harold Wilson had made his *volte face* on Europe under left-wing pressure), and 244 MPs voted against it, 33 of them Conservative.

On 21 November the Queen opened a new session with a speech introducing the instrument of accession to the EEC, to be signed in January 1972. The speech also proposed a Housing Finance Bill which would make local authorities charge economic rents for their council houses, and which was to lead to the defiance of the law by the so-called Clay Cross martyrs, and their support by the Labour Government – a deeply disturbing constitutional phenomenon.

In January 1972 Heath went to Brussels to sign Britain into the EEC. The fulfilment of his greatest ambition was in sight. If Disraeli was 'the man who made Victoria Empress', and Lloyd George 'the man who won the Great War', and Churchill 'the man who beat Hitler', he would go down in history as 'the man who took Britain into Europe'.

That January also saw the miners' strike for more pay, which spotlighted and struck at the Achilles' heel of Heath's Government – the first symptom of the malady which was to prove fatal to it.

In the manifesto of 1970 one of Heath's most important pronouncements was :'We will subject all proposed price rises in the public sector to the most searching scrutiny. If they are not justified, they will not be allowed.' Now a mighty demand was being made on the most vital part of the public sector, which could not but cause an intolerable 'price rise', and which could not by any sophistry be 'justified', and which therefore could not conceivably be 'allowed' by the Government. It was not 'allowed'. The Coal Board, statutorily independent but in reality the creature of governments, had to resist the demand. The effect of the strike upon industry and commerce and the domestic life of the private householder subjected to the inevitable power cuts was devastating.

It was the general view of ministers and their advisers that a total breakdown in the life of the nation – water supplies, sewage disposal and all the essential services being ultimately dependent upon the production of coal – was imminent, and they had no plans for averting it.

On 9 February Heath declared a state of emergency. The Coal Board was driven next day, and presumably 'allowed', to make a humiliating concession by doubling its original offer to the miners, only to have it contemptuously rejected. With rising unemployment and loss of production exacerbated by violent picketing of power stations and elsewhere by miners and their militant supporters, the Government was forced on 11 February to appoint a court of inquiry presided over by a Chancery judge, Lord Wilberforce. The choice was significant. It had been Wilberforce who to the dismay of the then 'tough' Government, had a year before heaped upon the striking electricity workers an over-generous eighteen-per-cent pay-rise. The result was total defeat for the Government in the most important aspect of its economic policy. Wilberforce recommended yielding to the miners an increase of five to six pounds as compared with the four to seven pounds they had originally demanded. The justifying of this surrender by the court on the grounds that the miners were a 'special case' deceived no one. The miners were out for seven weeks before they settled.

Eight months of talks with the Confederation of British Industry and the Trades Union Congress, and both together, ensued. This was the life-and-death struggle for Heath and his Government. Their purpose was, as was the purpose of the Industrial Relations Act, to establish in Britain a *modus vivendi* whereby the same sort of constructive and productive partnership as prevailed in the other countries of western Europe, notably Western Germany and America, would be created between 'the two sides of industry'. It is to Edward Heath's eternal credit that he did try to achieve this transformation. His perception of the need (which Wilson also saw, though he failed to satisfy it) marks him out as a statesman of vision in this respect at least. His attempt to solve the intractable and perennial problem was realistic and courageous. Whether or not he is to be blamed for it, however, the fact is that he failed, and the juncture at which his failure became apparent and irreversible was the point at which the long series of talks with the CBI and the TUC broke down.

On 6 November, to the chagrin and anguish of Conservative front- and back-benchers alike, he rose in the Commons to say:

'The responsibility for action now rests with the Government. We have come to the conclusion that we have no alternative but to bring in statutory measures to secure the agreed objectives of economic management in the light of the proposals discussed in the tripartite talks . . . the Government propose to introduce tomorrow an interim Bill to provide for a standstill on all increases in pay, prices, rents and dividends . . . I deeply regret that last Thursday's disagreement has forced us to take action which I regard as less satisfactory than a voluntary arrangement could have been. I profoundly believe that the course upon which we had embarked was the right, rational and sensible course for Britain. I therefore hope that this setback will not be allowed to stand in the way of our resuming discussions between the three parties in due course on the objectives and problems of economic management.'[2]

This was the 'U-turn' for which he was to be slated and mocked by supporters and opponents. It represented the reversal of the policy emphatically stated throughout the general election and the succeeding two years, and the embracing of the statutory incomes policy which he had so mercilessly derided when imposed by the preceding Labour Government.

More formidable than the malicious glee of opponents was the denunciation by the saturnine figure two benches behind him. Enoch Powell could now say, 'I told you so.' He had consistently maintained that the Industrial Relations Bill had been irrelevant, and that no cosmetic remedies, but only the organic one of eliminating the budget deficit, would ever cure inflation. True, when the kind of deflationary measures he advocated had in the past created unemployment at a level no political leader could tolerate, Powell had conspicuously refrained from drawing attention to the relationship between this dreaded ill and the remedy he advocated for the other; but this did not make the pain of his lash any less sharp upon his Leader's back. Nor was Powell's lone voice raised in the cause of the monetary solution. He had allies among the ablest and most promising of the back-benchers.

The interim Bill to which Heath had referred was the Counter-Inflation (Temporary Provisions) Bill which was in due course succeeded by the Counter-Inflation Act of 1973, and the Prices and Pay Code established under it, and the whole apparatus of state control of prices and wages. He was on the road to disaster.

Triumph, however, had been his in another sphere. On 1 January 1973 Britain had joined the European Community.

During all this time the troubles in Ulster which Heath had inherited from Wilson, and regarding which it would be idle to attribute blame, continued unabated. Heath had decided the previous March to impose direct rule on the Province and dismantle the half-century-old apparatus of Stormont government. In this difficulty alone, of all his major difficulties, Heath asserts, did Wilson have no party motive for reversing the policy which he had pursued while in power, and the Opposition – with a few exceptions, increasingly muted – was not disposed to embarrass the Government. At the time of writing, in 1975, within earshot of the random bombing of civilians by IRA terrorists in London and with no coherent policy being advanced by either political party to solve the historically insoluble problem of Ireland, no mature judgement can be made on Heath's role in this drama. But he did not give way to the temptation over Ulster, as he maintains Wilson did over Europe and industrial relations, to exploit the situation for party political motives. Had he chosen to 'play the Orange card', in Lord Randolph Churchill's phrase, he would have reaped the harvest of enough Ulster Unionist MPs accepting the Conservative Whip and returning to Westminster in the February 1974 general election to have enabled him to form a Government[3]. It would of course have cost him his Lord Chancellor, Lord Hailsham, the former Quintin Hogg and the best man in his Cabinet, and possibly others, but a less scrupulous party leader might have been prepared to pay that price, and more.

In October 1973 the shadow of fate fell across Edward Heath. The Israelis and the Arabs went to war. This resulted in serious oil shortages for British industry and the quadrupling of the price of oil by December. It was at this moment that the coalminers decided to impose an overtime ban and demand an increase in wages which if granted would have been in breach of 'Stage Three' of the counter-inflation policy announced by Heath on 8 October. The combined effects of the shortage of oil, its rise in price, and the coalminers' action, which rapidly developed into a strike, led inevitably to the partial shutting down of British industry, and, as in 1972, the threat of ultimate chaos. Twelve days before Christmas Heath again declared a state of emergency, and put industry and commerce on a three-day week.

Pointing to the sixteen million trade unionists who had submitted to the limit for pay-rises imposed by 'Stage Three', the Government refused to yield to the miners and dress up surrender once again as a 'special case'. Eventually Heath decided to dissolve Parliament and appeal to the electorate on the issue of whether the country was to be ruled by Parliament and Government or by militant trade union leaders. Wilson countered with the slogan, 'Back to work with Labour'. Polling ended with Labour winning 301 seats and the Conservatives 296 seats, although in fact Labour had fewer votes than the Con-servatives.

Heath's three years and nine months in office were over. For three more days he stayed on in 10 Downing Street as Prime Minister in an effort to achieve an anti-Labour coalition with the Liberals on the grounds that the anti-Labour parties had a majority of the votes cast.

It is hard to imagine that historical judgements of the future will deny that the issue on which Heath went to the country was a fundamental one which sooner or later would have to be decided one way or the other. It is tempting for Conservative partisans in general, and those who champion Heath in particular, to say that his judgement was sound and his conduct in calling the election courageous, and that blame lies not with him for having asked the wrong question at the wrong time, but with the British people for failing to respond to the challenge he put to them. What Heath and his

Government would have done about the still unresolved problem of the defiant miners and the energy crisis had the electorate supported him, is one of those hypothetical questions which it is fruitless to pursue. The economic issue of pay claims enforced by union power against Government policy has become a constitutional one. Neither party has yet met the challenge.

Wilson, of course, could not hope to govern comfortably with so small a majority. By September he felt confident enough to call another general election. Heath's dilemma was crucial. On what issue should he fight? 'We were right, and you were wrong. Think again!'? He might have done; but in the end he plumped for 'national unity'. The nation did not respond. Candidates who had managed to hold their seats in February were swept away – Labour was in again with a majority of forty-three seats over the Tories, and the disparate parties which secured the remaining seats were obviously never going to form a coherent anti-socialist opposition.

The immediate cause of the fall of the Heath Government, and later of Heath himself, was the confrontation with the miners, just when the Arabs had quadrupled the price of oil, during his attempt to cure inflation. In that confrontation he failed to secure public support at the polls and had to cede power to an Opposition which at once yielded to the miners' demands with every appearance of joy.

The appearance was, however, deceptive. Responsible Labour party leaders had long been as aware as Heath himself and the Conservative party of a deeper cause of his defeat – the fact that one part of the industrial organism, namely organized labour, is capable of wrecking the national economy, and that the democratic national institutions, such as Parliament and the Government, are incapable of bringing the trade unions under control. The reason why neither Wilson nor Heath could prevail upon the trade unions to help prevent the inflation which threatened to destroy the existing structure of society was that such destruction was the very end to which some of the most influential and assiduous trade union activists were as confessed Communists or men of the extreme Left specifically dedicated.

Wilson's Government had recognized the threat posed by over-powerful trade unions, and analysed its nature and prescribed a remedy, in its White Paper 'In Place of Strife', at which only a captious

Conservative could have cavilled. His subsequent attempt to apply the remedy, which consisted of introducing legislation calculated to limit the power of irresponsible trade union leaders to undermine the economy by enforcing inflationary wage demands and disrupting production by a process euphemistically referred to as 'industrial action', failed. This legislation, presented to the Commons by Mrs Barbara Castle, had to be withdrawn because of trade union pressure in a Labour party peculiarly susceptible to such influence.

It was against this background that Heath had offered the electorate a virtually identical, if somewhat less drastic, remedy in his 1970 manifesto. It was against this background that he had pushed his Industrial Relations Bill through the Commons against Labour opposition led by Mrs Barbara Castle eating her words of three years before from the Government dispatch-box. It was against this background, rich in irony, and offering a sceptical public some grounds for its traditional cynicism about politicians that Heath's vanquishers of February 1974 faced the foe which had laid him low, and from whom they had themselves been obliged to flee.

It is against this background too that a judgement must be made on Heath as a national leader. He had, if not the right idea, at any rate the same idea of the same remedy for the mortal disease as his opponents, he made the same effort to put it into practice, and was thwarted by the same forces.

But was it the right idea? Should, or could it have been put into practice differently? If the difference is a question of timing, and if it is alleged that the legislative control of trade unions should, and could successfully, have been attempted a decade or more earlier, then it might be said in Heath's defence that he was not responsible for such decisions. Perhaps, however, he was even then seized of the problem and armed with the remedy he later tried to use too late?

I can offer some evidence on his point, because it so happens that on 31 July 1957, my husband moved for leave to introduce a Bill which adumbrated the essence of Heath's Industrial Relations Act. Labour's frenzied opposition could be taken for granted. More instructive was the intense hostility to the idea evinced by the then Conservative Chief Whip – Edward Heath. On two subsequent occasions my husband urged upon two successive Ministers of Labour the importance for the nation's economic future of some such measure as he had proposed. Each was emphatically antagonistic to the idea – their names were Iain Macleod and Edward Heath. So whether or not the two Macmillan governments could have anticipated the Industrial Relations Act, whether or not it would have been acceptable to the electorate had they done so, and whether or not a framework of law around the privileges accorded to British trade unions would have prevented the 'crisis of capitalism' developing as it has done since, at least it is established that Edward Heath was not in the vanguard in pressing for it. It could be argued that had this measure been introduced then, thirteen years before it actually was, when trade union leaders were possibly more amenable and the Conservatives were headed for a hundred-seat majority, the troubles of 1974 would have been avoided and Edward Heath would have enjoyed a second term as Prime Minister.

Yet was it the industrial conundrum in conjunction with the oil crisis which had defeated him, or was it the man who had destroyed himself? Was it that Heath had had no stomach for the battle, that he was in fact a half-hearted leader for such a cause? More natural to him perhaps had been that later call for 'national unity', which had brought him no support. National unity is only, after all, a variation of the coalition theme, beguiling and always (except briefly in war) a deadly trap for a national party leader. Had Heath learned nothing from the fates of Grenville, Aberdeen, Lloyd George and MacDonald? Had he failed to appreciate Baldwin's and Attlee's motives for pulling out of coalitions? Had he forgotten, or had he never realized, that a coalition alienates friends and never placates enemies? Heath himself resents any charge of being a 'consensus' coalitionist, and points to the fierce opposition he evoked on industrial relations, Europe, taxation, local government reform, housing, finance and immigration.

Or was it perhaps, as he himself sometimes wonders, that the very activity of his reforming administration damaged him? He is sure that his Government got the priorities right, and did a very great deal in its three and three-quarter years. Yet he asks himself whether 'the change was too much and too rapid for the citizen to digest all at once'.

Or was the trouble really Heath's personality, and his inability to communicate, even to strike a chord, let alone to rouse? Would the nation have responded to a call to resist trade union tyranny if it had been sounded by one capable of inspiring it to sacrifice and endeavour? Had the people been rejecting him rather than his policies, refusing to follow a conductor they considered tone-deaf to life?

Who can be sure of the answers? Not Edward Heath. But he and his Government, he has insisted, did suffer a crippling and unique handicap, in having to deal with an Opposition 'so dishonest' as to change its policies on major issues, and to refuse to work with the Government on matters of vital national importance on which there was no genuine disagreement. Wilson had, Heath says, behaved disingenuously about Europe, about statutory incomes, and about the trade unions. As Heath saw it, he had been sold down the river in a way no other Prime Minister had ever been. He believes that such volatility is a threat to the entire democratic system, which cannot survive unless parties remain true to their policies wherever fundamentals are concerned.

So much for Heath's rejection by the nation. There remains the question of his historic rejection by his own parliamentary party, the most complete since the 'Balfour Must Go' campaign, and which took him, by his own admission, completely by surprise. With unusual frankness, considering Heath is still alive, many have asked whether this was the fruit of his lack of appreciation for, or even tolerance of, anyone not cut in his own image or likely to promote his interests, together with his lack of magnanimity towards those who had ever crossed him. It is true that those who had fallen out with him, or who had been insultingly ignored by him, suddenly reappeared as giants on the scene in February 1975 – Thorneycroft, Maude, du Cann and Neave, for instance.

Heath's contention is that some eighty per cent of Conservative constituency and national party officers wanted him to remain. This would not, however, mean that Conservative party members everywhere, let alone voters and potential voters for the party, shared the feelings of those who are habitually most loyal to the leader, whoever he may be. Conservative MPs, too, would reply that their responsibility was to look deeper and see further than constituency officers, and that they had made thorough and conscientious soundings in their constituencies.

Did his rejection in fact originate among the grass-roots of the party because of his failure to get on with the Lord Randolph Churchill of his day? If he had brought himself to accommodate or contain Enoch Powell, could he have saved himself, his party, and possibly the country?

Certainly it was thought and said that it was because Heath had not proved to be a 'gut' Conservative (as his opponents in his original selection stakes had feared) that his own party had rejected him after he had lost three elections out of four. No statement of distinctively Conservative belief or faith had been heard for a decade, people said, except in the columns of the *Telegraph*. The Tory leadership had turned its back on its own people, so its own people had turned their backs on it. It was symbolic that the only memorable phrase Heath coined was 'the unpleasant and unacceptable face of capitalism' – gratuitously kicking into his own goal.

Other critics asked whether the fact that he was so out of sympathy with women, in the very midst of the struggle for sex equality, was not more of a handicap than he realized. That he could be capable in that atmosphere of criticizing women MPs as not having made a specifically feminine contribution spoke volumes and passed belief. Had his attitude to women not been so painfully apparent perhaps his handling of the nomination for the redistributed Bexley seat might not have had so shocking an impact, and the famous one-sentence letter to *The Times* ('Time was in Bexley when a gentleman gave up his seat to a lady who was standing') would not have echoed round the nation. To many it seemed poetic irony that he should have been toppled by a woman – and by a woman who made no physical concessions to masculinity and asked no intellectual quarter because of her gender.

For every Prime Minister the overriding consideration on assuming office is how best to handle the reins of power. Edward Heath says, however, that although a great deal of work was put into considering the machinery of Government in opposition, it was always regarded by him as a means towards carrying out his policies and not an end directed to increasing the power of the Prime Minister.

During the 1966 Parliament, in anticipation of the formation of a Conservative administration, Heath had delegated to two of his young henchmen the task of collecting ideas about this machinery of government, and they had visited Canada and America to study the systems in operation there. Their basic contention was that there should be a strengthening of the 'centre', that is of the Prime Minister, *vis à vis* the departments and their respective ministers.

In 1970, apparently taken by surprise by the Conservatives' electoral victory, they rather hurriedly put together their ideas, which had not been canvassed with Heath or among MPs – ideas which Heath's civil service advisers at least found 'somewhat half-baked'. They were concerned with the fact that power in the British system is with ministers once they have been appointed by the Prime Minister, though he retains the residual and ultimate authority of being able to dismiss them. Macmillan rather stretched this in the 'night of the long knives', since when prime ministers have been wary of using their powers of dismissal. Thus a Prime Minister finds that once he has exercised his initial power by making his appointments there is a dispersal of power, and it has gone out of his hands. He is in a quandary about how to pull it back without going to the extreme of dismissals.

The first question, however, that Heath had to answer concerning the organization of government was how many departments there should be. If it were decided to have fewer, the next problem was how to coalesce and regroup existing departments. Heath was in favour of reduction because he wanted a smaller Cabinet, of under twenty. But in attempting to achieve this there is inevitably a dilemma. If a Prime Minister is to avoid having a Cabinet of about thirty, which is unmanageable for discussion and decision-making, he has to establish a grading of departments into first and second ranks. A form of amalgamation had in fact been going on over many decades; the Foreign Office, for example, had become an external relations department, as in other countries, whereas there had originally been the Foreign, the Colonial and the India and Burma Offices.

Heath discussed this problem with top civil servants before the 1970 general election, as the Leader of the Opposition had been entitled to do since 1964. He was preoccupied with the question of whether he should decide to amalgamate in advance of his possible accession to office when he would have an opportunity to assess the situation at close quarters, or whether to leave the departments as he found them, take his time in deciding how to amalgamate, and then have a painful uprooting of already established ministers.

Heath resolved the dilemma by deciding to take six months to study what amalgamations would be best, and he warned ministers from the beginning that they were appointed for only a six-months' term since he would be having a major reorganization at the end of that period. He was the only Prime Minister to do this, thereby retaining power in his own hands even after appointing his ministers. In the end, he accomplished all his amalgamations in the first few months, and so arranged for all departmental heads (except for the Minister for the Post Office and Telecommunications) to be in the Cabinet.

Having resolved this first question, Heath was left with the other, of how to develop the strength of the centre. The proposition was that in a modern Cabinet each minister goes to Cabinet meetings with his department behind him, fully briefed, and with the injunction that the department's interests must be defended. The only man (apart from the Leader of the House and the Lord Chancellor, who have narrower and attenuated responsibilities in such respects) who has no brief is the Prime Minister. Edward Heath was not of the class of Prime Ministers, of whom Macmillan is the best recent example, who are unconcerned by this. He was not happy without a brief.

This problem, his travelling henchmen suggested, could be dealt with by the first of their two main proposals, viz. that there should be a 'central capability staff', on the American pattern, to brief the Prime Minister. This appealed to Heath and he adopted it, but widened it to the extent of providing that there should be briefs not only for the Prime Minister but for all departmental ministers from the same neutral source on every departmental question before the Cabinet. This was how the Central Policy Review Staff, or 'Think Tank', came to be formed. It also had the task of providing the basis for discussion at the regular six-monthly meetings, which Heath chaired, of his Cabinet, his middle-rank ministers, and all his junior ministers. The purpose of these meetings was to discuss the Government's objectives and the progress being made towards their realization. Never before, Heath claims, had there been so comprehensive a briefing of an entire Government. 'The lower the tier the more sparking-off of ideas there was', he observes.

The second proposal put to Heath for strengthening the centre was that the functions of the Treasury should be rearranged. The UK Treasury is a mixture. It is central in the sense that it deals with other departments and not the public. It is thus like the Cabinet office or the Civil Service Department. But it is also a department which deals with the public, as in taxation. The proposal was that this duality of function should be broken up, on the model of the American system, in which the Bureau of the Budget, which deals with taxation, for example, is separate from (and a minor department in comparison with) the American Treasury, which deals with the control of public expenditure, and is therefore of fundamental importance in affecting the economy. The central function, it was proposed, should be moved to the Prime Minister, leaving the Chancellor a comparatively minor departmental head. In the event Heath came out against this proposed shift of power and responsibility. Whatever the merits might be in theory, no Chancellor of the Exchequer of any calibre would have been prepared to surrender the Treasury function as the principal economic department. In one form or another, for example in the Department of Economic Affairs experiment by Wilson and George Brown, this breaking up of the Treasury has long tempted all those concerned with the machinery of government.

Heath himself was troubled by the way good and desirable projects were put in hand by governments, and rolled on of their own momentum for decades without ever being looked at, though with the passage of time they might become less desirable or less economically justifiable. To examine such projects in every department, he formed PAR, his Programme Analysis Review, with, as he says, 'a simple objective, but one very difficult to achieve'.

Heath, ever the efficient administrator, left the machinery of government better adapted to its purpose for his tenure of office. If he achieved no revolutionary developments in the office of Prime Minister, he had never had any such ambition.

Ought one to hazard an assessment, premature as it must be, of Edward Heath, with the wisdom of a little hindsight? Heath himself would wish to be remembered for Europe; for initiating an Ulster constitution; for laying the foundations of the tax credit system which he feels is bound to come eventually; for the Barber tax reforms; and for holding the party together for a decade. The Powell dissensions seem not to affect his judgement on the last point. He regrets only that he did not realize the head of steam behind the inflationary pressure; and that he did not succeed in communicating to the nation his sense of being embarked on a 'great adventure to bring the country up-to-date, modernize it and put it on a steady course for a mixed and expanding economy'.

To be harsh, one might accuse him of being deficient in vision and resourcefulness, two of the three prime requisites for a successful leader. He failed to anticipate and prevent the miners' power to defeat a government, by building up coal stocks and creating an emergency corps to keep the electricity supply going for water and sewage. He failed to invent a constitutional device for reversing the ratchet effect of successive Labour Governments' irreversibly creating a collectivist state. He failed to see the potentialities of the referendum device, both for preventing further nationalization and for providing security against renationalization, the lack of which had made de-nationalization impossible. He failed to appreciate the impotence of local authorities as guarantors of education in the national interest and apply the education voucher system as an alternative. He failed to secure the institution of private property as an essential element in liberty, which he could have done by vesting council house freeholds in their tenants, and replacing security of tenure under the Rent Acts by a new system of 'shorthold' tenure. He failed to inspire managers to change their attitude towards their men so as to forestall syndicalist worker-participation by true participation based on realistic teamwork and common interest.

One whose judgement of Edward Heath as Prime Minister must be considered among the most weighty has said, 'He has a fundamental belief in rationality and reasonableness. He believes that men round a table must be able to get to a solution. This failed him, for example with the TUC and at Sunningdale. It is an occupational hazard of a Prime Minister to think that he can achieve things and make people see sense. Heath's flashpoint was touched by irrational bloody-mindedness. But then, that is basic to human nature, and the handling of it is what politics is all about.'[4]

Notes

1. Ralph Harris and Brendon Sewill, *British Economic Policy 1970–74, Two Views* (Institute of Economic Affairs 1975), pp. 29–32.
2. *Hansard*, 6 November 1972, col. 627.
3. *The Times Guide to the House of Commons, February 1974* (Times Newspapers Ltd), pp. 250–7. MPs elected: Labour, 301; Conservative, 297 (including the Speaker); United Unionist Coalition, 11.
4. Opinions quoted in this chapter and attributed to Edward Heath are taken either from a Thames Television programme, 'People and Politics', broadcast on 26 March 1975, or from a personal interview with him on 17 October 1975. His article, 'Downing Street and Whitehall', printed in the *Daily Telegraph* on 17 April 1975, is also relevant. Unattributed quotations are from interviews with other responsible persons under the 'Chatham House rule'.

Harold Wilson

John P. Mackintosh

Sir Harold Wilson had two periods as Prime Minister. He was a brilliant opposition leader who edged his party into power after thirteen years in the wilderness, yet by the end, after his resignation in 1976, he was a lonely, dispirited figure. A brilliant economist at Oxford, a man who had made his case to govern on grounds of his professionalism as opposed to Conservative amateurishness, he had presided over the longest and most serious slide in the history of the British economy. Yet he was an expert party manager and communicator, he was a product of the Labour Movement and his leadership was never seriously challenged from within the party.

Exactly when Wilson decided to pursue a political career is hard to pinpoint, but his own account, that it was an unwavering determination ever since he was twelve, when his father had described the career of Sir Henry Campbell-Bannerman, appears to be correct. He had told his future wife in 1936 that he would enter Parliament after he had established himself in academic life, probably sometime in his thirties. It was during his period as a don at University College that he broke his formal links with the Liberals, began to lean towards 'Keynesian socialism' and agreed to help G.D.H.Cole with work for the New Fabian Research Bureau. The more positive commitment to the Labour party probably occurred in the early years of the war when he worked closely with the leaders of the Miners' Federation on miners' wages and his abilities also became known to Labour ministers. This led to a number of offers of adoption as a candidate for the party and he accepted one from Ormskirk Constituency in 1944.

Carried into the House of Commons by his own hard work in his constituency as well as by the 1945 Labour tide, Mr (later Earl) Attlee appointed him Parliamentary Secretary at the Ministry of Works. His Minister was George Tomlinson, who was not interested in departmental matters, and Harold Wilson was left to, make the running. His activities were resented and resisted by a few civil servants, but Attlee placed great confidence in his judgement and one official was moved. Wilson rapidly revealed his customary high degree of assiduity together with a determination to have agreed plans pushed through. But though he carried out his tasks with precision and authority, at this stage he lacked parliamentary ability. His speeches were delivered rather rapidly, without much variation of pace or tone, and were often overloaded with facts.

In these years, he was not known for any particular ideological slant, having an open, rather academic approach to problems. But he did admire Aneurin Bevan from afar, probably because his own religious background made him feel the force of Bevan's moral appeal and, though it was not part of his approach, he respected, perhaps almost wished he could evoke, the sentimental response which Bevan drew from his hearers.

In 1946 Harold Wilson was promoted to a post of ministerial rank as Secretary for Overseas Trade at the Board of Trade. The major event during his short tenure of this office was a mission to Russia. Wilson himself has often recalled this episode. The main objective was 700,000 tons of grain and the Russians offered 500,000 tons. Wilson asked for two million, called for his plane and threatened departure on several occasions, the final offer being 1,250,000 tons. He eventually came home without the complete agreement signed rather than concede certain points where he felt the Russians were asking too much. The arguments on the most minute details lasted till the early hours of the morning over a period of three weeks, and both Mikoyan, the Russian representative, and Wilson appeared to enjoy these contests and derived a healthy respect for each other.

At home, Sir Stafford Cripps was put in charge of a Ministry of Economic Affairs in 1947 and Wilson was appointed in his place as President of the Board of Trade and one of Cripps' economic team along with Gaitskell, Marquand and Jay. In this office, he again rapidly demonstrated his command both of technical details and of personnel, one senior official being moved because Wilson regarded him as obstructive. Informed observers had mixed views of his record as President. To many, he appeared as an able statistician or research worker who had somehow managed to become a minister, a judgement made easier in that his political speeches were still like short research papers and in that he had taken over a department which, above all others, could allow him to revel in a sea of reports and statistics. The Board of Trade also encouraged his usual approach of tackling problems in a pragmatic manner and Wilson began to scrap many wartime controls which he felt were no longer necessary,

Still a relatively little-known man, though with some reputation in Whitehall, he aroused tremendous surprise and interest when he joined Aneurin Bevan in resigning from the Labour Government over the question of priorities in expenditure in 1951.

Any interpretation of his career has to account for this episode but it is possible that there was an impulsive element in the action; Wilson's record has shown that he is not always a cold and methodical calculator of the odds. On the other hand, in as much as his action was thought out, it was both risky and courageous. After all, he was the youngest Cabinet minister in modern history and, though Gaitskell was elevated above him (becoming Chancellor of the Exchequer), he was still ten years Gaitskell's junior so that the decision to cut himself off from the Leadership of the party was a momentous one. Probably Wilson's motives were a mixture. There was a strong practical basis in that he doubted whether the 1950 rearmament programme of £3,000 million over three years was realistic and he saw that it would lead to cuts in expenditure on health and housing which were both deplorable and unnecessary. When the rearmament programme was raised by Hugh Gaitskell in late 1950 to £4,700 million, Wilson thought that this was patently impossible and would at once undermine the Government's capacity to provide proper social services.

But there was probably also an element of admiration for Bevan, an acceptance of his attacks on United States pressure for such a large, rearmament programme, an acceptance of his passionate attachment to a free health service and a feeling that the Labour party would have at some time to accept Bevan's left-wing attack on the declining vitality of the Government. There was a strong feeling that the Attlee regime was finished and Wilson wanted to be part of the new, not the old guard.

As it happened, when the crisis came to a head, Attlee was ill and

Bevan's old enemy, Herbert Morrison, was presiding over the Cabinet. In order to husband resources, Hugh Gaitskell, as Chancellor of the Exchequer, proposed charges on aspects of the Health Service and said he would resign unless this was accepted. Bevan opposed and also threatened resignation, Herbert Morrison doing nothing to narrow the gap. A majority of the Cabinet supported Gaitskell and Bevan decided to go, but far from dragging a reluctant Wilson with him, Bevan showed little interest in Wilson's actions, but did try to persuade him to remain in office. Nevertheless Wilson, rather embarrassingly, insisted on resigning also and later helped to persuade Bevan to widen his reasons for resigning from the Health Service cuts to the whole cost of the rearmament programme.

On this precise point, events soon proved Wilson's estimates correct as one of the first actions of the Conservative Government was to scale down the rearmament programme. But, having resigned with Bevan, Wilson soon found himself classed with the wide-ranging group of left-wingers who became known as Bevanites. This was his first experience of the rough and tumble of internal party struggle and gave him, for the first time, a chance to establish a real political position in the Labour party and to woo mass support among the rank and file of the party, which soon showed itself in the shape of election (in 1952) to the National Executive. Thus Wilson found himself in the curious position of a pragmatic believer in a mixed economy, a decontroller in the conditions of 1950–1, a man with no ideological conviction that more and more public ownership was the proper policy for Labour, accepted as a lieutenant of Bevan by the Left.

On the other hand, he agreed with the Left's dislike of aggressive commercialism and the over-selling of the 'American way of life' associated with John Foster Dulles. He accepted their fear of a rearmed Germany. He resented Conservative claims that they alone were fit to run the country and he could fairly attack the swollen rearmament programme and erosion of the social services as the issues on which he had resigned. So there was no great difficulty when he carefully made himself a place as a Bevanite with Barbara Castle and Richard Crossman and when he later refused to take a doctrinaire position on the abandonment of nuclear weapons. The facts of the 1951 political position, the decline in the Labour Government, and his deep admiration for Bevan had carried him into a group two or three of whom were far to the left of his actual political opinions but he realized that, in opposition, this had given him a place and position in the party which he would never have achieved had he not resigned and had he continued simply as the able, full-of-facts young ex-minister.

As the internal struggles in the Labour party became increasingly bitter, Wilson placed considerable emphasis on the need to maintain a semblance of party unity. On the other hand, he did dislike United States policy in South-East Asia, he attacked an excessive emphasis on rearmament, defended the value of existing nationalized industries and left the front bench of the Opposition in order to speak against German rearmament. But, though these views, taken with his original act of resignation, served to convince the left-wingers in the party that he was one of them, Wilson always believed in a mixed economy and on the need to solve social problems by using the extra wealth created by greater efficiency and productivity. Above all, he was one of the Labour leaders who believed that the main task of the party was to return to power.

As a result, when Aneurin Bevan resigned from the Shadow Cabinet in April 1954, Wilson (who was runner-up in the elections) defied Bevan's threats and decided to step up and take Bevan's place. He said that he agreed with Bevan's reasons for resignation (dislike of the SEATO pact) but said that 'what matters in the last resort is the unity and strength of the Party'.[1] This led to a breach between the two men and Wilson moved closer to Gaitskell. It became clear, first, that Attlee would soon stand down from the Leadership of the Labour party and, second, that in this case Wilson was prepared to support the selection of Gaitskell rather than Bevan, though with some reservations.

The chief reservation was over Gaitskell's tendency to decide what was correct, to spell out the precise points on which he disagreed with other elements in the party and then force a vote, the majority conclusion being adopted as party policy. To do this gave Gaitskell a great reputation as a man of principle but Wilson did not consider it was the way to lead as diverse an organization as the Labour party. The party was a coalition, a federation of diffuse elements, and what was needed was to emphasize the common objectives and not to fight unnecessary battles over precise points of policy when an election was so far off that the issue might well have changed by the time the party won power.

Apart from this one reservation, Wilson was ready to work with Gaitskell and shortly afterwards Bevan returned to the front bench so that the Labour party gave an appearance of unity in the years leading up to the 1959 election. Wilson was Shadow Chancellor and his debating style improved greatly. By careful study he equipped himself with 'impromptu repartee' and set jokes which the House began to enjoy. Respected rather than liked, he was clearly regarded as one of the mainstays of any future Labour government.

But, despite the new harmony, the Labour party suffered the shattering defeat of the 1959 general election. Soon thereafter, Bevan died. Gaitskell, having analysed the causes of the defeat, decided that one of them was a popular misunderstanding of the policies of the Labour party. These were essentially reformist and based on a mixed economy. Gaitskell therefore felt that Clause Four of the Party Constitution, which demanded the public ownership of the means of production, distribution and exchange, was out of date and should be altered. He also met the claims of the Campaign for Nuclear Disarmament (CND) with a meticulous account of his reasons for supporting the retention of nuclear weapons.

Through both these controversies, Wilson maintained that the drawing of precise lines which invited tense ideological battles was unnecessary. The party's attitudes to a mixed economy and nuclear weapons should be adjusted in the interests of unity. The Left detested Gaitskell and his policies. They decided to oppose his Leadership and to put up Wilson as their vote-getter. He was reluctant to run but yielded to the pressure of Barbara Castle and others, gaining 81 votes to 166 for Gaitskell.

For some time thereafter, Wilson's personal standing in the party declined, but with Gaitskell's premature death in 1963 the Leadership race was reopened. Wilson had left-wing support; he also appeared to be the most reliable, electorally presentable candidate and, in the intense contest for votes, he made many personal overtures and promises which later greatly influenced his Cabinet-making. As a result of this combination and helped by some rather clumsy canvassing by George Brown, Wilson edged ahead, finally defeating

George Brown by 144 votes to 103. At once Wilson began to put his own stamp on the Labour party. By a policy of continual activity and comment, he drew some of the attention normally bestowed on the Prime Minister. He strove to present Labour as the party of 'moderation', the party that understood science and technology, the party that would improve Britain's lagging performance in many fields of endeavour and raise it to the levels of growth and modernization being achieved by most other major nations.

At the general election of October 1964, Wilson kept all the reins in his own hands, making the major pronouncements, taking the press conferences and guiding the tempo of the campaign. His guiding ideas had by now been made clear in three books, all written by himself: *The New Britain: Labour's Plan*; *Purpose in Politics*; and *The Relevance of British Socialism*. When, with two weeks to go, the polls showed a Conservative lead, he had sufficient flexibility to change his style and draw attention to the current very serious economic position. Even then there were hesitations and the campaign slackened in the last few days, but the Labour party managed to scrape home with a majority of four. Some commentators complained that the Labour campaign had good tactical points but no strategy, that no themes emerged and that there was little sense of direction. On the other hand, despite the Profumo affair and the Conservatives' evident fatigue after thirteen years in office, to defeat a party which was associated with a long period of prosperity and which had had the lion's share of publicity, patronage and power for so long was an achievement.

Directly he assumed office, Harold Wilson found the country in the midst of an acute economic crisis with a deficit on the balance of payments running at £800m a year. As Prime Minister, Wilson's first decisions were not to devalue the pound or to make any political concessions to the small group of Liberal members but to push on with a purely Labour programme. In November 1964, there was a run on sterling which was not halted by a seven-per-cent Bank rate and some deflationary measures but the close links Wilson had made with the United States Administration bore fruit when American bankers gave considerable assistance in negotiating sufficient international support for sterling to tide it over this crisis.

By the spring, the Government's policies were beginning to take shape. Plans for improved social services were brought forward and old age pensions were raised. George Brown at the head of the new Department of Economic Affairs (DEA) persuaded both the TUC and the CBI to accept the principle that prices and wages should not rise faster than productivity and it was agreed that claims for increases should be submitted to a new Prices and Incomes Board. A National Plan was prepared, showing the contributions that would be required from each industry if the three-and-a-half-per-cent growth rate was to be maintained until 1973. Richard Crossman at the Ministry of Housing carried a new Rent Act and increased housing subsidies. A new Ministry of Technology was established. The Budget of April 1965 increased taxation to pay for the higher social service benefits but it also introduced a Corporation Tax and a new Capital Gains Tax.

During this first year, both the Labour Government's morale and popular support fluctuated, but the Prime Minister remained extremely cool and self-confident. In December 1964, the Foreign Secretary, Patrick Gordon Walker, contested a by-election at Leyton and was defeated in what had been a safe Labour seat so that the early collapse of the Government was widely predicted. While most of the Labour party clung to the Prime Minister, left-wing members were worried by the close association with the United States and in particular by support for the Vietnamese war. In Rhodesia, the outlook of the white settler minority was becoming increasingly independent and racialist so that Britain's residual responsibility for this territory began to absorb some of the Prime Minister's attention.

Meanwhile, at home, the nationalization of iron and steel had been part of Labour's programme, but many held that it could not be forced through Parliament when the government's majority was only three. There was a tense situation over the passage of a preliminary White Paper (two MPs threatening to defect) but this was eventually accomplished. There had to be some further deflationary measures in the summer of 1965 and, as the end of the session drew near, Labour backbenchers were extremely down-hearted, wondering if the Government could survive the coming winter or the ensuing election. On 29 July, facing a motion of censure, the Prime Minister, in one of the finest speeches of his career, restored their spirits with a detailed recital of the achievements of the Labour administration and scathing comments on the Conservatives' record.

During the summer recess, speculation was renewed when the Speaker, Sir Harry Hylton-Foster, died, since the Conservatives were likely to insist that his replacement came from the Labour side, which might have reduced the Government's majority to one. Again, showing great calm, Harold Wilson offered one of the non-voting posts in the House of Commons to a Liberal, thus restoring the position. When Jo Grimond, the Liberal Leader, made a conditional offer of support at his party conference, it was ignored by Harold Wilson. But no sooner had Parliament reassembled than there was a further challenge to the Government, the leaders of the European minority in Southern Rhodesia deciding to make an illegal unilateral declaration of independence. This was met by economic sanctions and Harold Wilson explained that only if Rhodesian leaders accepted a steady and acceptable progress towards majority rule would Britain recognize Rhodesian independence.

Over the winter of 1965–6 unemployment remained low; the deflationary measures taken by the Government had had very little effect. Nevertheless the economic situation appeared to improve and the Chancellor of the Exchequer forecast that the balance of payments deficit would be over by the end of the year. George Brown, determined to maintain full employment and the growth of the economy, kept calling for restraint over wage claims but the level of earnings continued to rise. Then a good result in the marginal seat of Hull North indicated that a general election victory was possible and Wilson gave five weeks' notice of polling day, which was to be 31 March 1966.

The election strategy Wilson devised was that he should remain in the background at first and continue to govern as Prime Minister while the Conservatives, led by Edward Heath, spent themselves in partisan attacks. Then, when Harold Wilson entered the fray ten days before the end, he expected that all attention would focus on him, on his defence of Labour's record and on his request for a full period of office to carry out Labour's programme. In fact, this strategy misfired. Heath, after a bad start, made most of the running and when the Prime Minister did intervene, the public appeared to be losing interest and he was tired. While Labour was asking for a full period of office to complete its programme, Heath had concentrated on criticism of Labour's economic record, on proposals for more selectivity in welfare policies and on pressure for a new British application to join the Common Market.

In fact, the Labour party had won before the campaign started, not because of any arguments on either side, but because it had governed for eighteen months when there had been continuous and increasing prosperity. Wilson's own contribution was the aura of confidence and competence he had created during these months which, together with the correct timing of the election, brought their reward in a majority of 98.

Setting out on his new ministry in April 1966, the Prime Minister made few changes of personnel and laid himself open to the criticism that he was still paying off too many political debts by his appointments to senior positions. The atmosphere on the Government benches lacked enthusiasm and, by Whitsun, Wilson was having to come in person to address his backbenchers who were deeply disturbed over Britain's defence programme, particularly on men and bases east of Suez and over the continued defiance of Britain by the rebel government in Rhodesia. It soon became evident that Wilson had been able to handle an 'impossible' majority of three with far more skill and confidence than he showed in dealing with the huge majority he had acquired in the 1966 election. Also, on a knife-edge majority, everyone realized that he had to live from hand to mouth. Now, with a huge majority, his supporters waited for the overall strategy to emerge, but it never appeared.

In the 1966 Budget the Chancellor decided to obtain the required measure of deflation not by traditional taxes but by a new Selective Employment Tax falling chiefly on the service industries. A practical weakness was that the tax was to start in the autumn by which time it was already too late. By June it became clear that the problems which the Budget had been designed to tackle were accumulating rapidly. The National Plan targets were not being met, production was lagging, wages were rising too rapidly and the balance of payments was not showing the expected improvement. On top of this, the National Union of Seamen began a strike which the Government had to resist to maintain any credibility in its incomes policy, but where the price of resistance was a further deterioration in the balance of payments.

The combination of these factors produced a run on the pound in July. The Prime Minister, who had so often attacked Conservative policies of deflation (he had contemptuously labelled them 'stop-go' policies), at first hoped that this could be tided over with the existing reserves, but by the middle of the month the crisis had assumed major proportions. While Wilson was on a largely fruitless visit to Moscow, a series of severe deflationary measures and a compulsory wages and prices freeze was hurriedly prepared by senior civil servants.

While he was away, some ministers began to discuss devaluation as an alternative. This had been advocated in a Treasury paper over a year earlier but the document was suppressed on Wilson's orders and the subject became known in Whitehall as 'the unmentionable'. Nevertheless, while the Prime Minister was in Moscow, it was mentioned and he returned to find that a number of senior ministers, including James Callaghan the Chancellor of the Exchequer, were now devaluers. But the policy was still opposed by Wilson as he had unhappy memories of the 1949 devaluation. He felt that this was capitulation in the face of Britain's economic enemies and he feared a serious political reaction.

On his return, Wilson sized up the situation and began by reconverting Callaghan. Having succeeded there, he then faced Roy Jenkins, Anthony Crosland and five others as well as George Brown. After surprisingly little argument, only Brown was left and he withdrew his resignation after receiving a letter from a hundred backbenchers begging him to stay. In the meantime, on 20 July, the Prime Minister announced to a stunned House of Commons a series of measures to cut domestic demand by over £500 million.

One consequence of the severe deflation was that the Prices and Incomes policy adopted in 1965 had to be stiffened, the National Prices and Incomes Board being given statutory powers to enforce delay in any wage claim. The idea that a Labour Government should take powers to intervene in labour relations so as to deny workers a rise in pay gave the very deepest offence to the left wing of the party. Frank Cousins, who had resigned as Minister of Technology before the announcement of 20 July because he was opposed to a state-enforced

Prices and Incomes policy, thereafter led the attack on the Bill, twenty-six Labour MPs abstaining in the crucial divisions.

Harold Wilson conceded in his speeches that the Government had been 'blown off course' but during the summer recess he recovered some of his composure. With the aid of the Canadian Prime Minister, Lester Pearson, the Conference of Commonwealth Prime Ministers was prevented from breaking up over the Rhodesian question, the communiqué stipulating that Britain would never recognize Rhodesian independence unless African rule were guaranteed. At home, Wilson began to argue that deflation made possible a necessary redeployment of labour and that the British economy must 'sweat it out' in the drive for higher productivity.

With the recovery in his confidence and an attack on conservatism with a small 'c' as the source of all Britain's economic weaknesses, he carried the 1966 Labour party conference without much difficulty because the party was still popular in the country. During the conference, stories were published that there had been plots to replace him during the July economic crisis and there were defeats on resolutions over defence costs east of Suez and over British support for the war in Vietnam but these amounted to little.

Nevertheless, Wilson began the 1966–7 session with his reputation as an economic expert, and above all as a technocrat in government, seriously tarnished. The Rhodesian problem proved a continuous embarrassment. After further talks, the Prime Minister made a major effort in December 1966 to obtain a settlement in a direct meeting with Ian Smith, the Rhodesian leader, on HMS *Tiger* in the Mediterranean. But when Smith returned to Salisbury he abandoned the agreement and his party, the Rhodesian Front, moved steadily to the right. In mid-1967 a Preventive Detention Bill was passed in Rhodesia and by early 1968 a new constitution was adopted which rejected any notion of progress towards majority rule. Thereafter talks were held at intervals but made no progress and Harold Wilson was left applying the mandatory sanctions called for by the United Nations but with less and less hope of having any decisive effect.

In late 1966, Wilson was coming round to the view that Britain should make a new application to join the European Common Market. The motives underlying this conversion are not clear, despite the long passages devoted to the subject in Wilson's memoirs. He does not appear to have made up his mind as a result of a reassessment of Britain's role in the world and of relations with the United States and the Commonwealth. The arguments which he put with most force (for all the possible lines of advocacy appeared in his speeches) were the benefits of pooling technology in Europe and the advantages of a wider market in reducing overheads. The French Prime Minister, M. Pompidou, on a visit to Britain had told his hosts that, while the outcome was not certain, an application was more likely to be successful if it was for full membership rather than for any form of association. Wilson, accompanied by George Brown (who had been moved to the Foreign Office after the July 1966 crisis), toured the capitals of the six member states in early 1967. On 11 May a formal application for membership (together with Ireland, Norway and Denmark) was made, though only after some dissension in the Labour party and a vote of 488 to 62 (the Conservatives supporting) in favour of the application. Almost at once it became clear that General de Gaulle would raise objections and, after doing so in May, the final French veto was delivered in November 1967.

Probably the diplomatic venture which excited Wilson most was the attempt to mediate between Russia and the USA over a bombing pause in Vietnam. The Prime Minister recalled his early successful trade negotiations with Russia; he badly needed to show he was against the war without antagonizing Washington, and President Johnson was prepared to let the British (as well as the Poles, Italians and Yugoslavs) try to act as intermediaries. The efforts reached a climax in February 1967, when Kosygin visited London, but came to nothing. George Brown's view was that the time was not appropriate and that the episode, if anything, revealed Wilson as over-eager to 'play a role', and made Britain seem almost 'foolish'.[2]

The Government also tried to moderate Egyptian pressure on the Straits of Tiran but this likewise had no effect. After Israel's overwhelming victory in the Six Days' War, it became clear that British influence in the Middle East was negligible and it was President Johnson's announcement of a bombing pause that led to direct peace talks with North Vietnam.

Meanwhile the effort to achieve a positive balance of payments seemed to be meeting with some success and in early 1967 the Chancellor of the Exchequer talked of a 'period of controlled growth' of three per cent a year. This policy involved a new Prices and Incomes Bill which was resisted by the left wing and carried with twenty MPs abstaining but once again, after reassurances from Wilson and an able speech by Callaghan, the Party Conference acquiesced. Then, during the autumn, the trade returns became worse, a run on the pound developed, and in November 1967 Wilson was forced to devalue by 14.3 per cent (from $2.8 to $2.4 to the £).

This represented an immeasurable defeat for Wilson. As the Civil Service advisers, economists outside the government and most other influential sections of opinion (except the Conservative Opposition) had come to the conclusion that the pound was over-valued, it became more and more evident that the refusal to contemplate this policy was due to the Prime Minister and the Chancellor of the Exchequer. Afterwards Callaghan publicly accepted that he had been driven to adopt an expedient he had long resisted and, having in this sense failed, he insisted on leaving the Exchequer for the Home Office. But Wilson, who bore the main responsibility for the economic policies of the previous three years, could not move or purge himself in this way.

Following on devaluation, Wilson had to abandon his view of Britain's world role. Aden was evacuated in the same month, the Persian Gulf was to follow and it was decided that British forces were to leave the Far East by 1971. Extensive cuts were announced in public expenditure, including a slowing down in housing, no purchase of American strike aircraft and the reintroduction of prescription charges. With the resignation of Callaghan, Roy Jenkins became Chancellor of the Exchequer and the major figure in the government besides Wilson. But, though the salient policies pursued since 1964 had been abandoned and in March 1968 there was talk of a 'Mark II' cabinet, the Prime Minister made no sweeping changes. Roy Jenkins, Barbara Castle and Richard Crossman became the most important figures in place of Brown (who finally resigned in March 1968) and Callaghan. The illusion that the country was still a world power was finally buried but, despite the change of emphasis, there was little new sense of cohesion or direction.

The price of economic failure, of the lack of growth and of the restriction on wage increases was acute unpopularity. As early as June 1966, a new electoral phenomenon appeared in the loss of a Labour seat to a Welsh Nationalist at Carmarthen to be followed by one to a Scottish Nationalist in November 1967. Losses to Conservatives began in March 1967 (Pollok), the swing against the Government reaching eighteen per cent in September 1967 when Walthamstow West was lost and 21 per cent when Dudley was lost in March 1968. The local elections of 1967 saw a twelve per cent swing against Labour, leading to the loss of the Greater London Council, while in 1968 Labour was cleared out of most of its remaining local strongholds.

Such acute unpopularity, particularly as it focused on the Prime Minister, affected his conduct. From 1963 to 1966 Wilson's relations with the press had been of the best. He studied the papers and understood the needs of journalism, while most commentators could not avoid open admiration for his dexterity and capacity to communicate. At the same time, he appeared often on television and dominated these occasions as effectively as he did Question Time in the Commons. But when the fortunes of the Government declined, this relationship deteriorated, attacks on Wilson intensified and he retaliated by accusing the *Daily Express* of a breach of the D-notice security system in June 1967. He also summoned editors, complained about alleged misrepresentations by their political columnists and even demanded the dismissal of specific journalists. Pleased with Lord Hill's chairmanship of the Independent Television Authority and on poor terms with the BBC, he transferred Hill from the chairmanship of the ITA to the BBC and appointed a former Cabinet colleague, Herbert Bowden (Lord Aylestone), to the ITA.

At times in 1968, the attacks on Wilson in the press reached heights unparalleled in recent history and he reacted by showing some loss of confidence, intense suspicion of all critics and self effacement in that he appeared little in public or on television for the first half of 1968.

In the Parliamentary Labour party, the failures and unpopularity of the government led to much heart-searching and several periods when there was talk of replacing Wilson. The month after devaluation, when Wilson's popularity was at a low ebb, a crisis arose over a proposal to sell arms to South Africa. This had come from the Ministry of Defence, had been endorsed by George Brown at the Foreign Office and, according to him, had been accepted by Wilson as Chairman of the Defence and Overseas Policy Committee of the Cabinet. But when backbenchers heard of this, there was an outcry and the Chief Whip, who was close to Wilson, suddenly began to encourage these backbenchers to put pressure on the Cabinet to reject the proposal. After several tense meetings (with George Brown fog-bound in Brussels) the project was abandoned but the result was a period of mutual suspicion among the senior ministers concerned. Wilson's own account of the episode is obscure but he does say that 'it was the first and the last time in our near six years of office that I had to fight rough with any of my colleagues'.[3] In January, April and June 1968, there was active canvassing of support for alternative leaders but in every case agreement was impossible. Wilson still retained the support of the left wing, while the lack of a generally acceptable alternative on the right and the patronage always at the disposal of the Prime Minister, together with his own skilful handling of the party, made him unassailable.

For the earlier part of 1968, Wilson was preoccupied with his position and most of the work of the government was left to other ministers. Barbara Castle carried a major Transport Bill and Callaghan at the Home Office became the centre of a storm over a Bill to reduce the flow of Kenyan Asians possessing British passports. The Home Secretary failed to restore his credit with the liberals in his own party a few months later with the introduction of a Race Relations Bill. Roy Jenkins at the Exchequer, having cut public expenditure in January, cut private consumption by the record figure of £923 million in his Budget and it was evident that the fate of the Government turned on whether devaluation would work – whether there would be a sizeable and steady balance of payments surplus by the end of the year.

By mid-1968 the trade figures appeared better. Wilson emerged from his exclusion and made two speeches, one condemning racialism and the other forecasting 'an economic miracle'. Then at the party conference in Blackpool in October 1968, the Prime Minister rallied the delegates to the attack in 'Labour's decisive year'. Despite an adverse TUC vote on the Government's Prices and Incomes policy shortly before, Wilson affirmed that unpopular but necessary policies would not be abandoned. For the first time in almost a year he appeared on television to answer questions. Within the week, he was to snatch the headlines again on the opening day of the Conservative conference by engaging in yet another attempt to reach a settlement of the Rhodesian question. These talks aboard HMS *Fearless* were as fruitless as the previous negotiations, because Mr Smith would not contemplate any terms which pointed even nominally towards majority rule.

In the autumn, the economic situation failed to improve and uncertainty over sterling led to further severe restraints on consumer spending in November. At the start of 1969, the Labour party and Wilson's popularity seemed to have reached rock bottom, and this at a time when an election was probably only about eighteen months away. Devaluation had not yet produced the desired results while the Prices and Incomes policy was both unpopular and unsuccessful. Rhodesia remained defiant, Britain had been excluded from the Common Market and the government's support for the Federal Government of Nigeria in its war with secessionist Biafra had encountered bitter opposition. Knowing that the Donovan Commission report on industrial relations had to result in a bill, and eager to take any step which was both electorally popular and economically helpful, Wilson was easily persuaded by Mrs Barbara Castle, the Minister of Employment and Productivity, that some action was necessary to improve industrial relations and to reduce the number of unofficial stoppages.

The policy, very much that of Wilson and Castle, was set out in a White Paper, 'In Place of Strife'. In addition to a charter for trade unions, it proposed sanctions against those involved in certain categories of strikes. The TUC was hostile and sixty-two Labour MPs voted against the White Paper. Meanwhile, nearly a year earlier, the Government had decided to reform the House of Lords by abolishing the hereditary element and relying on a nominated chamber. All-party agreement on this reform had been reached in the summer but Conservative support was abjured by Wilson after a quarrel over a Rhodesian order. As a result of 'the usual channels' not operating, the Parliament (No. 2) Bill ran into formidable backbench opposition from both sides of the House. Because it was not a party measure, because the fate of the Government was not at stake and because the Labour party's morale was low, the Bill limped slowly through days of debate.

At the same time, the Cabinet felt it could no longer maintain its Prices and Incomes policy and was also sensing the growing resistance to any bill based on 'In Place of Strife'. Because of the Government's position, Wilson was less able to dominate the Cabinet but he and his colleagues felt that their collective authority had to be asserted and decided to abandon the Parliament (No. 2) Bill in order to concentrate on pushing through a short Industrial Relations Bill by the end of the session.

This decision provoked intense dissension within the party and brought Wilson into the most exposed position he had occupied since his election to the Leadership. All sorts of grievances had accumulated but one target, particularly for the loyalist centre of the party, was the Chief Whip, John Silkin. He was a smooth and pliable man, chosen by Wilson because he was in touch with the left and because he believed in the kind of mild discipline which would prevent any showdown with Wilson's old supporters on the Left. This permissiveness infuriated many MPs and to appease them John Silkin was replaced by Robert Mellish but this did not halt the disaffection. The Left, Wilson's old base in the party, was incensed; the right-wing members who had come to dislike Wilson's style of leadership were hostile and the solid centre of the Parliamentary Labour party was disturbed by the conflict with the unions. Mellish eventually told the Cabinet that he could not guarantee the passage of the procedural motions essential for the progress of an Industrial Relations Bill that session. The Cabinet then deserted Wilson and Castle, and the Prime Minister was left to get what face-saving formula he could out of the TUC, emerging with a 'solemn and binding undertaking' from its leaders to try to conciliate in disputes and thus prevent stoppages.

This was the most serious and humiliating defeat Wilson had suffered as Prime Minister. The forced devaluation was the abandonment of a policy which had also been close to Wilson's heart but it could be alleged that it had been imposed on him and on the country by external pressures, by speculation and by such evil creatures as 'the gnomes of Zurich'. But the defeat in this case was imposed by his own Cabinet and showed a misjudgement in an area where Wilson normally would not have miscalculated, in his hold on his own colleagues and on the Labour party. However, once Wilson backed out of the minefield he had laid for himself, his position was restored, the backbench efforts to remove him faded away and he was left powerful and remote but also bruised and deflated.

On the credit side for the Government, a balance of payments surplus was at last achieved during the summer of 1969, while on the debit, the policy of sending arms to the Federal Government of Nigeria seemed to yield little except the hatred of the vocal supporters of Biafra. Britain's general reputation overseas was hardly enhanced by the dramatic despatch of paratroops to quell gangsterism and revolt on the little Caribbean island of Anguilla. The Government's thoughts were clearly turning towards the coming general election and the Cabinet decided to set aside the report of the Boundary Commission (whose proposals, it was thought, would cost Labour fifteen to twenty seats) on the grounds that constituency boundaries would be better readjusted after rather than before the forthcoming re-organization of local government boundaries.

During the summer, the situation in Northern Ireland became serious, with riots in Londonderry and Belfast. The problem was ably handled by the Home Secretary, Jim Callaghan, who sent troops to these areas, started investigations of the police and of discriminatory practices against Catholics and insisted on the Stormont government beginning a process of reform.

By the time of the autumn party conference, Labour's unpopularity appeared to be declining. The Conservative lead grew again in the winter but so did the balance of payments surplus. Politics were increasingly dominated by the forthcoming election and the Conservatives began to show their fears that Wilson's political agility and sense of timing were once again capable of turning the tide. After an unexciting Budget in which the Chancellor of the Exchequer was able to give relief amounting to £200 million, Labour's standing steadily improved in the polls until, in April, the party went into the lead with good results in the GLC and municipal elections while Wilson's personal rating was far ahead of that of Edward Heath.

As the signs that an election victory was possible accumulated, the pressure on Wilson grew. Since the GLC successes he had favoured a summer rather than an autumn election and in late May announced that 18 June would be the polling day. Wilson went on to fight a supremely confident campaign in which he stressed neither the positive achievements of the Labour government (for instance in education or regional development) nor the broader political issues. Wilson's entire concentration was on the improvement in the economic position and on the choice between himself and Edward Heath as Prime Minister. During the campaign, Labour's lead in the polls increased until the last few days and most commentators and politicians on both sides took a Labour victory for granted.

But when the results came in they showed a remarkably uniform swing averaging 4.7 per cent to the Conservatives, which gave that party an overall majority of thirty. In retrospect, it seemed that events in the last week of the campaign, a £31 million trade deficit for May, talk of another devaluation and continual Conservative reiteration of economic dangers ahead, all served to remind electors of the distaste many of them had felt for the government until the previous few months. As against this, there was no positive, obvious case for voting Labour as Wilson had fought an almost totally negative election campaign simply asking for a vote of confidence in himself.

The result, coming after this kind of campaign and as a complete surprise, seemed to stun Wilson. His aides, clearly echoing his views, blamed the BBC but subsequent academic investigations found no evidence of bias, much less of the kind of distortion which could swing an election. Wilson half retired, busying himself writing a vast defence of his Government called *The Labour Government, 1964–70: A Personal Record*. He did the work of Leader of the Opposition in a rather low key, living close to the House in Lord North Street during the week and retiring to a country house he had bought near Chequers at weekends.

Meanwhile, the Labour movement was quiet for a time, contemplating its defeat. But the unions were moving to the Left, with such men as Jack Jones and Hugh Scanlon becoming leaders of the Transport and General and of the Engineers. Heath had re-opened negotiations for British entry to the Common Market and with General de Gaulle gone, the result was an agreement in June 1971. The Left in the Labour party and the unions, disliking all the Heath Government did, feeling that entry would 'write capitalism into the British constitution' and also evincing an element of English nationalism or xenophobia, all turned against joining the Community.

This pulled Wilson back into active politics. What was he to do, given the many speeches in which he had said that the details of entry did not matter, that he 'would not take "no" for an answer', that Britain's future lay in Europe and that he 'meant business' with his application? Also those concerned with the abortive Labour negotiations, George Brown and George Thomson, said the terms Heath had obtained were very similar to those Labour had hoped to get. At first, Wilson seemed to agree with this view.

He met the problem with characteristic ingenuity, calling for a 'great debate' and in July 1971 there was a special party conference, which reached no conclusion, but where Wilson's own speech was preponderantly anti-European. By the time of the October party conference, Wilson had decided to overcome his problem by saying he favoured entry to the Community but not on 'Tory terms' and his speeches became more and more anti-European. Though the Conference supported this compromise, sixty-nine members of the Parliamentary Labour party voted with the Conservatives for the acceptance of the terms when Parliament reassembled.

This whole episode put great strain on party unity and confirmed the pro-European section of the party's belief that Wilson had no principles, no long-term view of Britain's place in the world and that his sole objective was to retain his position. There was active discussion in 1971 and 1972 as to whether he should be opposed in the annual elections for Leader but Roy Jenkins, the main pro-European candidate, felt the time was not ripe. In May 1972, the *New Statesman* said of Wilson that 'his very presence in Labour's leadership pollutes the atmosphere of politics'. The *Daily Telegraph* had a cartoon of two ships, one containing Labour pro-Marketeers and the other Labour anti-Marketeers both sailing away from a rodent struggling in the water with the caption 'the ships desert the sinking rat'.

Yet Wilson survived all this. He went along with some of the criticisms of his own Government as too pragmatic and too reformist. The National Executive Committee came more into the centre of policy-making. It appointed a series of working parties which began to put together a 'mid-term manifesto' which was much more positively socialist. At one committee meeting on a proposal to nationalize the twenty-five largest companies, the motion was carried by seven to six with Wilson abstaining, but he was able later to modify this to a vaguer committment to a broad extension of public ownership through a National Enterprise Board.

The European issue continued to divide the party and a serious split was averted when Tony Benn's suggestion of a referendum on British membership was adopted in April 1972. At the 1970 election, Wilson had rejected this device firmly, saying that referenda were contrary to the spirit of parliamentary government, but now he was prepared to reverse his position in order to prevent a showdown over Europe. Roy Jenkins (and two other Shadow Cabinet members) resigned in protest. Dick Taverne, MP, was dismissed by his local party for voting for Europe, resigned his seat and won it against an official Labour candidate in March 1973.

Again, Wilson managed to survive and to pour some oil on the troubled waters. By the autumn of 1973, the party was in a very different stance from that of 1966–70, but was still substantially intact. Wilson had agreed to no statutory control on incomes, extensive further nationalization and renegotiation of the European terms followed by a referendum. He had also managed to mend fences (breached since the 'In Place of Strife' episode) with the unions and the first talk was heard of some kind of contract with the unions.

Meanwhile, at the end of 1973, the Heath Government was becoming embroiled with the miners. They were clearly out to break Phase III of the Incomes Policy and the Government's reaction was uncertain. It alternated between attempts to show that the miners were a special case and tough action, cutting street lighting, cutting TV time and reducing industry to a three-day week. Eventually, caught between the miners' determination not to compromise and the Conservative party's determination to know 'who governs the country', Heath called an election for 28 February 1974.

Wilson had not wanted an election on this issue. He feared a strong pro-Government, anti-union reaction but, at the same time, he had his new-found contract with the unions to consider. After a very uncertain start, he realized that the Conservative campaign was running into difficulties and he stepped aside from the issue of inflationary wage settlements and the power of the unions. He began instead to concentrate on Heath, as the man of confrontation, the man who invited hostility with his Industrial Relations Act, the man who put industry on a three-day week. Gradually, the Conservative lead fell. The public wanted a rest. Heath was difficult to understand, and abrasive. Yet the voters did not swing to Wilson and the Labour percentage of the poll fell from 43 per cent in 1970 to 37.1 per cent. Six million voted Liberal in a rejection of both major parties but the result was to leave Labour just ahead of the Conservatives with 301 seats to their 297. There were also 14 Liberals and 25 Northern Irish and Nationalists.

Heath hesitated over the weekend and then resigned, Wilson taking over for his third premiership this time as the Leader of a Government with an actual minority of seventeen votes in the House. Some wondered if he would perform, once again, with the brilliance of his 1964–6 period. But Wilson was ten years older than the days when he had talked of a brave new future. Compared with a 1964 deficit of £800 million, it was now £4000 million; in comparison with a three per cent inflation rate before, it was now nineteen per cent. Also, Wilson was much more hemmed in. In 1964, only two ministers had previously held Cabinet office, now it was thirteen. Also he was tied to an elaborate, very left-wing manifesto and a 'social contract' with the unions which gave them considerable say in policy.

So, operating much more as the leader of a team, Wilson guided his Government towards the general election which could be only a few months away. The miners were given their money, the three-day week was ended and industry returned to normal. Wilson was troubled by revelations that his office manager, Anthony Field, had been investing in slag-heaps and had used a letter with a forgery of Wilson's signature. Mr Field's sister was Mrs Marcia Williams, Wilson's political secretary, and he responded by promoting her to the peerage as Lady Falkender.

Meanwhile, the Government prepared for the election. Prices were rising but wages rose faster. The social contract laid down no guidelines for wages, simply urging the unions not to ask for wage increases that went beyond the general level of price inflation. The Conservatives' Industrial Relations Act was repealed and the Pay Board abolished. Rents were frozen, £500 million spent on food subsidies and pensioners were given the largest increase on record.

Then, in October, the general election took place. In many ways, it was a continuation of the February election except that Heath was portrayed even more vividly as the man who could not avoid conflict with the unions. The Conservatives, according to Wilson, stood for industrial chaos whereas Labour had a special contract with the unions which would allow peaceable, orderly government to continue. As a result, Labour's share of the poll crept up from 37.1 per cent to 39.2 per cent, the party winning 319 seats, an overall majority of three.

This was a disappointment to Wilson, but he set off on his new Government carefully balancing pro- and anti-marketeers in the Cabinet. The lines with the unions were kept open by making Michael Foot Secretary of State for Employment. There were two immediate tasks – resolving the European problem and trying to get the economy on to a healthier basis. On Europe, Jim Callaghan, the Foreign Secretary, had begun the process of demanding renegotiation before the election but the other EEC members were not prepared to let Britain break a treaty unilaterally – any new concessions would have to come as part of the normal process of change in the Community. This whole episode was seen by the rest of the EEC as simply a method by which Wilson hoped to get over internal party difficulties; it caused considerable irritation, did Britain's reputation considerable damage and, in the end, produced marginal results of no significance. By April 1975, the process was complete. The Government recommended acceptance of terms, Wilson allowed Cabinet members who disagreed to campaign on the other side and the referendum was fixed for June 1975. Two sides were organized but Wilson stood back a little from the campaign. He made one or two speeches but left the bulk of the battle to the consistent pro-Europeans, the result being a two-to-one popular majority for Britain's remaining a member of the Community.

The other major issue was the economy, with inflation moving up towards twenty per cent and unemployment rising over a million. The Labour Government was committed to no attempt to control wages, yet sterling was weakening. The pound was floating and in mid-1975 dropped for the first time below $2. Also Tony Benn as Minister for Industry was alarming the private sector. Various nationalization Bills were being pushed through the House but the result of the European Referendum was a severe setback for the Left. Wilson took advantage of this and of speeches which were barely in line with Cabinet policy to move Benn to Energy and replaced him with Eric Varley, who was not only a moderate but a protégé of Wilson's.

At the same time, the decline of sterling forced Wilson and the Cabinet to turn to an incomes policy, though it was stressed that it was totally voluntary. Through the winter of 1975-6, the economic situation deteriorated. Varley and Wilson, in the early autumn, announced a new policy which merely amounted to a declaration that the Government would support successful rather than failing industries. But this was immediately followed by a long wrangle over the possible collapse of the Chrysler car factories which ended with the Company receiving a subsidy of £162 million.

To try and restore external confidence in sterling and to ease inflationary pressure (caused by high interest rates needed to hold money in Britain), it was felt that public expenditure had to be cut and, after much heartsearching, cuts of £1,000 million were announced. Thus on all fronts, Wilson was pulling this Government round to the same stance as that of his 1964-70 administration – moderate, pro-European, trying to get industry to expand and shelving doctrinaire approaches.

Then to the surprise of all except Lord Goodman, the Queen and his closest entourage, on 11 March 1976, he announced his intention to resign. No one is quite sure why he came to this decision but there is no reason to doubt his own explanation that he was tired, that he had decided to go when he was sixty and was doing so. He waited while the Parliamentary Labour party chose a successor, took a Garter, so becoming Sir Harold Wilson, and caused a flurry over his resignation honours list. This contained a number of unexpected names from business and it was clear that Wilson and his secretary, now Lady Falkender, were thanking all who had helped them in the recent past. But it was said that the Scrutiny committee had objected to a number of the names (to no effect) and the episode left a bad taste in the mouths of many Labour members.

In assessing Wilson's period as Prime Minister there is, first, the question of his political philosophy. For some genuine socialists, such as Jack Mendelson, MP, till at least the last year or two, Wilson was one of them, a real socialist. He certainly kept the support of the Left till virtually the end of his period in office. On the other hand, to Paul Foot he was always a liberal, he had no belief in an alternative, non-capitalist economic system and he never sought one. Foot quotes a conversation between Wilson and John Junor, editor of the *Sunday*

Express in the late 1950s, about Harold Macmillan. 'You know, John,' Wilson said, 'the man's a genius. He's holding up the banner of Suez for the Party to follow, and he's leading the Party away from Suez. That's what I'd like to do with the Labour Party over nationalization.'[4]

In reality, the truth is more complex. Wilson never wanted or even contemplated a totally publicly owned economy. But he did regard many of those connected with the management of industry as upper class, incompetent and ineffective. If the situation was hopeless (as in the mines), public ownership was the answer. Otherwise Wilson was an interventionist. He was a great believer in the idea that a National Plan or a bunch of little Neddies or a 'shake out' due to a recession would somehow alter the conduct of British industry. Perhaps the best definition of Wilson's socialism is his own:

> Socialism, as I understand it, means applying a sense of purpose to our national life: economic purpose, social purpose and moral purpose. Purpose means technical skill – be it the skill of a manager, a designer, a craftsman, an engineer, a transport worker, a miner, an architect, a nuclear physicist, a doctor, a nurse, a social worker. If you fly the Atlantic in a jet, you want to be sure the pilot knows his job, that he's trained for it. If you're in hospital, you feel more confident if you know that the surgeon has given his lifetime to fitting himself for his work. Pilot or surgeon: it matters not who his father was, or what school he went to, or who his friends are, yet in Government and in business we are still too often content to accept social qualifications rather than technical ability as the criterion.[5]

This was written in 1964 when Wilson was going for the middle-class vote, when he was contrasting his own professionalism, assiduity and technical competence with the impression of old-fashioned, unconcerned inefficiency presented by the Tories under Macmillan and Douglas-Home. Slightly rephrased with the implication that public ownership was the ultimate answer to capitalist incompetence, it could sound quite socialist enough to please the Labour Left. But in 1964 Wilson gave his views a different twist and one which certainly excited and won over many in the groups at which he was aiming. Opening the Science debate at the 1962 Labour party conference, he had said:

We are re-stating our Socialism in terms of the scientific revolution. But that revolution cannot become a reality unless we are prepared to make far-reaching changes in economic and social attitudes which permeate our whole system of society. The Britain that is going to be forged in the white heat of revolution will be no place for . . . outdated methods on either side of industry.

For the commanding heights of British industry to be controlled to-day by men whose only claim is their aristocratic connections or the power of inherited wealth or speculative finance is as irrelevant to the twentieth century as would be the continual purchase of commissions in the armed forces by lordly amateurs. At the very time that even the MCC has abolished the distinction between amateurs and professionals, in science and industry we are content to remain a nation of Gentlemen in a world of Players.[6]

Once a Labour Government led by Wilson had taken over and there was steady growth, then the surplus could be applied to eradicate poverty and to end slum housing. Had British industry done as well in the 1960s as German industry – under the overall direction of a Labour Government – it is quite possible that Wilson could have achieved the hope he put to John Junor. He was no nationalizer for its own sake. Wilson's two main sentiments were contempt for traditional Tories and lower-middle-class egalitarianism. Had there been the growth envisaged in the 1965 National Plan he would have been able to keep both Right and Left in the party happy and achieve his objectives. He was a reformer who knew how to use left-wing language.

The tragedy for Wilson was that the economy did not respond. How, after 1966, could he go on about inefficient Tories, scientific revolutions and so on, when every economic indicator was worse under Labour than it had been before 1964? It was this that soured his whole philosophy, that left him with nothing to say so that he had no come-back when the Left said the only answer was a more full-blooded socialism. He agreed with them in Opposition and slowly reverted to his old position in Government, but it was all no good if the British economy continued to drift downhill.

It was also typical of Wilson that, faced with what became a decade of relative economic failure, he never considered the broader problems of how a left-wing party, tied to the unions, hostile to private enterprise and to profits, can get the private sector of a mixed economy to operate with vigour and confidence. Nor, for that matter, did he think through the rules that would be necessary if the public sector was to be efficient and profitable. He was not interested in this kind of question. He was too political in the most immediate sense and thought all the time about being one up on the Conservatives. Joe Haines relates how Wilson said he was worried in 1953 that Hillary's conquest of Everest and the Queen's Coronation might enhance the popularity of Churchill's government. Haines said he was too young then to think in those terms. Wilson replied, 'I have been thinking like that since the day I was born.'[7]

Foreign affairs were always secondary to domestic politics for Wilson. But he was a child of the 1940s and had a rugged patriotism. One reason he was so reluctant to devalue after 1964 was that he felt this was a defeat for Britain. His early period at the top in the 1950s was a time when the Left were opposed to German rearmament and to the more aggressive aspects of United States policy under John Foster Dulles, both views which Wilson shared.

But when John F. Kennedy was elected, Wilson was captivated by his image of youth and modernity, which was just what Wilson wanted to convey himself. He would have been very happy to rely on the special relationship with a President of this kind, Britain operating still as a minor world-wide power. In 1966, when he said 'Britain's frontiers are on the Himalayas', he undoubtedly meant it.

But Johnson was not Kennedy and the Vietnamese war created all sorts of difficulties for Wilson. He wanted to maintain the special relationship and yet convince the Left that he was pressing Washington to stop the war. Once again, he fell into the idea that his own cleverness could produce a solution and he thought up Common-wealth Peace Missions and the despatch of special envoys to Hanoi, and he engaged in assiduous brokerage between the Russians and the Americans, all of which came to nothing. He did not rethink Britain's role in the world given the country's changing circumstances.

At first, his attitude to the Common Market ('obtaining a marginal advantage in selling washing machines in Dusseldorf') was a combination of his doubts about the Germans and about what he called 'the candyfloss society'. But, by the mid-1960s, he saw that the Community had been made into an effective base by General de Gaulle and was enhancing Germany's standing. His desire to 'make Britain great again' led him to think that this country could be similarly promoted and so he applied for membership.

Yet this was not a fundamental matter for him and he did not think Britain would suffer much if it did not come off, so that when domestic political pressures made an anti-Market stance more convenient, he moved in that direction. He was disturbed later by the utter contempt felt for him by the leaders of the German SPD (whom he had pressed again and again to use their influence with de Gaulle to get Britain into the EEC) and he left most of the renegotiation of terms to Jim Callaghan.

In Commonwealth affairs, Wilson's deep and genuine distaste for racialism helped him to hold the heterogeneous group of countries together, but his main problem was over Rhodesia. When he had decided not to use force (and he never seriously contemplated it), he thought once again that his own abilities as a negotiator together with economic sanctions would be sufficient. But Ian Smith was more than a match for him. Time and again he led Wilson on, only to abandon any agreement once he got back to Salisbury.

Turning from Wilson's views to his domestic political skills, his first and pre-eminent ability was his capacity to manage the Labour party. At the time of his election as Leader in 1963, George Brown was backed by most of the union leaders but Wilson presented the image thought most likely to unite the party and win an election. In this, he showed great skill. Though one of the best 'firsts' of his period at Oxford, he was never labelled by the most damaging of all tags in the Labour party – he was never called an 'intellectual'. The pipe-puffing, the slight north country accent, the talk of bottles of HP sauce on the table, the preference for the little upstairs parlour at No. 10 Downing Street rather than the large, handsome drawing-room, all had both a certain value and a certain authenticity. Wilson managed to be the man who could out-debate the Tories, perform at the highest international level and yet speak on television as 'one of us' in a manner which went right through to the audience in working men's homes and clubs.

Once chosen as Leader, he had to manage the party at three levels:

there was the Annual Conference and all the other meetings of activists during the year, the National Executive Committee and Transport House and the party in Parliament. As far as the meetings of activists were concerned, Wilson was indefatigable. Throughout his period as Leader, he journeyed round the country, weekend after weekend, speaking to gatherings of the faithful. He seemed to derive strength from these contacts and from the warmth with which he was received. It encouraged his view that it was in Parliament and in London and among the south-east upper classes that there was a tacit agreement to run him down.

In the case of the party conference, Wilson had taken the line that Gaitskell was too adamant, too precise. What this amounted to was that Gaitskell had a concept of leadership that took the party conference intensely seriously and he wanted to convince delegates of certain policies so that the party had a basic unity. For Wilson, the conference was an occasion where he wanted the maximum personal support and no defeats for official policies but, if there were a gap between the members and the leaders, he was not unduly disturbed. In 1963, 1964 and 1965, he was wildly acclaimed. His first setbacks were in 1966, when Government policy was repudiated on defence, public expenditure and unemployment, but when Wilson was asked what he was going to do about it, he simply said 'go on governing'.

Each year thereafter he spelt out the Government's record, laid into the Tories, stressed such questions as concern for the disabled and for the thalidomide babies and wound up calling for a united effort by the party. Each year he received a standing ovation and then the conference went on to attack his policies. In 1968, for example, the Prices and Incomes policy was defeated by five million to one million. It became clear that Wilson had made some sort of separation between his position and conference decisions; in a sense he did not take the occasion all that seriously. He was not concerned to mould the thinking of the party or to explain the realities of politics to the delegates; he was concerned simply to get by and this he always did with considerable skill. If he knew he could not get by – which happened only once – his tactics were rather different. In the Special Conference called in 1975 to consider the government's recommendation to vote 'Yes' in the referendum on the EEC, Wilson knew he would lose. Also, he could not talk about other matters. So he made a very low-key speech and then went away leaving Jim Callaghan the task of winding up against a hostile audience.

His relations with the National Executive Committee and Transport House were never so straightforward. He had been elected as an anti-establishment candidate in the Bevanite upsurge of 1952 but now members were being elected because they were opposed to his policies. He did what he could to maintain a favourable majority by appointing MPs on the Executive to ministerial posts when they were supposed to take the Government view. As has been described, he had trouble with Jim Callaghan when the latter used his NEC position to indicate his dislike of the 'In Place of Strife' proposals. Later, during the 1974–6 Government, Tony Benn often sailed very close to the wind. Wilson's difficulties with the NEC increased when the party went into opposition, partly because the NEC swung further left (only Denis Healey of the non-Left could win a place in the constituency section), partly because no patronage was available and partly because the new General Secretary of the party elected in March 1972, Mr Ron Hayward, regarded himself as the custodian of party conference decisions.

On the whole, the NEC succeeded in pulling the party to the left in the years 1972–4 and it started a mammoth consultation exercise which, in fact, allowed left-wing activists to write the much more socialist 'Labour's Programme 1973' which became the party manifesto. During this period, Wilson as Leader attended the NEC and its committees but played little active part, often exercising what he claimed to be the Leader's right to abstain if there were any votes. When Labour came to power, Wilson was meticulous that precise commitments included in the manifesto should be implemented. (He seemed to feel that a legitimate complaint against his previous Government was that some pledges had not been fulfilled.) But, once in office again, he had more weapons against the NEC. Where there were doubts about just how much public ownership the National Enterprise Board should initiate, he came down on the moderate side. Ministers on the NEC were ordered to toe the Government line and, though relations were difficult by 1975–6, they never reached the levels of disagreement and acrimony that occurred later under Callaghan.

The other section of the party which Wilson had to manage was in

Parliament. At first, his relations with Labour MPs could not have been better. His successes were their successes. They identified totally and in the 1963–6 period and, on occasion, in later years, he could be devastating as a baiter of the Tories and a raiser of Labour morale. After the 1964 and 1966 elections, Wilson made some effort to meet new back-benchers, but this was not really necessary. He was leading the party with skill, he had won two general elections and he had over eighty posts in his Government to offer. He came to meetings of the Parliamentary Labour party and, though he read his papers and signed letters throughout, he also replied effectively if the debate was important.

At the same time, Wilson had little feeling for the life of a backbencher – he had never been one himself. He had always been on the front benches and, in opposition, had always earned a good deal more than the standard MPs pay. So he was not interested in talk about improving backbenchers' conditions. (He once said to the author more than the standard MP's pay. So he was not interested in talk about idea what to do with a secretary'.) In July 1964, he made a speech on parliamentary reform and Richard Crossman pressed him to act on these lines but he instinctively felt that if an MP was any use, he would be in office (or shadow office) and if he was no use, why complain? After the 1966 election he announced the creation of two 'specialist committees' to keep the new members, many of whom were parliamentary reformers, happy. But as soon as Whitehall became hostile, he was ready to let them be dissolved.[8]

In practice, Wilson regarded the Parliamentary party as a body to be managed and sometimes he let his impatience, bordering on contempt, show very clearly. After the 1966 election, the Left tried to force votes on a number of motions at Parliamentary Labour party meetings. Wilson intervened to say that this was damaging and must stop. But if a vote were forced, then a private whip went around the hundred ministers (Labour peers could vote) asking them to attend so that any critical motion would have required the support of seven-tenths of the remaining backbenchers to be carried. Normally Wilson was a mixture of persuasion and firmness. Sometimes he added an attack on the press or a reproach that fellow Labour MPs should choose to make their objections to lobby correspondents or in speeches and not to his face. Once, when Richard Crossman had had a rough time as Leader of the House, he went up to the party meeting just afterwards and said: 'Watch it. Every dog is allowed one bite, but a different view is taken of a dog that goes on biting all the time. If there are doubts that the dog is biting not because of the dictate of conscience but because he is vicious, then things happen to that dog. He may not get his licence renewed when it falls due.' This was a rather foolish threat, the Parliamentary party's reaction was hostile, and Wilson tried to pass it off as a joke; but it did represent one facet of his feelings towards backbenchers.

In many ways, the first sign of a turning-point in these relationships came in July 1966. Then the abandonment of the growth targets and therefore of most of Labour's plans meant that there were critics on the Left who disliked the cuts and critics on the Right who blamed Wilson for supporting sterling rather than devaluing. Once Wilson sensed anything less than total support, he rapidly became a prey to fears of conspiracies and coups. Significantly, he first feared such plots in July 1966 when he said there was a City plot to get a National government and a Ministers' plot to force him to devalue. He also feared a plot to remove him when Ray Gunter resigned in mid-1968. The one real plot, and it was woefully weak, was in April and May 1969 when he was pushing the 'In Place of Strife' legislation.

Then, the Left felt he might have to go, the trade union centre of the party was deeply disturbed and the Right, who had come to dislike his values and his style, saw an opportunity to strike. But the attempt was crippled for lack of an agreed alternative and no one in the Cabinet would move. Douglas Houghton, as Chairman of the party, was keen on killing the Bill – the leadership issue could take second place – and he said he would accept no motion at a Parliamentary party meeting calling on Wilson to go unless it had a hundred signatures. This prevented any move and then Wilson ended the whole situation by reaching his 'solemn and binding' agreement with the unions that they would, on their own, reduce the number of unofficial strikes. Once the situation was over, the plot collapsed and Wilson was never again threatened in any of the time he spent as Prime Minister.

As time went on, his relations with the Parliamentary Labour party became more remote. He had this vast amount of patronage which was of great help and he regarded it as such. Wilson's constant attack on the Conservatives in 1963 because of their amateurishness was in contrast to his own professionalism; he did not mean that he intended his Government to be based on specific ability or professionalism. Wilson realized that the capacities of six or eight ministers were crucial to the success of the Government and he moved them round to ensure that there was no 'crown prince'. But below them, his chief trust went to the senior, sympathetic civil servants and all the rest of the jobs were filled so as to gather support – so many Left, so many Right, some from each region and each interest group. Once, when the trade union group was restless on prices and incomes, the next batch of three junior jobs went to its leaders. This approach was a pity because it failed to recognize that, for certain groups, what matters is the quality of the junior minister in charge and if he is there for internal party reasons and has no ability, then it can damage the Government.

By the 1974–6 Government, Wilson had lost many of his skills in the House, his capacity to rally and comfort his supporters and to score off the Opposition. He was unchallenged as Leader because there was no generally accepted alternative; no side of the party was ready to remove Wilson if it meant that the other side's candidate would take over. But his speeches lacked fire; they were always long, often boring, and sometimes trivial. Although he was unchallenged in these years there was no evidence of regret when he announced his resignation.

Apart from his skills in managing the Labour party, Wilson as Prime Minister had to govern the country. In the period of 'institutional optimism' of the early 1960s when Wilson was leading an increasingly aggressive and confident opposition, he talked a good deal about the machinery of government and about how in 'the first hundred days' after Labour took office, a new atmosphere would sweep through Whitehall.

In this respect, his ideas concentrated on two areas. One was the central direction of government where he wanted to strengthen the Cabinet office and the No. 10 Downing Street secretariat. The other was the need for some new, large departments, one to counterbalance the Treasury, the others to collect and upgrade certain aspects of administration that he thought were of special importance. On the first, he did in the end go some way towards a 'Prime Minister's department'. In addition to the Cabinet secretariat, he strengthened the No. 10 staff (by two or three people) and set up a special political office under Mrs Marcia Williams. In practice, Wilson found that this arrangement, plus his press secretaries, gave him all the advice and briefing his quick mind needed.

Mr Heath added the Central Policy Review Staff (the 'Think Tank') and Wilson kept it when he won the 1974 election, adding in a Special Policy Unit under Dr Bernard Donoughue, largely because the Think Tank had become part of the official machine. To create a full Prime Minister's department, all that would have been needed would have been to add in the Civil Service department and the section of the Treasury that monitors public expenditure. But Wilson did not find this necessary. His control was sufficiently effective in those areas where he took an interest, though if these crossed departmental boundaries they were often made the responsibility of special 'Cabinet units' – examples being Northern Ireland, the coordination of services for the disabled and devolution.

Wilson had thought a good deal about the structure of government while he was in opposition.[9] It was a view fairly widely held at the time that the 'stop-go' policies Wilson was attacking were due to the Treasury's over-absorption with sterling and the balance of payments. So the main idea, which also sprang from George Brown, was the creation of a second economics ministry, capable of rivalling the Treasury and dedicated to growth. This was set up with real zest and took control of regional policy and of framing the National Plan.

Other ministries were created to meet the requirements of Labour's manifesto. One was a Ministry of Overseas Development to look after aid. A Ministry of Technology was established. The commitment to set up a Land Commission caused a little difficulty as neither Crossman nor Dame Evelyn Sharp (the Minister of Local Government and Housing and the Permanent Secretary) wanted to have anything to do with it, so a separate Ministry of Land and Natural Resources was set up but it never came to anything.

The DEA never recovered (i.e. the Treasury won) after the July 1966 cuts ended all the forecasts on which the National Plan was based and the ministry was wound up in 1969. Later, Wilson tried making some amalgamations, though this was done more in consultation with William Armstrong, the Head of the Civil Service, than with any ministers. As a result the combined Department of Health and Social Security was created, the Board of Trade and Technology became a Department of Industry, while a mammoth Department of the Environment was created out of Housing, Local Government and Transport. All this was part of the reforming atmosphere of the period. It had also led to the appointment of the Fulton Committee on the Civil Service (Cmnd 3638, 1968), but its report contained little that the Civil Service was not already doing or which it could not accommodate. The real problem was that the key issue, the Civil Service's relations with Parliament, was not included in the Committee's report.

Heath continued some of these changes but, by the time Wilson returned to office in 1974, the mood had totally altered, there was little or no enthusiasm left for institutional change. In a sense, national problems were too serious for this and no changes in the machinery of government, other than the creation of Dr Donoughue's unit, were contemplated.

On top of the civil service side of administration, there was the political layer culminating in the Cabinet. Given all Wilson's 1963–4 talk of professionalism in government, one might have expected him to go for a 'ministry of all talents'. In fact, his emphasis on professionalism was a contrast between himself and Sir Alec Douglas-Home. The next few people around Wilson were unavoidable – Brown and Callaghan in 1964–6, then a more mixed group including Jenkins after he went to the Exchequer. After the return to office in 1974, there were quite a number of established leaders to whom he conceded larger roles. But below these men, largely necessary for political reasons, Wilson used the posts at his disposal as patronage, to buy NEC votes, to square the unions, to keep certain sections happy and he always took the view that the actual government was done by the top half-dozen ministers and by the civil service.

When it came to handling the Cabinet, Wilson's methods have been described in detail in the three volumes of Crossman diaries. Wilson never had an inner Cabinet. He was too lonely or too suspicious a man for that. (One of his colleagues, who sat with him in the Cabinet from 1964 to 1970, has said that at the end of the six years he did not feel that he knew Wilson any better.) However, he did have to work with Brown and Callaghan in the period immediately after victory in 1964. By late 1966, Brown was excluding himself and in 1967 Callaghan insisted on going to the Home Office. Those in close or powerful positions were less easy to identify, though Mrs Castle and Crossman thought they had more influence. In 1974–7 clearly Michael Foot played a very important role and some senior trade union leaders, notably Jack Jones, might well have been senior members of the Cabinet, given their influence on the Government's policy.

Over Wilson's handling of the Cabinet, there is some dispute. Lord Gordon-Walker, in his book *The Cabinet*,[10] says that every issue of any moment was decided in full and free discussion round the Cabinet table. But he also admits that the retention of British bases east of Suez was never explicitly considered (though it was a burning topic in the party, in Parliament and in the press) till the decision was forced on the Cabinet by the devaluation of 1967. The real explanation is that the Government inherited a number of on-going policies, which had been endorsed or accepted without discussion before the Cabinet was even formed (by the Wilson–Brown–Callaghan triumvirate) and it would have been a bold Minister for Wales or for Transport who sought to overturn such a policy. The same was true of devaluation. When Wilson decided to defend sterling, this became known as 'the unmentionable' in Whitehall and, if it came up, it was only at crises such as that of July 1966 when the Government's policy and position were, for a moment, in the melting-pot.

Richard Crossman in his *Diaries of a Cabinet Minister*,[11] watched Wilson very carefully at his Cabinets. The picture that emerges is very similar to that under other Prime Ministers. There were some principal themes of government policy set by the key figures in the Government, and these only came up for discussion if there was a major reason for altering course. Otherwise, it was disputed business that came before the Cabinet. Wilson laid down a rule that there was no automatic referral from a Cabinet committee; this could only be with the consent of the chairman. No disputes of fact could come to Cabinet; it had to be issues of principle.

Within this framework, Wilson was a competent manager and, if he had a strong view, he usually got his way. He could be defeated. The major instance was when the Cabinet deserted him and Barbara Castle over the 'In Place of Strife' legislation. Wilson did not, in this case, concede defeat, but went once again to meet the TUC. If he had returned and said 'They offer nothing; I will bring in a Bill and those who do not like it can resign', no one can say what would have happened, but it would have precipitated a leadership crisis and Wilson preferred to concede. Gordon-Walker suggests that Wilson and Brown wanted to use the navy to keep open the Straits of Tiran before the Six Days' War but were overturned by the Cabinet.

Yet such situations were exceptional. Most often, Wilson was using the Cabinet in the normal way to establish priorities and reconcile conflicts between spending departments. On such occasions, the chief criticism of his methods was his desire to get general consensus by 'going round the table'. It was said that this encouraged ministers to think too much of their own departments and too little of the overall policy of the Cabinet. In the early years, Bert Bowden, who sat beside Wilson (as Lord President of the Council) kept the score.[12] 'Usually these were on minor issues but sometimes Wilson used this on bigger questions and on expenditure cuts.' Crossman records a series of decisions on Prices and Incomes policy: 'On all these issues votes were taken and Harold wrote down the score. At one point it came to 12–9. Willie Ross switched his vote and it came to a tie, and Harold said, "What shall I do, it is a tie?" I said *sotto voce*, "Be a Prime Minister", and Richard Marsh giggled. But Harold repeated plaintively, "What shall I do, it's a tie?" '[13] On the other hand, if the issue mattered, Wilson could be decisive. In December 1967 he, George Brown and Denis Healey, at a Defence and Overseas Policy Committee of the Cabinet, had agreed to sell certain arms to South Africa. This reached the backbenchers and Wilson's sensitive antennae told him it was going to be very unpopular. So he let the Chief Whip run a motion against the project, switched sides and the Cabinet finally agreed. As Wilson said himself 'It was the first and the last time in our near six years of office that I had to fight rough with any of my colleagues'.[14]

The main defect of Wilson as a governor, an administrator, a leader of a ruling team, was that he had no overall strategy. This complaint is made time and again by Crossman and was very evident to contemporaries in the House. He was an absolutely brilliant Leader of the Opposition, he was a superb rallying-point for a Government living from hand to mouth on a majority of three, but once he had his big majority and could map out a broad strategy, there was none.

It may be understandable that he was not prepared to remould the Labour party or British society but, compared for instance with Lloyd George (who had little strategy), he did not tackle the main problems that forced themselves on his attention. Lloyd George saw the poverty of his period and brought in national insurance, old age pensions and unemployment relief. Wilson saw the major burning issue of bad industrial relations, tried to act, was defeated but thereafter pretended it did not exist. If he could have adapted the Conservative Industrial Relations Act after 1974 or if he could have worked out other, more gradual approaches to the problem, there would have been one major item of legislation to his credit. But in fact, there is none. The other weakness Wilson had, which got worse in his later years, was to imagine that the announcement of a committee, the tackling of a problem in a speech, was equivalent to action. So he presided over conferences to 'regenerate' aspects of British industry and then claimed this had happened. He ran over lists of Bills passed and then felt that he had done something to alter British society though the country, when he resigned in 1976, was much the same (barring lower confidence, lower investment, higher inflation and higher unemployment) as the Britain he had taken over in 1964.

The final role of a modern Prime Minister is as the Government's public relations officer. The Prime Minister appears in eight or nine times as many news reports as any of his colleagues; for many his character and personality epitomize the government. Wilson welcomed this from his earliest days as Leader of the Opposition and he was a real professional. He knew all about the press; when the last stories had to be in, who wrote which column and so on. He was also a brilliant performer on television, exuding ability, confidence and knowledge, but not upper-class remoteness. He ran rings round Alec Douglas-Home and Ted Heath. In his early days as Prime Minister, he often presided at the confidential weekly briefings of lobby correspondents and he was always accessible to journalists. As a result of this and his own successes, he got a superb press in the 1963–6 period. At the 1966 election the *Economist* said there was only one issue, 'were you or were you not for Britain's clever little man?'

Once again, as might be expected, the turning-point came for objective reasons, when the Government was 'blown off course' in July 1966. Then Wilson began to resent critical stories. A little later, in mid-1967, relations became worse over the D-notice affair and Wilson began to resent the critical tone of the leading articles in *The Times*. He and his staff would collect evidence of what they considered to be bias and then summon editors or proprietors and protest, or even ask for changes in their staff[15] and the amazing thing is that sometimes editors and proprietors conceded, though overall relations did not improve.

These difficulties were paralleled by a rift with the BBC. Even as far back as the 1964 election night, he gave an interview on the train to an ITA team, but not to the BBC. He accused some BBC interviewers (Ian Trethowan and Robert Mackenzie) of pressing him harder than they pressed Conservatives. As a result, when Bert Bowden wanted to leave the House, he was made Chairman of the ITA and Lord Hill, the incumbent, was moved to the BBC with the implication that he would teach them their place. When Wilson rose to address the 1968 Labour party conference and got a cheer, he said 'thank you for what the BBC, if they are true to their usual form, will tonight describe as a hostile reception'.[16]

This relationship settled more or less at rock bottom. Wilson accused the BBC (through Joe Haines, his press officer) of being a major reason for his defeat in 1970 and Ron Hayward accused the BBC of bias in 1974. What is peculiar is first that a man who was so skilful on the media should have got into this state and second that a politician as knowledgeable as Wilson could have attributed such influence to the media – even if they had been biased (and no one has shown that the BBC was biased). The answer, really, is that Wilson was dogged by failure and was both puzzled by it and resented it. Also, his constant dislike of the upper middle class, the south of England Establishment, combined to make him want to blame the media and to pick on the BBC in particular. This obsession will probably never leave him. He was always worried about burglaries, which he said were attempts to get at his private papers. He constantly suspected the press and one of the only two speeches he made in the Commons in the year after his resignation was an attack on the *Daily Mail*, while he also accused a 'mafia' of former members of MI5 of conspiring against him in league with 'certain elements in the press'.

In attempting any assessment of Harold Wilson as a Prime Minister, it is necessary to mention two other aspects of his period in office. One is his entourage. He had as private secretary Mrs Marcia Williams, later Lady Falkender and several other members of her family worked for him. Then there were press officers Gerald Kaufman and Joe Haines and a number of other advisers and helpers such as Lord Balogh, John Allen, Lord Wigg and later Bernard Donoughue. There is nothing unusual or wrong about the presence of such a 'kitchen cabinet'. Some premiers rely more on their senior colleagues and political friends. Wilson was a lonely man and it was understandable that he should therefore be more dependent on a group who had little political standing but who were there because he trusted them. But there have been accusations that assign a larger role to this group. Crossman often says that Mrs Williams was more powerful than any Cabinet minister. Wilson himself responded by saying that she never saw Cabinet papers, but the *Sun* printed a memo to an official (Derek Mitchell) in which it was agreed that she was to see some Cabinet papers. The controversy was blown up by Joe Haines – Wilson's last press secretary – who asserts that but for the malign influence of Mrs Williams, Wilson would have been a great Prime Minister.[17] Mrs Williams herself wrote her version of her role in *Inside Number Ten*.[18]

There is little to be said about all this except that the entourage reflected Wilson's personality. Joe Haines asked himself how Mrs Williams had such a hold on Wilson and concluded, 'I do not know the answer, except, perhaps, that it lies deep in his own insecurity'.[19] Certainly, she encouraged his fear of plots, she believed that the Civil Service was 'against Labour', but she could also argue with Wilson about the Common Market (she was opposed) or about deals with Ian Smith. It is hard, after careful study, to see any specific actions of the Wilson premiership that owed more to his entourage than to him. He was his own man and they fulfilled his needs.

This leads to the question of Wilson's style. In his later years, many attacked his whole approach to politics and he was Prime Minister during a period when the British people's confidence in the political system and in politicians underwent a steady decline. The aspect of his style that became the subject of criticism began with Wilson as a conscious theory of leadership. He had come through the 1950s when the Labour party had torn itself apart over so many issues, most of which he saw as unnecessary. So when there was a contest for the leadership in 1955, Wilson turned to Gaitskell and said: 'I'll back you for it wholeheartedly so long as you stop trying to force every issue, by always trying to get a majority decision on everything that crops up. If you'll really try to work with the *whole* party and take a unifying not a divisive view of your responsibilities, you can count on my complete support.'[20] This was an admirable doctrine until the party came to power. For instance, Wilson defused the terrible battle over nuclear disarmament with a commitment to produce some sort of multilateral force (the formula was soon forgotten) and, once he was in office the nuclear weapons stayed. But this approach was harder to maintain in a Government that had promised a list of specific economic achievements and was not delivering. It is one thing to produce a formula to cover some disagreements; another to cover actual failure. Increasingly after 1966, Wilson's great skills were devoted not to giving a lead to this set of zealots rather than that, but to getting by the next round of political controversy, usually by pretending that all was well. For instance, when patently beaten by the Cabinet and the TUC over labour relations, he came to the Parliamentary party and flourished some 'solemn and binding' agreement that meant absolutely nothing. His style grated on no one more than on Ted Heath, who decided that if he won the 1970 election he would be as different from Wilson as possible. He wrote in the introduction to his election manifesto:

> During the last six years we have suffered not only from bad policies, but from a cheap and trivial style of government. Decisions have been dictated simply by the desire to catch tomorrow's headlines. The short-term gain has counted for everything; the long-term objective has gone out of the window. Every device has been used to gain immediate publicity, and government by gimmick has become the order of the day. Decisions lightly entered into have been as lightly abandoned.

It is a measure of Britain's problems that, despite Heath's desire to be totally different in policy and in style, the overall relative decline that had baffled Wilson continued under his successor.

In Opposition again, Wilson once more resorted to his tactics of 1963, but it was a different matter after he had been in office for six years. To be against Tory terms, and then virtually against British membership of the Community was such an evident *volte face*. So was the adoption of a referendum. So was the acceptance of much of the 1974 manifesto. So was the out-and-out condemnation of all industrial relations legislation and of any attempt by the Conservatives to run a Prices and Incomes policy.

Wilson's reputation never really recovered from these shifts of front. He was accused of leaving the Labour party without idealism or a sense of direction. Among the middle and senior rank ministers he brought on there is a mixture of ability, but too many think that politics is the capacity to score off the Tories, to get a rousing cheer at a conference of the faithful, to prevent a split in the party over some vote; but beliefs, idealism, issues come nowhere. On the other hand it has to be recognized that Wilson was also a product of the Labour party. Could it have been any other way? Why was he left there, by the end unloved and barely respected but not challenged?

The verdict on Harold Wilson's period as Prime Minister and on his own performance will always be mixed. He was brilliant in the 1963–6 period. He had praise lavished on him from every quarter. Yet his whole time as Leader of the Labour party – 1963–76 – was one when Britain's relative position in the world declined. But although he left behind him no major legislative or diplomatic triumphs, he nevertheless did have his achievements, and they were in party and electoral terms. He made a warring set of factions look like an alternative government in 1963. But for great skill and resilience, Labour could have lost that election and been out of office for a fourth consecutive Parliament. After 1964, Wilson made Labour the party of government. For a while, it attracted all the talent. The Conservatives, in their policies, their tactics and even in their choice of Leader, were merely reacting to what Wilson did. Though he lost in 1970, he held the Labour party together through another period of divisive in-fighting and brought it back to power in a way which again demoralized the Conservatives.

Whether these positive factors are held to be of great importance, whether they mitigate or outweigh the defects that have been described really depend on how much value is placed on holding the Labour party together and keeping it in government. If, after the next election, the Labour party goes into opposition and tears itself apart, then it will be said that Wilson only delayed these developments and his capacities in this field will be discounted. If Labour wins and remains an effective and progressive force in British politics (or loses but retains its unity and contributes more to national life at a later stage), then he will retain some credit as a skilled party manager, an adroit tactician, a brilliant publicist, a tough political infighter; but not as a statesman.

Notes

1. The *Daily Telegraph*, 24 April 1954.
2. George Brown, *In My Way* (London 1971).
3. Harold Wilson, *The Labour Government, 1964–70: A Personal Record* (London 1971), p. 471.
4. Paul Foot, *The Politics of Harold Wilson* (Harmondsworth 1968), p. 127.
5. Harold Wilson, *The New Britain: Labour's Plan* (Harmondsworth 1964), pp. 14–15.
6. Harold Wilson, *Purpose in Politics* (London 1964), pp. 27–8.
7. Joe Haines, *The Politics of Power* (London 1977), p. 186.
8. He told Norman Hunt (*The Listener*, 6 April 1967) that 'they have taken the bit between their teeth a little'; and Richard Crossman, in *The Diaries of a Cabinet Minister*, Vol. II, explains how he had no support from Wilson in trying to keep the experiment going.
9. See *Whitehall and Beyond: Three Conversations with Norman Hunt* (BBC Publications 1964).
10. P. Gordon-Walker, *The Cabinet* (London 1970).
11. Richard Crossman, *The Diaries of a Cabinet Minister*, Vols. I and II (London 1975 and 1976).
12. *Ibid.*, Vol. II, p. 80. Wilson is conscious of this criticism and denies that he took votes, saying it only happened over the expenditure cuts of January 1968 (*The Labour Government, 1964–70*, p. 481), but there is instance after instance recorded in Crossman's *Diaries*.
13. *Ibid.*, Vol. I, p. 591.
14. Harold Wilson, *The Labour Government, 1964–70*, p. 476.

15. *The Cecil King Diary, 1965–70* (London 1972), p. 145.
16. *Report of the 1968 Annual Conference of the Labour Party*, p. 164.
17. Joe Haines, *op. cit.*
18. Marcia Williams, *Inside Number 10* (London 1972).
19. Joe Haines, *op. cit.*, p. 159.
20. Leslie Smith, *Harold Wilson: the Authentic Portrait* (London 1964), p. 114.

James Callaghan

Brian Redhead

'And what would Houdini have done?'

The speaker was the Prime Minister, Jim Callaghan. His question, which required no answer, was directed to his predecessor, Harold Wilson. The occasion was the publication of the agreement which came to be known as the 'Lib-Lab Pact'. It was a year, almost to the day, since Callaghan had become Prime Minister and he knew that he had achieved a deal which not even the past master himself could have bettered, a deal which would sustain his minority Government in office. A year before, on the morning after the day upon which he had become Prime Minister, his name, which was in everyone's mouth, had been pronounced in three ways within an hour on one radio channel. Callahan; Callagan; Callacan. A call had been made to Downing Street to inquire which was correct, or at least preferred. Downing Street had settled for Callahan, with the stress on the first syllable. The need to check might have amused, but more probably would have annoyed, Callaghan's father. He too was James, but he had changed his surname from Garoghan to Callaghan both that it might the more easily be accommodated in English mouths and that it might the less easily invoke anti-Irish (and anti-Catholic) prejudice.

The confusion over its pronunciation, though a trivial matter in itself, pointed to an interesting paradox. The holder of that surname, the man who had just become Prime Minister, was no stranger to high political office. He was, in the strictest sense, uniquely qualified for the post of Prime Minister. No other man in British political history had ever held all four of the major offices of state – Chancellor of the Exchequer, Home Secretary, Foreign Secretary, and now Prime Minister. (Rab Butler was the only other politician in this century to manage the first three, but he never achieved the top job.) Nor had Callaghan's preferment over the other five candidates for the Labour leadership in succession to Wilson come as a surprise. He had first been named as 'crown prince' to Wilson nearly ten years previously. He was the favourite in the election for the leadership of the Parliamentary Labour party from the start. If there were any surprise that he should now be at No. 10 it arose not from his grasping of the opportunity but from the creation of that opportunity. The only unexpected happening had been Wilson's resignation, not Callaghan's succession. Once Wilson had decided to go, Callaghan was his obvious successor. And yet commentators were hesitating over his name as if he were some newcomer to the political scene. Further, if they could not pronounce his name with assurance, no more could they pin upon him the handy labels of political demarcation. He was simply Callaghan, however it was pronounced. But who was Callaghan? He was clearly someone of much greater substance than the Sunny Jim of the headlines. Beneath the bonhomie which characterized his public appearances there was evidently a man of relentless political ambition. Jim Callaghan was not an unknown, but he was not known. And both his character as a man and his behaviour as a politician had contributed to his recondite reputation.

He had never been a man to talk about himself in public. When two eager young journalists[1] set about writing a book on his road to No. 10 he made the pressures of office an excuse for not seeing them. Over the years, although he had given many interviews about events, he had given only a handful of interviews about himself, and in all of them he had said much the same, in much the same words, and not very much at that. And yet his upbringing, poor but honest, was one which he, as an ambitious Labour politician, could, had he so chosen, both have described and augmented to his advantage. His father James Callaghan (Garoghan) was a sailor, a chief petty officer, who nearly went with Scott to the Antarctic. (Evans went instead and never returned.) He had been persuaded by his young wife to accept an alternative offer to join the crew of the royal yacht, the *Victoria and Albert*. She had argued very sensibly that, as the Queen disliked sailing, the royal yacht would spend most of its time tied up at Portsmouth, where they lived, so they would be together. It was, they were, and their son, who was christened Leonard James, was born on 27 March 1912. He was Leonard or Len, not James or Jim, for his first thirty years. If he had stuck to Len, one of his Cabinet colleagues observed years later, would Len Murray have been compelled to stick to Lionel?

Callaghan was brought up Protestant, not Catholic. In changing his surname his father had also changed his denomination. His parents were married in the Church of England but Mrs Callaghan was more Protestant than Anglican and brought her son up a Baptist. It is said to have helped when he appeared before the selection committee in Cardiff South in 1944. Had he been Roman Catholic he almost certainly would not have been the chosen candidate. His disposition however was ecumenical. He would never become the prisoner of dogma, nor a man to give hostages to fortune. His father was seriously injured in the Battle of Jutland and invalided out of the Royal Navy. He became a coastguard and the family moved to Brixham in Devon. But he died in 1921 at the age of 44, and his pensionless family of widow, son and daughter returned to Portsmouth. Three years later, thanks to a Labour MP, Mrs Callaghan got the widow's ten bob a week. Some say she voted Labour ever after, but she certainly had no intention of offering up her son as a political sacrifice. She had only one ambition for him – that he should get a safe job and hang his hat on a pension. And who, as her son has said himself on several recorded occasions since, could blame her? So he left school at sixteen and got a job as a junior clerk with the Inland Revenue at 33s. 6d. a week and the safe prospect of a pension. Had he stayed in the civil service to draw it, it would have been index-linked.

To get a safe job in the Inland Revenue two years after the General Strike and at a time when the dole queues were lengthening was neither a socialist baptism nor a standard first step to the Labour leadership – which may explain Callaghan's reluctance to discuss his early years except in the broadest terms. But Labour's establishment has many mansions, and one of them is the Inland Revenue Staff Federation. The young Callaghan joined the union soon after he started work, became a local official, then (at the age of only 22) a member of the National Executive, and in 1936 Assistant General Secretary. He had made his way up largely by speaking up when he knew what he was talking about and shutting up when he didn't. His reputation was built upon his ability to speak his mind: his career was built upon his ability to know when not to. He wrote well in the union journal, was seen to be both ambitious and sensible, and was picked out by Harold Laski as a young man to be encouraged in the Labour party. The two corresponded for some years and Callaghan always acknowledged his debt to Laski as a tutor. But in truth, though Laski could teach Callaghan about ideology, he could teach him nothing about politics. When Attlee finally decided that the egregious Laski's best contribution to the Labour party would be a period of silence, Callaghan was already safely launched in Parliament.

That was in 1945. Callaghan had joined the navy in 1943. He had attempted to enlist at the outbreak of war even though his job was classified as a reserved occupation. He had been marked down for the army but had protested to the Admiralty that as the son and the grandson of a sailor he ought to be in the navy. Eventually he got his wish and when the naval censor noticed that he was corresponding with Laski he deduced not that Callaghan was a trouble-maker but that he was a potential officer. Ordinary Seaman Callaghan became Lieutenant Jim Callaghan. It was the lieutenant who met the selection committee in Cardiff South in 1944 and was adopted parliamentary candidate. It was the lieutenant who attended the Labour party conference in December 1944 and supported a resolution proposed by an old friend from his school-days in Portsmouth, Ian Mikardo, calling for an extensive programme of public ownership. The resolution was carried and Herbert Morrison was convinced that it would cost Labour the next election. It didn't. Lieutenant Callaghan was flown home from Rangoon to conduct his campaign and he took the seat from the Conservatives with a majority of 5,944. He was one of 393 Labour MPs.

In the quarter-century between 1945 and 1970 Labour had two spells in office, each of six years, with thirteen years of Tory rule (or, as they say in Labour circles, misrule) between. Callaghan held junior office through most of Labour's first spell and Cabinet office throughout the whole of its second. He spent the Tory years distancing himself from factions within the Labour party and establishing himself as a man of the party.

Attlee made him a PPS the moment he entered the Commons, but just before Christmas 1945, in an uncharacteristic moment of rebellion, Callaghan voted against the Bretton Woods agreement and quite unnecessarily resigned. It was an act of youthful folly that he was never to repeat. He spent the next two years a a backbencher, but he only voted against the Government once more and that was over the price of cocoa. He attended the Keep Left lunches but declined to sign the Keep Left manifesto. He knew the Left but was not of the Left, and towards the end of 1947, when Attlee offered him a 'real' job, he jumped at the chance. For the next four years he was a Parliamentary Secretary, first for Transport and then, to his delight, with the Admiralty. He established a reputation for competence and confidence, clear-headed and plain speaking in debate in the Commons, sensible and decisive in the work in his departments. In short, he was a good man to have in government.

But he was more than that. He had emerged as a very real politician of the kind that politicians best understand, the kind for whom politics is not only the art of the possible but also the science of the control of the power to do that which is possible. He had emerged as the kind of politician who attends to things, who, when others weary, keeps on, who is not distracted by false visions of a promised land. When Labour lost the 1951 election, Jim Callaghan, by now almost 40, was seen by his party to be a man, not a boy. No one ever called him the darling of the constituencies or of the Parliamentary Labour party, but year after year in the interregnum he was there, voted on to the National Executive by the constituencies, voted on to the Shadow Cabinet by the PLP. And he was not there by chance. He was neither a man of the Left nor a man of the Right; he was a man of the party. When Wilson challenged Gaitskell for the leadership of the party in 1960 Callaghan plumped for Gaitskell, not because he was a Gaitskellite but because he knew that Gaitskell commanded the greater support in the party. The election proved him right and in the same month he stood himself against George Brown and Fred Lee for the deputy leadership not because he thought he could beat Brown (he knew he could not) but because he needed to demonstrate his strength within the party. Brown won on the second ballot but Callaghan was rewarded by topping the poll for the Shadow Cabinet. When Gaitskell died in January 1963, Callaghan faced an even more interesting contest.

He and Wilson had much in common as politicians. To label Callaghan a man of the Right was to diminish him. To label Wilson a man of the Left was equally to diminish him. Their personal styles were very different but their occupations of the party very similar. Each could command a wing, but both could command the centre. A straight fight between them for the party leadership would have been very close. But it had come too soon for Callaghan. George Brown as Gaitskell's deputy was bound to stand. As Gaitskell's loyal lieutenant Brown commanded considerable support in the party, but he alarmed several moderates as well as irritating the Left. If the moderates were faced with a straight choice between Brown and Wilson, Callaghan believed they would opt for Wilson. He even toyed with the idea of trying to persuade Brown not to stand in the belief that the moderates would welcome the chance to vote for him, Callaghan, rather than for Wilson, but Brown naturally was not to be persuaded. Callaghan still stood to indicate that he would be there when needed and the election went pretty much as he had forecast. On the first ballot the result was Wilson 115, Brown 88, Callaghan 41. Callaghan's support split 2-1 for Wilson and the final result was Wilson 144, Brown 103. Callaghan, it can be assumed, voted for Wilson on the second ballot.

The struggles for the leadership of the party had revived Callaghan's interest in his political career just when it had begun to sag. There are Labour politicians who prefer opposition to Government (it frees them to exercise their consciences without the responsibilities of office) but Callaghan was not one of them. He had come into politics not only to get on, but to get on with things. He wanted to be doing, not preparing. He saw himself as a practitioner, not as a prophet. He despised doctrinaire denominationalism within the party. He wanted a united party in order that it might be seen to be fit to get on with the job of running the country. And in 1962 he had very nearly given up in despair. He thought the party had been too long out of office and for once he made no secret of his own ambitions, which were to be in, and of, a Labour Government. He had not enrolled, he said, to spend his life sitting in a waiting-room. After the election for the leadership which Wilson had won, he did not have to wait much longer.

Labour won the 1964 general election, though only just, and Wilson appointed Callaghan Chancellor of the Exchequer. The job came as no surprise because he had been Shadow Chancellor appointed by Gaitskell, although it is always said that Gaitskell intended to switch him elswhere when Labour came to office, being apparently of the opinion that although robust in opposing Tory economic policies, Callaghan had too little grasp of economics to be confident and secure at the Treasury. Subsequent events suggested that there was some truth in that judgement. But Wilson allowed himself no such misgivings and Callaghan found himself, at the Treasury, splendidly placed to get on with things. From the start things went badly, however. It is true that he and the Treasury together, by the simple device of keeping a firm hold on the purse-strings, won the battle against George Brown and the newly created Department of Economic Affairs for control of the economy.

They had an unexpected ally in Dame Evelyn Sharp, Permanent Secretary at the Ministry of Housing and Local Government. She insisted that her Minister, the Pepysian Richard Crossman, have inserted the word 'economic' before 'planning councils' in the regional structure George Brown was creating. She saw his new councils as a threat to the control of land-use planning, and her intervention pushed them further towards advisory and neutered status. But if George Brown's imaginative enterprise was crumbling, Callaghan at the Treasury was discovering that it was one thing to have control of the economy and quite another to control it. What went wrong in his three years at the Treasury has been amply chronicled. Essentially it was a reluctance to devalue.

When Labour got a first look at the books in 1964 it was obvious then, as indeed it had been to those in the know since 1962, that the pound was overvalued. But actuarial evidence is not necessarily political wisdom. Wilson would not devalue, and Callaghan, though of the opinion that Wilson was rejecting the possibility too hastily, agreed. There were economists for, and there were economists against, and the Treasury was cautioning delay. But it was not the economic arguments one way or the other which swayed Wilson and Callaghan. Both believed that a Labour Government with a tiny majority could not afford to get itself labelled the party of devaluation. It had been the undoing of the Attlee Government, the cause of the humiliation of Stafford Cripps. The party that had just come to power promising a white-hot technological revolution could not be seen to begin by devaluing the pound in the pocket. So they put off the evil day until well after the 1966 election, and even when it had to happen in 1967

Wilson almost pretended that it hadn't. The postponement gave Callaghan three troubled years. The bloom of his bonhomie faded. He looked very unhappy. And even though he described it to his colleagues as the unhappiest day of his life, it must have come as a relief when he broke it to the Cabinet on 16 November 1967 that he had decided the pound must be devalued. The world was informed two days later, on the Saturday, and in the eyes of the world that weekend Callaghan appeared cast down and discredited. A lesser man, a lesser politician, might have departed public life, taken a peerage, and gone off to the City. But not Callaghan.

He resigned, it is true. On the very evening of the devaluation announcement he wrote to Wilson a letter of resignation taking upon himself the blame for what had happened. Wilson was grateful for that. In return he agreed that the resignation need not be made public until the devaluation procedures had been seen through Parliament. And in the devaluation debate in the Commons on the following Wednesday Callaghan made a speech, universally judged one of his best, which the *Daily Telegraph* actually headlined: 'Bid by Callaghan for Premiership'. He had done nobody down, but he had put himself back up. The resignation letter was published and Wilson announced that Roy Jenkins and Callaghan would exchange jobs. So Jenkins went to the Treasury and Callaghan to the comparative safety of the Home Office. It had been the fastest come-back in recent British history.

Jenkins had been an appropriate Home Secretary in a permissive age, a serious and eloquent supporter of reforming legislation which gave both greater freedom and greater protection to minorities. But there were rumblings within the Labour movement that things had gone too far. One old Labour warhorse, recently ennobled, commented that these things might be helpful in Hampstead but did nothing for Labour in his constituency where he knew of only two homosexuals and neither of them voted Labour. If there were genuine misgivings within the party then Callaghan was the man to allay them. For many years he had augmented his Parliamentary salary as paid adviser to the Police Federation and his public manner always had a touch of Dixon of Dock Green. As Home Secretary, however, he was to prove too much of a blunt instrument. There was a bad moment in the Commons early on when he described a man who had been arrested as 'the man who committed the murder', and at that moment the man had not been charged, let alone convicted. He got himself into a tangle over immigration, the patrial principle and the Kenyan Asians which did nothing for the nation's liberal reputation. But he kept his head over the Vietnam demonstrations in London, and essentially, as many commentators have observed, was better on cases than on principles.

As Home Secretary he was also landed with Northern Ireland. The discontent in the Province, which had been quiet or supressed for some years, erupted in demonstrations in 1968 and in violence the following year. Although it was the Home Office's responsibility the department was ill prepared to handle the crisis, so Callaghan chose an ecumenical approach, trying to coax and wheedle the two communities into tolerating each other. It looked at first as if his method might work. In his presence the Catholic minority no longer felt as if they were second-class citizens and the Protestant majority appeared to enjoy his bluff style. He tried to treat the Province as if it were one constituency – his – and he talked of a future in which the political conflict would be the normal to and fro of Labour and Conservative. But every relaxation of Stormont's hold in response to legitimate claims for the extension of civil rights encouraged the extreme Republicans to push harder to achieve a break with Britain, and this in turn inflamed extreme Unionist fears that the Province was about to be cast off from the United Kingdom. Callaghan was compelled to send in the troops to keep the two sides apart. It was said later that he was only rescued from the consequences of his policies by the defeat of Labour in the 1970 election, but at the time his policy was judged to be a success. And when Labour was out of office he took the opportunity to defend his policies in a book[2] in which, far from being on the defensive, he argued that his had been the right approach. There is some truth in that, but his policy, or more accurately his method, had needed to be accompanied by a clear statement from the British government about the permanent status of the Province, with no ifs and buts. As long as the position of Northern Ireland within the United Kingdom were open to argument, even speculatively, the extremists on both sides could find a justification for their activities. In his book Callaghan virtually admitted this to be so. The Irish dimension was too much, even for a man with an Irish dimension.

He was on safer ground back home at Westminster. In spite of the occasional mishap his period at the Home Office so restored his political confidence that between 1968 and 1970 he ganged up with backbenchers to defeat the Government, of which he was a senior member, on three major issues: the reforming of the Lords; the control of incomes; and the curbing of strikes. All three were interesting episodes, but the third was enthralling. Callaghan's popularity within the party had declined, for obvious reasons, during his years as Chancellor. His position in the annual poll by the constituency section for the National Executive had been falling steadily. In 1967 therefore, when the opportunity presented itself, he got himself elected Treasurer of the party largely by the block votes of the trade unions. From then on his place on the NEC was no longer at risk, and as the recipient of the trade unions' subscriptions he was centrally placed in the Labour party. At the party Conference that year, barely a month before devaluation, he defended his policies as Chancellor with such courage and conviction that he emerged in the eyes of many commentators as unmistakably second only to Wilson in the party hierarchy. Indeed it may well have been his success at Scarborough in October 1967 that gave him the strength to survive and to surmount the devaluation in November.

In 1968 he sounded off at the Fire Brigade Union Conference about the need to replace a statutory incomes policy with a voluntary policy, which, as Home Secretary, was strictly none of his business. Wilson ticked him off in the Cabinet but Callaghan was unmoved. He saw coming a conflict between the unions and the Government and he had already decided which position to adopt. The conflict came with the publication of Barbara Castle's White Paper 'In Place of Strife.' Its fate is already a well chronicled episode in the history of the first Wilson Government, with more to come when Mrs Castle's memoirs are published. The White Paper proposed legislation to make compulsory strike ballots, cooling-off periods, the imposition· of demarcation solutions, and other nostrums unwelcome to trade unionists. At a crucial meeting of the Labour Party National Executive Committee Callaghan voted against them even though they were government policy. In an attempt to win him round Wilson invited him into an inner Cabinet of seven who were supposed to be united in purpose and policy. But Callaghan was not to be seduced. As Treasurer of the party he was convinced not only that the unions would never wear the policy in the White Paper but that it represented a departure from Labour orthodoxy which the leadership would shortly repent. He, Callaghan, he implied, was not being disloyal to the Government: the Government was being disloyal to the party. And he, Callaghan, would get it back on to the true path. At a joint meeting of the Cabinet and the NEC he made the point. Wilson was not amused. He dismissed Callaghan from the inner Cabinet. The press jumped up and down in excitement. Callaghan let it be known to them that he was not seeking to topple Wilson, only to set him right. The TUC called a special conference and rejected the penal measures in the proposed legislation by eight million votes to one million. It offered in their place a measure of persuasion which Mrs Castle, growing increasingly piercing in her frustration, denounced as feeble. But Callaghan had judged the mood of the party aright. At a special Cabinet meeting in June 1969 the Chief Whip, Bob Mellish, advised the Prime Minister that he could not deliver the necessary votes in the Commons. The next day, in place of 'In Place of Strife', there was a 'solemn and binding' agreement that bound no one very tightly. And it was left to Heath's stubborn Government to come to grief in the face of union recalcitrance.

Encouraged by the opinion polls which led him to believe that he could not lose, Wilson tried to free-wheel to victory in the 1970 general election, and instead came a cropper. The Conservatives, other than Heath, had been equally misled by the opinion polls and had been backing away from Heath throughout the campaign ready to pin the blame upon him and upon him alone when they lost. Consequently when Heath won he found himself in a position of splendid and powerful isolation and he set about at once fulfilling his principal political ambition which was to get Britain into Europe. He wasted little time and Britain became a member of the European Economic Community on 1 January 1972. Callaghan had long been opposed to Britain's entry but he had never been a strident anti-Marketeer because it was not in his political nature to become the prisoner of any policy. The day might come when the party would need to change its mind, or when it might have to adopt one policy in opposition and another when in office. While Heath was negotiating entry Callaghan thought it in the party's best interest to be opposed to joining. But as the date of Britain's entry grew nearer, and it became more certain that Britain would be joining, Callaghan increasingly opposed Tory policy rather than the EEC. He began to decry not Britain's joining but the terms of her joining, and took to talking about renegotiating those terms. He had already realized that once Britain was in the Community it would be extremely difficult for her to get out again, but he knew that this dilemma could not openly be admitted without tearing the Labour party apart. In this judgement Wilson and he were in accord. The anti-Marketeers in the party played into their hands by demanding a referendum. Once they had persuaded themselves that the public would vote 'Yes' if the matter were put to them skilfully, Wilson and Callaghan knew that they could both keep the party intact and keep Britain in Europe. Wilson wisely entrusted the renegotiations to Callaghan who had become Foreign Secretary when Labour won the first of the two 1974 general elections. Callaghan banged his demands upon the table like a trade union leader making the first claim in a wage negotiation. It went down well at home, especially among the party faithful, and although his method frightened a few Europeans, Willy Brandt got the message. It worked just as Wilson and Callaghan had planned, and there was never a time when they worked more closely or more sympathetically. Callaghan, as they had planned, gradually toned down Britain's demands until the Six had no difficulty in accepting them, yet he kept them seemingly firm enough to convince all but the most passionate and suspicious anti-Marketeers at home that Britain was getting what she wanted. The referendum campaign in Britain was more like a teach-in than a contest and 67 per cent of the voters obligingly voted 'Yes'. There was only one unexpected development. Callaghan himself got the Common Market bug. It was not an outbreak of unaccustomed idealism, but a new bout of *Realpolitik*. It had suddenly dawned upon him that the EEC was a power base too, and one which gave Britain's Foreign Secretary an added dimension.

He confessed that he was enjoying the job more than any that he had had before, and at the beginning of 1976 as his sixty-fourth birthday approached he had reason to believe that he was at the summit of his career. Wilson was four years younger and although he had mentioned to Callaghan before Christmas that he was thinking of retiring, Callaghan did not believe him. He thought it was out of character. So Callaghan was as taken aback as anyone when Wilson told him just before the Cabinet meeting on 16 March that he was going to resign as soon as a new Leader of the Parliamentary Labour party could be elected. Throughout the short campaign that followed, Callaghan was the favourite in the sense that he was the candidate whom most Labour MPs tipped to win whether they intended to vote for him themselves or not. Faithful to his record of knowing when not to speak, Callaghan said nothing throughout the campaign. 'I am here, if called,' was his message, though elbows were being squeezed systematically behind the scenes. The other candidates were less reticent and Tony Benn issued daily bulletins on the state of his personal ideology. But the figures, round by round, tell the story:

First ballot:	Foot	90
	Callaghan	84
	Jenkins	56
	Benn	37
	Healey	30
	Crosland	17

Crosland had to drop out, Benn always planned to, Jenkins decided to, and Healey refused to.

Second ballot:	Callaghan	141
	Foot	133
	Healey	38

With no majority overall there was one more vote.

Third ballot:	Callaghan	176
	Foot	137

So, on 5 April, Callaghan was home and dry. And if he had to have a close colleague representing the Left, who more agreeable and accommodating than Michael Foot?

With Callaghan now at No. 10 the press attempted, not for the first time, to explain him to the public – to answer the question 'Who is Callaghan?' They compared him to Baldwin and even to Mayor Daley of Chicago. They described him as instinctive, secretive, and (of course) pragmatic. Their judgements ranged from grudging admiration to contemptuous dismissal. Those who dismissed him were those who seemed least to understand the nature of politics, who wrote about it as if it were a sport, show jumping perhaps, with every event a jump-off against the clock. But politics is more like an endless pony trek on an unfamiliar route across a not unfamiliar landscape. What matters is not to fall off. And the politician will stay on only if he responds politically to events as they confront him. He is more likely to fall off if he is encumbered by premature decisions sometimes called principles. The only moral criterion of a political act is its consequence, not the motive that inspired it. Macmillan made the point unforgettably in an interview on television one evening shortly after his retirement. Asked what had worried him most during his time as Prime Minister, he thought for a moment and said: 'Events'. Callaghan would have agreed with the reply but would not have had the wit to put it so well. Callaghan's strength was his understanding of the essential nature of politics. His inspiration was his belief in the need to preserve the unity of the Labour party on a basis which would enable it to command wide support in the country. His weakness, which sprang perhaps from the insecurity of his youth, was his tendency to bridle and bluster when caught unawares. He would recover quickly but he preferred always to be prepared. This flaw in his temperament apart, he had proved himself a thorough politician who worked on the principle of what best could be made of the situation that confronted him: not what should be, but what could be; and always remembering that the unity of the party was paramount.

To Callaghan, therefore, being Leader of the party was every bit as important as being Prime Minister, and his first act when he took up office was to tell the assembled Parliamentary Labour party that no person or group within it held the ark of the covenant. Their first loyalty, like his, was to the party as a whole. He dismissed the fears of backbenchers that the party's effective majority over all other parties in the Commons would dwindle and vanish. They had a majority over the Conservatives of thirty and provided the Government could rely upon the unanimous support of the Parliamentary Labour party there would be no need for an election until they were ready for it, he said. When some innocent asked when that would be, he replied:

22 October 1979. And on that confident note he set to work as Prime Minister.

He confirmed Denis Healey in his post as Chancellor of the Exchequer and then had a look at the rest of the in-tray. Since the 1974 elections, normal service had been resumed in the country. The economic problems were still there – inflation, unemployment, lack of investment, inefficiency, and the rest – but the country was muddling through without the angry confrontations which had marked the last weeks of the Heath administration and there was no more apocalyptic talk about the country being ungovernable. Indeed it was doing better than muddling through. The trade unions had entered into a social contract with the Government whereby in exchange for rather loosely defined social benefits they had agreed to a period of voluntary wage restraint. Callaghan came to office two-thirds of the way through the first year of this contract (Stage One, or Phase One, as it was called) comfortable in the knowledge that the unions were abiding by the agreement and with every expectation that Stage Two for a further year would be equally honoured. And he made that the basis of his economic and industrial strategy.

He seemed rapidly at ease in his new job. It was reported that at his first two Cabinet meetings he was somewhat hesitant and nervous, but after that he was firmly in control. He allowed discussion in Cabinet to run on a bit (that had always been his style: to let the others have their say) but he was an active chairman of the meeting, initiating as well as responding, and above all appearing to his ministers to give them his support when they needed it. In return they gave an impression of unity and loyalty rare in Labour Cabinets. Even Mr Benn, whose opportunism appeared to know few bounds, seemed encompassed. Callaghan had restored him to some of the Cabinet committees from which Wilson had excluded him, but at the same time had made it clear that if he stepped out of line he would be dismissed. Callaghan was no less firm and straightforward in his handling of the party. He was more direct than Wilson had been with the National Executive and more prepared to use his authority as Prime Minister. He did not pretend that differences between them did not exist and he made clear the Government's policies. He was able to take such a firm stand not because he was Prime Minister, recently elected, but because the foundation of his strength was his relationship with the trade union leaders. They were not just his allies, they were his colleagues, or, to use Callaghan's own favourite description, his 'friends'. Friendship, in Callaghan's political vocabulary, was thicker than water. It was lasting and it was powerful. And he used friendships to disarm the Left both in the Cabinet and in the National Executive. Friendship also coloured his choice of ministers, inside and outside the Cabinet, but not anywhere near to the point where it could threaten the unity of the Party. He took to No. 10 for his private staff two old friends, his press officer Tom McCaffrey and his secretary Ruth Sharpe, but there was no question of creating a private office that would be a 'kitchen cabinet,' competing with Whitehall and becoming a centre of gossip and intrigue.

In the Commons too he looked comfortable and at ease. He leant on the dispatch box, said one backbencher, like a farmer on a gate. He was like a man in his own parlour, said another. Certainly he appeared to have little difficulty at Question Time. The answers got a little longer, their content a little thinner, as he settled in. His performance, especially when he took to patronizing Mrs Thatcher, the Leader of the Opposition, became almost a parody of his genial self, and it surprised some members to read in one newspaper that Question Time was something he hated. The only surprise was that he should have made such a confession, an indiscretion quite out of character. That he hated Question Time came as no surprise to most, for it could always produce the unexpected and Callaghan had a dread of being caught off balance. On most Tuesdays and Thursdays, it has to be said, he was not.

It has become a cliché of the media since the opening period of the Kennedy administration in the United States to pass judgement on the first hundred days of a new government. Wilson counted down his hundred days as if awaiting lift-off. Callaghan was more circumspect but on his hundredth day the press pronounced. Its collective judgement was best summed up by one old political opponent in the Commons who had witnessed Callaghan's career from the beginning. He was better at the top job, he said, than he had been at any other. And he was right. To be judged to have succeeded, a Prime Minister has to demonstrate that he can cope successfully with his Cabinet, his party, the Commons, the TUC and Whitehall. In the summer of 1976, after one hundred days in office, Callaghan was judged to be coping successfully with five out of the five. What no one could forsee then was that his unique political success as Prime Minister would be to do a deal with a sixth – the Parliamentary Liberal party – nor that in Jubilee Year the Crown would achieve a new political significance.

The autumn of 1976 was tricky. There was a run on the pound and the Government was compelled to negotiate a loan from the International Monetary Fund which further restricted its ability to deliver its part of the Social Contract. The unions, though remaining largely faithful to Stage Two of the pay restraint policy, were beginning to talk about an orderly return to free collective bargaining. And although both Healey and Callaghan continued to stress the importance of a Stage Three of the pay policy to take effect on 1 August 1977, they were also careful to designate it as one component of their industrial strategy, not as the only component. In the event, when the date drew near they had to settle for a goodwill agreement with the Government but not the unions saying 'not more than ten per cent'. The agreement was greeted with scorn by the Government's political opponents, but it caused scarcely a ripple in the money markets and was greeted by Callaghan himself with equanimity. He had been grateful for the interlude of Stages One and Two but he had known all along that it could not last. He also knew that a wages free-for-all would benefit neither the economy nor the members of many unions and the new agreement, with its promise of a twelve month gap between wage awards, afforded him enough purchase still to maintain his grip. Accordingly he was not dismayed because he was even more confident about his ability to sustain his government in office. Its ability to survive had been greatly improved since 23 March 1977. It was on that day that what came to be known as the 'Lib-Lab Pact', or in the smarter papers the 'Lib-Lab accommodation,' was reached.

In February the Government had been defeated in a guillotine motion of the Scotland and Wales Bill, the devolution legislation, when twenty two of its own supporters had voted against it and twenty more had abstained. The defeat had been unavoidable. Although its heart was not in it, the Government was committed to some measure of devolution. But many Labour MPs, not necessarily of the Left, were genuinely opposed to it. A Government with a reasonable majority could have shrugged off the defeat, but Callaghan's minority Government was looking very shaky. Callaghan had come to office confident that he could remain in power provided the PLP were united. The devolution defeat, even though it was brought about by Labour defection, began to reawaken the fears that even if the PLP were united the Government might still find itself without an effective majority. (On paper it had no majority over all the other parties.) The fears proved well founded on 17 March. On that night at the end of a debate on its public expenditure policy, the Government realized that even with the support of all the members of the PLP it could not win. It therefore instructed the Labour MPs not to vote. The result of the division that night was: Opposition parties 293, Government nil. Nobody could remember such a happening before. It was so unprecedented that it was farcical, and the Labour benches rocked with laughter when the result of the division was declared. But Callaghan knew that he might not laugh last. He did not call for a vote of confidence but challenged Mrs Thatcher to table one instead, while he set out in search of additional support from the Ulster Unionists or even, perhaps, from the Liberals. Mrs Thatcher had to accept the challenge. She could not be seen to shrink from the opportunity to bring about the Government's downfall at a time when both the opinion polls and the by-election results pointed to a substantial Conservative victory in a general election. It looked as if the end could be in sight for Callaghan, and yet throughout the six days between the lost expenditure motion and the no confidence motion there was scarcely anyone in Westminster on any side who could bring himself to believe that there would be a general election. The time was not ripe, the country was not ready, and somehow Callaghan would slip the rope that was supposed to be round his neck. He did, in a deal with David Steel, the Liberal Leader, and it saved the Government. It was done in a rush, but it was as adept a piece of political dealing as ever a Prime Minister achieved, and it was without precedent in recent political history. What is more, it was above board. Not until they publish their separate memoirs will it be known what went on behind the closed doors, but both Callaghan and Steel agreed that their understanding should be made public. Accordingly they published a joint statement which said that they had agreed a basis on which the

Liberal party would work with the Government in the pursuit of economic recovery. They would set up a joint consultative committee to examine government policy before it came before the House but this committee would not commit the Government to accepting the views of the Liberal party nor the Liberal party to supporting the Government on any issue. The arrangement would last until the end of the parliamentary session, when both parties would consider whether to continue it.

Only hours before the House divided on the no confidence notion the existence of the accommodation became known to almost every member of the Commons and the result of the vote was a foregone conclusion. The Government in fact had a majority of twenty-four. There was no more thought of a spring election and attention at Westminster turned instead to this new constitutional device which had saved the Government. What did it mean? It was not a coalition. It was not a realignment of the Left. The Liberals were with the Government but not of the Government. In exchange for Liberal votes and their support until the end of the session, Callaghan appeared not only to have conceded very little but to have gained additional benefits. He was now in a position where he could discard any unpopular measures proposed in the Labour manifesto on the grounds that he could not secure Liberal support for them; whereas the Liberals had joined with him in support of the very economic strategy to which he was committed. His only immediate worry was were it to prove necessary to shed a component of that strategy (Stage Three perhaps) would the Liberals be sufficiently flexible – to use his own favourite word – to accommodate him? But then Steel was in the position of the pupil rather than the teacher. What was in it for the Liberals? Steel had rushed it through probably against the better judgement of the majority of the members of the Parliamentary Liberal party. Those most in favour were those most likely to lose their seats in a general election. Grimond was sceptical from the beginning, and Cyril Smith was heavily against, but even he thought that almost anything was preferable to having Mrs Thatcher at No. 10. Steel himself, however, a brave and lucid man, was clear in his own mind about the purpose of the Pact. It was not simply to sustain the Government and to delay a general election; it was to implement some Liberal policies. He had never relished being the Leader of a party which contented itself with saying what should be done but which never succeeded in getting anything done. With only thirteen members in the House it was now, thanks to the Pact, going to be a party of government. The Pact took the Liberal party in the country by surprise and the Liberal candidate in the Smethwick by-election was the first victim. Steel's face fell on April Fool's Day when the result of the by-election for Roy Jenkins's former seat was declared and the Liberal came fourth behind the National Front candidate. Mrs Thatcher saw the result as just retribution. Labour and Liberal must hang together, otherwise they would hang separately, she said, or words to that effect. But she knew that victory in a spring election had been denied her. Weeks later she slapped down Steel in the Commons, dismissing him as 'this young man'. But this young man was proving resilient and the accommodation more resilient still.

The lengthiest clause in the original agreement concerned direct elections to the European Assembly and the Liberals' conviction that a proportional system should be used as a method of election. Callaghan understood that this one was the one Steel cared about most because it enshrined two hallowed tenets of Liberal policy – proportional representation and a European Parliament. Callaghan's problem was that there was considerable and unseducible opposition both to direct elections and to proportional representation within the PLP and the Cabinet. But having saved his Government with one political innovation – the accommodation with the Liberals, he sustained that accommodation with a constitutional innovation – a free vote in the Commons on an important matter of Government business with the freedom extended to members of the Cabinet. It was almost unthinkable. It had been done once or perhaps twice before in this century. It challenged a fundamental principle of government, the collective responsibility of the Cabinet. But when Mrs Thatcher chided Callaghan at Question Time about the constitutional impropriety of his decision and demanded to know when and on what grounds it could be countenanced, he replied jauntily: 'When I say so'. In July the government and the Liberals got a majority for the second reading of the bill to introduce direct elections to the European Assembly, but too late for it to become law in that session of Parliament. It was a handsome majority, 247, but 126 Labour MPs voted against the Bill, among them six Cabinet ministers, including Michael Foot, who had actually been responsible for the negotiations on the Bill with the Liberals. The choice between a system of proportional representation and the first-past-the-post system of election was left open. But the way was clear for an extension of the Lib-Lab Pact. The Government announced its new devolution intentions, another sacred Liberal cause, and promised both separate assemblies and separate Bills for Scotland and Wales. Both assemblies were to be given more freedom to arrange their own business than had been proposed in the previous abortive devolution legislation, but they were still to be funded by block grant without powers of their own to levy taxes. Steel accepted the new package as an improvement on the last but thought that the new assemblies would not long be content with the block grant and might coin the slogan 'No representation without taxation'.

In the last major debate before the summer recess Mrs Thatcher got the best of the rhetoric as she disinterred Healey's many budgets, but Callaghan, with the help of the Liberals, got his majority. The Liberal MPs met to decide the terms upon which they would agree to extend the accommodation into the next parliamentary session. They took a few days to make up their minds. Grimond and Penhaligon had serious reservations and Cyril Smith was firmly opposed to any extension of the Pact. In the end they settled not for a total commitment to support Callaghan's Government but for a conditional agreement founded on the continuing success of the Government's efforts to reduce inflation and to stand firm in the face of excessive wage demands. Indeed both sides to the agreement firmly understood that a collapse of the Government's pay restraint policy and a resumption of the rise in inflation would be regarded as grounds for the Liberals to disengage themselves. It took the Cabinet only ten minutes to endorse the extension of the Pact and to agree to the publication of its terms. Callaghan had given Steel one more sop, an imprecise commitment to the principle of profit-sharing in private industry. This too was a long-cherished Liberal policy which had never before been taken up by Labour. In the same week Callaghan appeared at a news conference alongside Len Murray of the TUC and together they presented a seventeen-page programme of policy proposals which purported to be the next stage of the social contract. It was entitled 'The Next Three Years and Into the Eighties'. Callaghan carefully stressed that it meant just that, and that several of the measures it proposed – the introduction of a wealth tax and the abolition of the House of Lords, for instance – would certainly not be turned into reality this side of a general election. The first priority, he kept repeating, must be to reduce the rate of inflation as the precondition for everything else. Almost on cue the departing Chairman of the Price Commission in his valedictory report announced that prices were indeed going down at last and the rate of inflation was falling.

Not all the loose ends had been tied up. The unemployment figures that were published in that last week of the parliamentary session were the highest since the Second World War. But Callaghan could depart for his summer holiday in the knowledge that things could have been much worse, for him and for his government. The Lib-Lab Pact had been renewed, albeit conditionally. There was something that he could still call a social contract and his own relations with the leaders of the TUC remained firmly founded on friendship. The Tories were still unready for office. And the nation, in Silver Jubilee Year, was in good heart.

Jubilee Year, in spite of its inevitability, had taken the nation by surprise. There had been so much talk about the need for economy to match the nation's economic fortunes that the feast of pageantry, both official and unofficial, which festooned the kingdom in June and July was unexpected and twice as enjoyable for that. But even more unexpected had been the outcome of the ceremony in Westminster Hall on 4 May when both Houses of Parliament had presented loyal addresses to Her Majesty to mark the beginning of the Silver Jubilee Year celebrations. In her reply the Queen began in an orthodox way reiterating that in a meeting of Sovereign and Parliament the essence of constitutional monarchy was reflected. It had provided the fabric of good order in society and had been the guardian of the liberties of individual citizens. These past twenty-five years had seen much change and those in Government and Parliament had to accept the challenges. Her audience listened politely as if nothing had changed. The problems of progress, she went on, the complexities of modern administration, the feeling that Metropolitan Government was too remote from the lives of ordinary men and women – these among other things had helped to revive an awareness of historical national identities in these islands. They provided the background for the continuing and keen discussion of proposals for devolution to Scotland and Wales within the United Kingdom.

Devolution. Suddenly, her audience was all attention. She continued:

> I number Kings and Queens of England and of Scotland and Princes of Wales among my ancestors and so I can readily understand these aspirations. But I cannot forget that I was crowned Queen of the United Kingdom of Great Britain and Northern Ireland. Perhaps this Jubilee is a time to remind ourselves of the benefits which union has conferred at home and in our international dealings on the inhabitants of all parts of this United Kingdom . . .

There was no perhaps about it. With that one sentence . . . 'I cannot forget that I was crowned Queen of the United Kingdom . . .' the Queen had turned a state occasion into a national event. Not only had she deflated the devolution debate (the Scots Nats blustered, threatened independence, and within a month were talking of offering her the Crown of Scotland), but she had also reminded her people of the importance of the nation as distinct from the state. In the next few weeks as she toured the kingdom in a royal progress without equal in public acclaim, it became clear that she had emerged after twenty-five years from her salad days, when she was green in judgement (as she put it herself), into a historic figure whose presence not only gave great pleasure to her people but identity and confidence too. Her Prime Minister was not a man to miss the significance of this national manifestation. He had known in advance what the Queen was going to say in Westminster Hall and he knew that her words would invoke a wave of genuine patriotism, which he would share and from which he would benefit. Callaghan, with his Irish name, his Welsh constituency and his English accent, had always been an emotional patriot. When the Queen reviewed the Fleet at Spithead at the end of June aboard the royal yacht *Britannia*, Leonard James Callaghan, son of the Chief Petty Officer who had served aboard the royal yacht *Victoria and Albert* sixty-five years previously, stood at her side. A week before he had been urged in the press to go to the people. In short, to get out. A week later he was telling the nation that over the next decade Britain would have the kind of opportunity that comes but rarely in the history of a people. And he said it with the air of a man who had every intention of being part of it.

Notes

The student of James Callaghan must, of necessity, bury himself in newspaper cuttings and copies of Hansard. If he is wise he will treat with a certain measure of misgiving the references to Callaghan in the Crossman *Diaries* and the Wilson memoirs. The two books mentioned in this essay, however, are essential reading. If and when Mr Callaghan retires he might decide not to produce full-scale memoirs. It would be in character for him not to. In which case his official biographer, when chosen, will have a difficult but enviable task.

1. Peter Kellner and Christopher Hitchens whose book *Callaghan: the Road to Number 10* (London 1976) is a brisk and perky narrative only spoiled by a strange squeamishness about political realities.
2. James Callaghan, *A House Divided* (London 1973). John Clare, who worked with Mr Callaghan on this book, reported that the author would dictate with 'cool, magisterial eloquence' for two hours at a stretch, rarely needing to refer to the four-foot high pile of cuttings provided by the Home Office.

Index